D0010896

OUT OF THE BEST BOOKS

OUT OF THE BEST BOOKS

AN ANTHOLOGY OF LITERATURE

VOLUME 3: INTELLIGENT FAMILY LIVING

Bruce B. Clark and Robert K. Thomas

1967

Published by Deseret Book Company, Salt Lake City, Utah

Library of Congress No. 66-29626

Lithographed by
DESERET NEWS PRESS
in the United States of America

To Alice L. Wilkinson,
our gracious prompter

Preface

The third volume of *Out of the Best Books* is a continuation of Volumes 1 and 2. In subject matter, Volume 1 emphasized individual values in our personal lives as explored through literature. Volume 2 focused upon home and family problems and ideals as also seen through literature, but with enrichment materials from the related arts. Now this third volume especially continues Volume 2—that is, the central focus is again upon love, marriage, and the family as seen through literature and art.

In method also the third volume follows the pattern of the preceding two volumes, emphasizing the critical approaches to literature presented in Volume 1 and continued in Volume 2. As in the past, so again, the emphasis is upon the works of literature themselves rather than upon authors' lives or historical background although pertinent biographical and historical facts are given as needed for interpretation. This emphasis on the work itself is intended to encourage stimulating discussion and exchange of ideas with all the insight into life and life's values that selections from the world's great literature can yield. Also, continuing concern is given to harmonizing literature with the Gospel, permitting a rich correlation between the ideals of our cultural heritage and the ideals of our religion.

Our obligation as members of the Church is first of all to study the scriptures and the words of our modern prophets for the fulness of the Gospel that they contain. But beyond these we are encouraged to study the best writings of the world for the supplemental knowledge and insight that these can give. At its best, literature is concerned with building faith and championing spiritual values—and with opposing and exposing selfishness, materialism, shallowness, and all things harmful to human personality or destructive in human relationships. We have not tried to limit the selections strictly to those that conform in every detail to L. D. S. doctrines and practices. In a larger sense, however, we have chosen those works that harmonize with and enrich the ideals of Gospel living. Many of the selections explore attitudes and practices to be avoided, but all are in a broad sense constructive and affirmative; for good teaching utilizes both the negative and the positive example.

As in the past, so also again, this third volume contains a sufficient number of selections that teachers can choose those most useful for their group. Some selections will appeal to some readers, and other selections to other readers. Some selections are especially demanding; others are less difficult. Which selections a teacher chooses will depend upon her own taste and background as well as the needs of the group; for no teacher can share enthusiasm that she does not genuinely feel, and every good teacher is sensitive to the needs of her class members. In any case, no teacher should try to cover all the selections in a section for one lesson. Such an attempt would inevitably result in superficial treatment. It is surely much better to cover only one story or one poem well than to rush over the surfaces of several selections. Also, whatever the selections covered, whether one or several, both teacher and class members should bring to their reading and discussion all of their own background in life's experiences. For literature is valuable not only because of the author's talent and insight but also because it stirs readers to think, evaluate, and aspire.

As we approach another volume it is also good to remind ourselves that reading a work of literature is a beginning and not an end. It opens doors rather than closes them. When we finish reading a selection we should be left thinking, not with all questions answered, but with sufficient insight that we are just a little better prepared to meet life's challenges and achieve life's eternal goals.

I have just two closing reminders before readers move into the rich selections that follow:

First, as we participate in the cultural enrichment program of the Church we should remember that the program will be fully successful only if we carry it into our homes, sharing the wonder and wisdom and beauty of good literature and art, as well as their delights, with our families. One of the most valuable things parents can give their children is a love of reading, music, and painting, plus some skill in analyzing these arts; and one of the best ways to do these things is to discuss literature and art as a family group in the home.

Second, as mentioned in the Preface to Volume 1, the principal idea behind this series of books is that the best way to study literature is to read it—that the work of literature itself is more important than anything that can be said about it, including all that we have said in our analytical discussions. So, readers, don't let anything stand between you and your personal experience with the literature itself.

May you have many hours of pleasant reading and stimulating discussion!

Bruce B. Clark
June, 1967

A Note about the Authors:

Bruce B. Clark, who has written the preface and sections 2, 4, and 5 of this third volume, is Professor of English and Dean of the College of Humanities at Brigham Young University. He has served twice as a bishop in The Church of Jesus Christ of Latter-day Saints, and three times as a high councilor. After seventeen years at B.Y.U. without a leave, he spent the summer of 1967 on a cultural tour of Europe, from which he sent the above preface.

Robert K. Thomas, who has written sections 1, 3, 6, and 7 of this volume, is Professor of English and Assistant Academic Vice-President at Brigham Young University. He has been a bishop and high councilor and is currently in the B.Y.U. 8th Stake presidency.

Acknowledgments

Selections under copyright are reprinted by permission and courtesy of publishers indicated below:

Appleton-Century-Crofts: for *And Now to Live Again,* by Betsey Barton. Copyright 1944 by Betsey Barton, reprinted by permission of Appleton-Century-Crofts, Inc., affiliate of Meredith Press.

The Atlantic Monthly: for "A Courageous Letter," copyright 1934 by The Atlantic Monthly Company, Boston, Mass. Reprinted with permission.

Brandt & Brandt, 101 Park Avenue, New York, N. Y.: for "Jacob and the Indians," by Stephen Vincent Benét.

E. P. Dutton & Co., Inc.: for "Farewell to Spring," "Farewell to a Friend," "Thoughts in Nan-shu," "The Pavilion" and "Methods of the Chinese Poet," by Wang Wei. From *Images In Jade* by Arthur Christy. Copyright 1929 by E. P. Dutton & Co., Inc. Renewal copyright 1957 by Gertrude N. Christy. Reprinted by permission of the publishers.

Harper & Row and Norma Millay Ellis: for "Love Is Not All" from *Collected Poems* by Edna St. Vincent Millay, copyright 1931 and 1958; and for excerpt from "Renascence" by Edna St. Vincent Millay, copyright 1912 and 1940.

Harper & Row, Publishers: for "The Happy Journey to Trenton and Camden" from *The Long Christmas Dinner and Other Plays in One Act* by Thornton Wilder. Copyright 1931 by Yale University Press and Coward-McCann, Inc. Copyright 1959 by Thornton Wilder. Reprinted by permission of Harper & Row, Publishers. Caution! "The Happy Journey to Trenton and Camden" is sole property of the author and is fully protected by copyright. It may not be acted by professionals or amateurs without formal permission and the payment of a royalty. All rights, including professional. amateur, stock, radio and television, broadcasting, motion pictures, recitation, lecturing, public reading, and the rights of translation into foreign languages are reserved. All professional inquiries should be addressed to the author's agent: Harold Freedman, Brandt & Brandt Dramatic Department, Inc., 101 Park Avenue, New York 17, New York. All requests for amateur rights should be addressed to Samuel French, 25 West 45th Street, New York 19, N. Y.

Holt, Rinehart and Winston, Inc.: for "Dust of Snow" by Robert Frost, from *Complete Poems of Robert Frost.* Copyright 1923 by Holt, Rinehart and Winston, Inc. Copyright 1951 by Robert Frost. Reprinted by permission of Holt, Rinehart and Winston, Inc.

The Macmillan Company and Ellen C. Masters: for "Lucinda Matlock" from *Spoon River Anthology* by Edgar Lee Masters, copyright 1914 and 1942.

The Macmillan Company and Harrison Smith: for "Love, Like a Drop of Dew" by William Henry Davies, published in *Chief Modern Poets of England*

and America by Gerald DeWitt Sanders and John Herbert Nelson, third edition, 1943.

Random House, Inc. & Alfred A. Knopf, Inc.; for "Giving" from *The Prophet* by Kahlil Gibran.

Charles Scribner's Sons: for "Richard Cory" from *The Children of the Night* by Edwin Arlington Robinson.

The Viking Press: for "The Waltz" by Dorothy Parker, from *The Portable Dorothy Parker,* copyright 1933, 1961, originally appeared in *The New Yorker;* and for "Clay" from *Dubliners* by James Joyce, originally published by B. W. Huebsch, Inc., in 1916; and "First Lesson," from *Letter From A Distant Land* by Philip Booth. Copyright © 1957 by Philip Booth. Reprinted by permission of The Viking Press, Inc.

TABLE OF CONTENTS

page

SECTION ONE

A Glad Heart

by Robert K. Thomas

A GLAD HEART

"With a glad heart and a cheerful countenance."
—Doctrine and Covenants

Introductory Comments

When we are "counting our blessings," we gain appreciation for what we have by contrasting our own situation with that of others less fortunate. Especially in our adolescence is this experience in perspective valuable. For we need to understand our strengths and prepare to take advantage of special opportunities. When we grow older, however, and have had some of the self-absorption of youth qualified by meaningful service to and from others, we no longer feel simple gratitude when we do not have to undergo another's misfortune. In maturity, our reactions to the problems of our associates are tempered by a realistic awareness that our advantages may be illusory or fleeting. All experience teaches the general lesson that the only control we may have over some circumstances in our lives is the ability and willingness to adapt skilfully to them. Accidents for which we have little responsibility may rob us of health, may limit our choice of vocation or may even take from us the very things which seem to make life most meaningful.

At such a time it is not particularly helpful to hear that everything will "work out in the end." In the most tragic circumstances the end seems to have arrived, and the pain of the present moment appears to numb our ability to find immediate comfort in a long view. Yet if we are not *given* all the consolation we need in a trying situation, we can always *make* enough happiness to carry us through. Most of the selections in this section will stress such achieved well-being.

Fortunately, not all happiness is dependent upon laborious effort. In his poem "I Wandered Lonely as a Cloud," William Wordsworth lets us share the quick change of mood which overwhelms him as he unexpectedly comes upon a field of daffodils. As he says, "A poet could not but be gay,/In such a jocund company." Even the memory of them gladdens later days. Leigh Hunt's "Rondeau" and Robert Frost's "Dust of Snow" similarly celebrate the sudden lift of the spirit which can be triggered by events outside ourselves.

With Emily Dickinson's "They May Not Need Me" we begin to shift from the external to the internal. The role of each person in modifying circumstance rather than merely accepting it begins to receive emphasis. "A Courageous Letter" gives advice for facing disappointment positively which transcends its particular setting. Thornton Wilder's homely little play shows us how basic a cheerful attitude can be in establishing individual and family well-being. Milton's *L'Allegro* is a famous statement of the advantages which a deliberately buoyant view of life generates.

The final selection, "The Flight of Betsey Lane" by Sarah Orne Jewett, introduces us to a trio of old ladies whose physical circumstances appear to be particularly distressing. Yet each manages some affirmation of life, and one, Betsey Lane, comes close to real victory.

Abstractions such as gladness, cheerfulness, and happiness are easily, if not very usefully, defined in terms of each other. What gives more than dictionary meaning to each of these terms is the illumination of experience. A glad heart is never locked in language; it is always manifest in the way we look and act.

I Wandered Lonely as a Cloud

William Wordsworth

I wandered lonely as a cloud
That floats on high o'er vales and hills,
When all at once I saw a crowd,
A host, of golden daffodils,
Beside the lake, beneath the trees,
Fluttering and dancing in the breeze.

Continuous as the stars that shine
And twinkle on the milky way,
They stretched in never-ending line
Along the margin of a bay;
Ten thousand saw I at a glance
Tossing their heads in sprightly dance.

The waves beside them danced, but they
Outdid the sparkling waves in glee;
A poet could not but be gay,
In such a jocund company;
I gazed—and gazed—but little thought
What wealth the show to me had brought:

For oft, when on my couch I lie
In vacant or in pensive mood,
They flash upon that inward eye
Which is the bliss of solitude;
And then my heart with pleasure fills,
And dances with the daffodils.

Rondeau

Leigh Hunt

Jenny kiss'd me when we met,
  Jumping from the chair she sat in;
Time, you thief, who love to get
  Sweets into your list, put that in:
Say I'm weary, say I'm sad,
  Say that health and wealth have miss'd me,
Say I'm growing old, but add,
  Jenny kiss'd me.

Dust of Snow

Robert Frost

The way a crow
Shook down on me
The dust of snow
From a hemlock tree

Has given my heart
A change of mood
And saved some part
Of a day I had rued.

Discussion of "I Wandered Lonely as a Cloud," "Rondeau," and "Dust of Snow"

These three short poems share an emphasis upon happiness which seems more provided than achieved. In all three situations the event appears to have a determining influence. The poet is less actor than acted upon. "I Wandered Lonely as a Cloud," for instance, is based upon an experience first described by Dorothy Wordsworth (William's sister) in her *Journal* for April 15, 1802:

The wind seized our breath. The lake was rough. There was a boat by itself floating in the middle of the bay below Water Millock. We rested again in the Water Millock Lane. The hawthorns are black and green, the birches here and there greenish, but there is yet more of purple to be seen on the twigs. We got over into a field to avoid some cows—people working. A few primroses by the roadside—wood-sorrel flower, the anemone, scentless violets, strawberries, and that starry, yellow flower which Mrs. C. calls pile wort. When we were in the woods beyond Gowbarrow Park we saw a few daffodils close to the waterside. We fancied that the lake had floated the seeds ashore, and that the little colony had so sprung up. But as we went along there were more and yet more; and at last, under the boughs of the trees, we saw that there was a long belt of them along the shore, about the breadth of a country turnpike road. I never saw daffodils so beautiful. They grew among the mossy stones about and about them; some rested their heads upon these stones as on a pillow for weariness, and the rest tossed and reeled and danced, and seemed as if they verily laughed with the wind, that blew upon them over the lake, they looked so gay, ever glancing, ever changing.

Wordsworth's friend, Samuel Taylor Coleridge, felt that the tone of this poem was pitched much too high for an experience of seeing daffodils. But, for Wordsworth, *bliss* was not too strong a word to describe a moment in which he felt himself to be in perfect tune with the universe.

Leigh Hunt (1784-1859) was the son of a Loyalist who returned to England after the United States declared its independence. Nine years younger than any of his brothers, he was under his mother's constant influence during his early years. This is worth noting, for in his *Autobiography* he states that he never remembers to have seen his mother smile. Fairly or unfairly, he ascribes his tendency to fits of depression to her example.

Yet the rather dreary circumstances in which he found himself most of his life undoubtedly contributed to the despondency he often felt. He edited papers and wrote books with extraordinary energy but with little financial reward. He was also an unsuccessful newspaper editor who spent two years in jail for libeling the Prince Regent. This much background helps us appreciate the almost extravagant tone of "Rondeau." Not technically a "rondeau" at all, for this French form must have at least thirteen lines and be confined to two rhymes, this small poem has a continuing appeal to those who treasure the spontaneous act which has a significance out of proportion to its size.

"Dust of Snow" has the hallmarks of its author, Robert Frost (see *Out of the Best Books,* Vol. 2, pp. 188-89 for biographical detail). Frost's concern for the relation of outer to inner weather is a major theme in his work. His use of the natural environment which surrounds him as both subject and object is equally typical. The deceptively simple language and rhyme scheme, the almost sing-song rhythm, might lull us if we hadn't learned to be alert to the carefully casual suggestions of Frost's poetry.

Note that we are not talking about just any bird. There is something a bit saucy and independent about a crow. Note also that the crow is not huddled down in his feathers as a hedge against the cold, but is actively adapting himself. Even the hemlock tree is necessary. For an evergreen seems least affected by season or climate and is appropriate station for a bird which intends to stay alive. The effect of these related images is to inspire a complementary integration in the human heart. We may only save part of the day, but the attitude we take, not the circumstances we face, is critical.

They Might Not Need Me

They might not need me; but they might.
I'll let my head be just in sight;
A smile as small as mine might be
Precisely their necessity.

—Emily Dickinson (1830-1886)

Discussion of "They Might Not Need Me"

When Thomas Wentworth Higginson visited Emily Dickinson in 1870, one of her cryptic comments to him was that she found "ecstasy in living." The well meaning but rather unperceptive Higginson didn't quite know what to make of this; but, in fairness, later critics have fared little better. There is something so bold and original about much of Miss Dickinson's poetry that it is difficult for commentators to avoid turning a hint into a declaration.

Fortunately, there are a number of poems in the Dickinson canon which need little explication; such a poem is the quatrain given above. If the attitude suggested here is much less intense than the connotations usually associated with ecstasy, the original sense of being beside oneself is not entirely lost. The feeling of modest detachment in this four line stanza, however, should not make us insensitive to its power. As we often find in Miss Dickinson's poetry, there is such an exquisite blending of tone and imagery that we may not remember how difficult such a harmony is to achieve.

Note, for instance, the deliberately tentative effect of the repeated "might." The smile which gives sudden illumination to this poem is thus kept in literal and figurative perspective. The opening "they" is also kept from too general a reference. A huge crowd would probably not notice so tiny and tentative a smile. Without limiting participation further, the poem thus keeps intimacy without narrowness. The non-assertive tone is reinforced by the seemingly casual detail that merely her head will be in view, and that only "just in sight."

One might wonder, at this point, if such reiterated qualification might not make the poem hopelessly indecisive. Perhaps one of the differences between talent and genius is the ability to make the questionable finally appear inevitable. In her use of "precisely" Miss Dickinson brings this little poem into triumphant integration. For it rescues the tentative from its usual connotations. Instead of suggesting vacillation or timidity—the Scriptural putting one's hand to the plow and then turning back—it reminds us that uncertainty may be simply a preliminary and necessary step toward certainty. For there is a point in most of our development when someone's brief smile of encouragement is just what we need. Too beaming a smile would appear either false or coercive. No smile at all would only reinforce our insecurity.

A glad heart need not be manifest in effusiveness, and we should not estimate the success of our encouragement by its heartiness. Someone who is uncertain may be alienated rather than heartened by our assurance. To let others know that we, too, are often discouraged and insecure, but that we can manage a little smile of hope and encouragement may do more for others than we realize. What we have is usually enough, if we are not afraid to use it.

A Courageous Letter

Dearest Elizabeth,—

You say in your letter, 'Do not scold or sympathize—I can do plenty of that for us both. Just tell me as completely as possible what you did and why, and whether or not it has paid.'

How could I scold you? Don't you suppose I know that a desperate woman is a mad woman, and that none of her reasoning will bear the earmarks of sanity?

And even though you forbid it, I do sympathize. I realize that this last blow is altogether merciless because it comes at the end of four almost unbearable years, and because it comes at a time when you believed that the worst really was over. It's all so futile—like the killing of a soldier in that last hour before the signing of the Armistice!

But, merciless or not, the emergency is here and has to be faced. Since you feel that my meeting of a similar emergency may have in it something of practical value for you, I am opening wide the book of my experience. What I did and why, and whether or not it has paid, is all here for you to read.

The first thing I did was to call the children into conference. Because of the gravity of our situation, it seemed to me to be the only way. I felt that our only hope for survival lay in complete cooperation.

I began by reminding them that their father is a man of rare ability, and that his record of achievement is such that we all have justifiable reason to be proud. I assured them that eventually a man of their father's ability and experience must find his place in the economic world. I warned them, however, that I did not know how long this readjustment might take, and I refused to hold out to them any false hope. Meanwhile, we were going right on being proud of him and having faith in him.

I felt this was of infinite importance to Jim and to me, for the children's pride and faith in their father have been very precious to us both.

Then I did a very prideful thing: I got out the history of their father's family and traced for them the part these men and women, whose name they bear, had played in the founding, the developing, and the perpetuating of this country. I said, 'You see, once upon a time this country had need for men and women like you. That need may come again. Consequently, I am not going to allow you to be wasted.'

I told them that the history of mankind was full of periods when just to survive was triumph. (And this, Elizabeth, is my answer to your question, 'If I can offer my children nothing but a bare existence, why bother with that existence at all?')

I admitted that, for the present, adequate shelter, the simplest of food, and something in the way of clothes were the very most we could do for them. With these bare essentials they must learn to be content, though naturally I neither expected nor wanted them to be satisfied with so little.

You see I was almost brutally honest, because I had to be. I knew that if I tried to play 'Pollyanna' and went about singing,—

> Just around the corner
> There's a rainbow in the sky . . .

and then that rainbow failed to make its appearance, I should no longer have the confidence of my children. I had to have their confidence if I was to see them through.

I told them that the fight for survival was always a grim business, but that we were not going to be one bit grim about it. On the contrary, we were going to be the jolliest group of soldiers that were ever put through a forced march.

I warned them that each one of us would have to develop great respect for a penny, but that we did not have to come to worship it. To me that has always seemed one of the most unpleasant characteristics of so many people of little means; they overestimate the importance of money and underestimate the value of everything else.

Frankly, I told the children that we were going to be poor,—this had been wished upon us,—but that we did not have to become impoverished unless we wished, because we were still rich in so much that made life worth living. I went over these riches one by one because it seemed to me that this was definitely a time for taking inventory.

'You children,' I told them, 'have more than average health and intelligence. There has always been harmony in your home and there always will be—something of which few children of this age can boast. You have beautiful memories of places, and your lives have touched interesting and worth-while people. You have always had the best in books and they are friends who will stand by you in the worst of days. You have a good radio which frequently brings you the best in music and sometimes splendid bits of drama as well. These are your riches; with them you will have to be content for the present.'

Then, since it was still inventory time, I told each one how I thought he was particularly well adapted to go through this adjustment period and where he might prove to be particularly vulnerable. I went even further and did what only a twentieth-century mother would do: I told them just where I anticipated trouble in myself.

'No crisis has ever yet found me lacking in courage,' I told them, 'but I am not certain that I have enough of the dogged, persistent kind of courage which can hold out day after day. If I am lacking in that, I shall have to develop it, and you children will have to bear with me and help me in every way you can while I am learning. In fact, our success in this new venture will be determined largely by the sympathy and understanding and tenderness we display toward each other.'

It was a big order I was giving my children and no one appreciated that fact more fully than I. First, no matter what happened, they were to keep intact their pride and their faith in their father. Second, they were to be content with existence, keeping in mind that people of their calibre were not so common that their country could afford to waste them. Third, they must learn the nice art of respecting money without worshiping it, and the equally nice art of being poor without being impoverished. Finally, though each one of them would be passing through a period of intensive change and adjustment, each must be patient and tolerant and kind to the other.

As I said, the order was large—much too large to hope to fill completely. But these children of ours have come so close to filling the order that our pride in them is colossal.

You want to know if the rewards have been worth the struggle. I do not know. It is too early to tell because I am still so close to it all.

There is a law of compensation. You and I both believe that. But whether the compensation is or is not proportionate remains to be seen.

My children know more about courage and steadfastness and self-control than many people learn in a lifetime of living. Besides that, they have gone far in tolerance and understanding. Never will they say as their mother used to do, 'How in the world did people like that ever get into such a jam anyway?' because they know too much about 'jams' to be impatient with anybody who is in one.

They have taken big strides in the art of cooperation, and it is no mean art to master. They have developed perspective, for, when one fixes his eyes upon the mountains, the molehills over which he stumbles slip by unnoticed.

I thought of that about Thanksgiving time when a girl whom I used to see often in the old days ran in tearing her hair because her Christmas cards were going to be a bit later than she had expected. I sat with my hands idle in my lap—they should have been doing so many things just then—and I thought to myself, 'No daughter of mine will ever take on about nothing.' I know it is true, too.

But still, with all this to their good, I wonder if it is best that my children should have to learn so much so soon. It is very like sending a ten-year-old child to college. It is possible that he could do the work, but why should he? I like an ordered existence, with everything coming along in its rightful place. I like childhood to be childish, and age to be dignified. This pushing of a child into adulthood—either in mind or in character—has no appeal for me.

As a family we have become genuinely fond of each other and beautifully friendly. Not many families can make a similar boast. I realized that the other day when a girl who seemingly has everything enviable in the world said, 'I'm so glad that Joan is old enough to take to the movies,'—Joan is four,—'because now I know what to do with her on Nana's afternoon out. She used to drive me so frantic that by the time it was seven o'clock I just fell into bed unconscious.'

Perhaps I am vainglorious, but I could not help contrasting that mother's experience with one of my own. Last fall when little David started off for his first day of school, he stopped at the drive, turned around, and came back to say to me, 'Mother, I just want to tell you that I think you and I've had a bully time here together.'

Mother complex? I don't believe so, for of all our children he has adjusted himself to school the most easily and the most happily. You see, he was fortified by his intensive course in cooperation here at home.

As a family we have become rank opportunists. Our faith in 'to-morrow' has been so often betrayed that we put no stock in it whatsoever. To-day is here. To-morrow may never come. So we set out to squeeze every last drop of pleasure and fun out of each day as it passes.

The other morning, while we were at breakfast, a gorgeous Kentucky cardinal perched on a snow-covered limb just outside the window. I carried that picture with me the whole day through, even when the washing machine broke down in the midst of the washing.

I know what you are thinking. You are thinking that it is just an affectation—this prizing of such simple and commonplace experiences. I used to believe that, too, in the days when my plate was so heaped with good things that my only dilemma lay in choosing. But, when the plate goes suddenly bare, one learns to appreciate the little that is left or else one spends his life in drooping melancholy. We, as a family, do not choose to droop.

In some ways it is easier to have a good time than it ever was before; first, because we are so eager for happiness, and then because we are no longer weighed down with the appurtenances of nice living. For example, picnics used to be the bane of my existence because there was so much to prepare and then to pack. Now, we take a meat pie out of the oven, put a couple of bottles of milk and a few apples into a basket, and with these very trifling impediments, wander down to the creek to eat our dinner. It's surprising how delicious this simple fare becomes when eaten under the trees.

Still, I miss nice living, and so will you. You will miss much else besides, such as folks that are stimulating, places that are new and different. You'll miss comfort and luxury, and, above all, you will miss the future. I have, anyway. Until I became an opportunist I never realized how much of my time I spent dreaming of the children's future. I wanted to do so much for them, especially for the girls—one feels that a man-child can get by somehow, if he has the proper stuff in him. Now all that has changed, and the change has been very difficult for me to accept. But I think I am a bit more reconciled than I was a few weeks ago, and all because of an experience which I know will interest you.

We were invited to the Town Club to a dinner party, and I did anticipate it, not only because that sort of thing is rare now, but because I very much wanted to meet one of the guests. If I were to tell you her name you would recognize her at once, for her father is a personage. The best of everything has gone into the making of that girl: the finest schools, extensive travel, unusual contacts—all that a mother most covets for her own daughters.

My dear Elizabeth, I have never in all my life been so thoroughly disappointed in anyone. She was most unprepossessing in appearance —thin and sallow and neurotic. Her voice was shrill and her manner shrewish. Her husband, who appeared to be a very likable fellow, bore the brunt of her ill temper. She "rode" him mercilessly and was anxious that we all should be an appreciative audience to the "riding."

In the same party was a girl who impressed me more than any stranger ever has. She was lovely to look at, she was beautifully poised, her voice was charming, she had the "grand manner" and yet was delightfully gracious. I kept thinking, 'Someone has made a mistake. Surely this is the girl with the many advantages!' But when I inquired I found that she had been her husband's secretary before her marriage and that her education had been confined to high school and a very short business course.

Now I have not lost my good common sense to such an extent that I instantly conclude that every secretary who marries her employer is a lady, and every girl of unlimited opportunity necessarily develops into a shallow, neurotic shrew. But this experience did remind me that the word 'educate' means to draw or lead forth, and, if there is nothing to lead forth, not one or a dozen schools can truly educate. On the other hand, if my daughters should have in themselves something worth while, it is possible that they will become true gentlewomen anyway.

That thought has been something of a consolation to me, and I pass it on because I know that your darkest hours will come when you allow yourself to contrast what you can do for your children with what you had intended to do.

There is another pitfall, too, against which I would warn you, and again I am going to tell you of an experience of mine which might help you. When a family of eight children moved into the house across the street I was all ready to throw up both hands and sink for the last time. I knew, of course, that there would be noise —quarrelings and wranglings and scoldings. And it was summer! To my surprise and delight, none of my fears were realized. In the whole time they lived there I never once heard the mother's voice raised in scolding. She was one of the calmest and most beautifully tranquil persons I have ever seen. I was both relieved and astonished, but much too busy to wonder how this new neighbor had come by so much serenity.

Then one day I saw my son looking at me speculatively, and presently he asked, 'Mother, do you think you could raise eight children without raising your voice?'

I confessed that I not only thought I couldn't but knew I couldn't. I said, 'Suppose you find out for me how it's done.'

After considerable sleuthing my son turned in his report, and what he discovered has stood me in mighty good stead. The mother of eight, he reported, was very wise in her choice of discards. Somewhere along the way she had come to accept the fact that she could not maintain the same standard of living with eight children that she could if she had but one. Jimmy reported that the house was always in order, but that often it was not dusted. The children wore serviceable clothes which did not show soil and were not too frequently washed, though the children themselves showed signs of frequent bathing. Furthermore the sheets were washed but not ironed, and the same was true of the towels. This sort of compromise went right on down the line.

To women like you and me, such a compromise is difficult to effect. Spotlessness—not just cleanliness—has been our birthright and the birthright of our children. But I warn you that in this new and changed world into which we have been thrust spotlessness comes at too high a figure. It is just another luxury which we must learn to do without.

Of course in fiction one does encounter women with unlimited strength, and, since authors of unquestioned integrity continue to write about such people, I am certain they must exist—somewhere. It has never yet been my privilege to meet one of these tireless souls. On the contrary, all the women I have known have had definite energy limitations. When they push themselves past those limitations, they become cross and unreasonable and not at all pleasant to live with. So I warn you that, unless you are certain you are one of these indefatigable souls, you must learn to compromise. If a film must gather somewhere, let it be on your windows and not on your spirit, which must be bright enough to show your children the way.

You and I, Elizabeth, have been dealt a no-honor hand. If ever we are able to take a trick, it will be because we have made such wise and careful discards. I think that we are going to take some tricks yet. When or how I do not know. But I am not ready to throw down my hand in disgust, and I feel confident that, when you have had a little longer to accustom yourself to your changed circumstances, you will want to go on playing the hand, too.

Meanwhile, I love you and believe in you.

Mary

Discussion of "A Courageous Letter"

This letter was submitted to and printed in the *Atlantic Monthly* for July, 1934. The author requested that she remain anonymous. That this is no usual letter-to-the-editor becomes apparent before we have completed the first few paragraphs. Being in personal letter form, it retains an intimacy which might be lost if it were presented as an essay, and the fact that the author refuses to be identified keeps us from having our reactions colored by the fact that the writer is too famous—or not famous enough. The further we read, the more we realize that this is just the kind of letter we would like to be able to write to someone in need. The fact that no author is given almost makes us feel as if we had written it.

If the occasion for this letter is rooted in the Great Depression of the thirties, its message is a universal one. In our day economic want may not be the most pressing burden for many (although there is probably no distress more pitiful than physical destitution in time of abundance), but no age has been characterized by greater need. For necessities and luxuries begin to blur under the coaxing of indulgence, and our needs expand to fit our affluence. As a result, we are trying desperately to fill the expanding hopper of need with *things*. It is easier to give money than sympathy and more convenient to make a contribution than offer service.

How gently—yet how firmly—this letter calls us home from Babylon. The needs of our time are great, but they are the same ones which have always existed, and no one of them is really material. The challenge of "A Courageous Letter" when it was first printed was how to live above poverty. The challenge of this letter for many today is how to live above plenty.

Note how little the basic problems discussed here are affected by circumstance. More than anything else the father who has lost his job needs the faith and support of his family. Surely the father who may have to change jobs several times to adjust to today's expanding technology requires similar faith and confidence. If having too little makes one selfish, having too much may have precisely the same effect. If too much sacrifice can make the heart a stone, too little may make it just as unfeeling. Poverty may force us to discard that which is superfluous, but plenty requires at least as many choices.

Beyond the continuing relevance of the problems recounted here is the manner in which the writer presents them. The tone is never one of resignation, which Thoreau defines as "confirmed desperation." In the midst of the most discouraging particulars there is a positive, on-going attitude. Nothing is ignored and nothing is over-dramatized. The negative effects on the children of assuming responsibilities beyond their years are recognized—and no attempt is made to explain them away. An even more subtle temptation, to insist that the gains "make-up-for" the losses, is similarly resisted. The tone of this letter never blurs into self-pity or self-righteousness. In fact the most remarkable single feature about this letter is its objectivity. Circumstances are faced without illusions, yet the writer does not assume a case-worker detachment. She is involved in the situation without being lost in it.

If this letter reflects a mother's point of view, it is just as successful in letting its readers see a mother's role. The author is not the head of her house—note how carefully she helps her family remember the father's position—but she is the rallying force whose own discipline and sacrifice are an inspiring example. This letter is peculiarly appropriate for this section because it lets us see clearly how little our material circumstances affect our happiness. The writer describes her family as being "eager for happiness" and exhorts her friend to let a film gather on the windows of her home if it must but not to let it collect on her spirit. In being the "jolliest group of soldiers that were ever put through a forced march" the family referred to here suggest the discipline and dynamic acceptance that prepares the ground in which happiness can flourish.

The Happy Journey to Trenton and Camden

Thornton Wilder

No scenery is required for this play. Perhaps a few dusty flats may be seen leaning against the brick wall at the back of the stage.

The five members of the Kirby family and the Stage Manager *compose the cast.*

The Stage Manager *not only moves forward and withdraws the few properties that are required, but he reads from a typescript the lines of all the minor characters. He reads them clearly, but with little attempt at characterization, scarcely troubling himself to alter his voice, even when he responds in the person of a child or a woman.*

As the curtain rises the Stage Manager *is leaning lazily against the proscenium pillar at the audience's left. He is smoking.*

Arthur *is playing marbles in the center of the stage.*

Caroline *is at the remote back right talking to some girls who are invisible to us.*

Ma Kirby *is anxiously putting on her hat before an imaginary mirror.*

MA. Where's your pa? Why isn't he here? I declare, we'll never get started.

ARTHUR. Ma, where's my hat? I guess I don't go if I can't find my hat.

MA. Go out into the hall and see if it isn't there. Where's Caroline gone to now, the plagued child?

ARTHUR. She's out waitin' in the street talkin' to the Jones girls.—I just looked in the hall a thousand times, ma, and it isn't there. (*He spits for good luck before a difficult shot and mutters:*) Come on, baby.

MA. Go and look again, I say. Look carefully.

Arthur *rises, runs to the right, turns around swiftly, returns to his game, flinging himself on the floor with a terrible impact and starts shooting an aggie.*

ARTHUR. No, ma, it's not there.

MA (*serenely*). Well, you don't leave Newark without that hat, make up your mind to that. I don't go no journeys with a hoodlum.

ARTHUR. Aw, ma!

Ma *comes down to the footlights and talks toward the audience as through a window.*

MA. Oh, Mrs. Schwartz!

THE STAGE MANAGER (*consulting his script*). Here I am, Mrs. Kirby. Are you going yet?

MA. I guess we're going in just a minute. How's the baby?

THE STAGE MANAGER. She's all right now. We slapped her on the back and she spat it up.

MA. Isn't that fine!—Well now, if you'll be good enough to give the cat a saucer of milk in the morning and the evening, Mrs. Schwartz, I'll be ever so grateful to you.—Oh, good afternoon, Mrs. Hobmeyer!

THE STAGE MANAGER. Good afternoon, Mrs. Kirby, I hear you're going away.

MA (*modest*). Oh, just for three days, Mrs. Hobmeyer, to see my married daughter, Beulah, in Camden. Elmer's got his vacation week from the laundry early this year, and he's just the best driver in the world.

Caroline *comes "into the house" and stands by her mother.*

THE STAGE MANAGER. Is the whole family going?

MA. Yes, all four of us that's here. The change ought to be good for the children. My married daughter was downright sick a while ago—

THE STAGE MANAGER. Tchk—Tchk—Tchk! Yes. I remember you tellin' us.

MA. And I just want to go down and see the child. I ain't seen her since then. I just won't rest easy in my mind without I see her. (*To Caroline*) Can't you say good afternoon to Mrs. Hobmeyer?

CAROLINE (*blushes and lowers her eyes and says woodenly*). Good afternoon, Mrs. Hobmeyer.

THE STAGE MANAGER. Good afternoon, dear.—Well, I'll wait and beat these rugs after you're gone, because I don't want to choke you. I hope you have a good time and find everything all right.

MA. Thank you, Mrs. Hobmeyer, I hope I will.—Well, I guess that milk for the cat is all, Mrs. Schwartz, if you're sure you don't mind. If anything should come up, the key to the back door is hanging by the ice box.

ARTHUR AND CAROLINE. Ma! Not so loud. Everybody can hear yuh.

MA. Stop pullin' my dress, children. (*In a loud whisper*) The key to the back door I'll leave hangin' by the ice box and I'll leave the screen door unhooked.

THE STAGE MANAGER. Now have a good trip, dear, and give my love to Loolie.

MA. I will, and thank you a thousand times.

She returns "into the room."

What can be keeping your pa?

ARTHUR. I can't find my hat, ma.

Enter Elmer *holding a hat.*

ELMER. Here's Arthur's hat. He musta left it in the car Sunday.

MA. That's a mercy. Now we can start.—Caroline Kirby, what you done to your cheeks?

CAROLINE (*defiant-abashed*). Nothin'.

MA. If you've put anything on 'em, I'll slap you.

CAROLINE. No, ma, of course I haven't. (*Hanging her head*) I just rubbed'm to make'm red. All the girls do that at High School when they're goin' places.

MA. Such silliness I never saw. Elmer, what kep' you?

ELMER (*always even-voiced and always looking out a little anxiously through his spectacles*). I just went to the garage and had Charlie give a last look at it, Kate.

MA. I'm glad you did. I wouldn't like to have no breakdown miles from anywhere. Now we can start. Arthur, put those marbles away. Anybody'd think you didn't want to go on a journey to look at yuh.

They go out through the "hall," take the short steps that denote going downstairs, and find themselves in the street.

ELMER. Here, you boys, you keep away from that car.

The Stage Manager *has moved forward four chairs and a low platform. This is the automobile. It is in the center of the stage and faces the audience. The platform slightly raises the two chairs in the rear.* Pa's *hands hold an imaginary steering wheel and continually shift gears.* Caroline *sits beside him.* Arthur *is behind him and* Ma *behind* Caroline.

CAROLINE (*self-consciously*). Good-by Mildred. Good-by, Helen.

THE STAGE MANAGER. Good-by, Caroline. Good-by, Mrs. Kirby. I hope y'have a good time.

MA. Good-by, girls.

THE STAGE MANAGER. Good-by, Kate. The car looks fine.

MA (*looking upward toward a window*). Oh, good-by, Emma! (*Modestly*) We think it's the best little Chevrolet in the world.—Oh, good-by, Mrs. Adler!

THE STAGE MANAGER. What, are you going away, Mrs. Kirby?

MA. Just for three days, Mrs. Adler, to see my married daughter in Camden.

THE STAGE MANAGER. Have a good time.

Now Ma, Caroline *and the* Stage Manager *break out into a tremendous chorus of good-bys. The whole street is saying good-by.* Arthur *takes out his pea shooter and lets fly happily into the air. There is a lurch or two and they are off.*

ARTHUR (*in sudden fright*). Pa! Pa! Don't go by the school. Mr. Biedenbach might see us!

MA. I don't care if he does see us. I guess I can take my children out of school for one day without having to hide down back streets about it.

Elmer *nods to a passerby.*

Ma *asks without sharpness*:

Who was that you spoke to, Elmer?

ELMER. That was the fellow who arranges our banquets down to the Lodge, Kate.

MA. Is he the one who had to buy four hundred steaks? (Pa *nods.*) I declare, I'm glad I'm not him.

ELMER. The air's getting better already. Take deep breaths, children.

They inhale noisily.

ARTHUR. Gee, it's almost open fields already. "*Weber and Heilbroner Suits for Well-Dressed Men.*" Ma, can I have one of them some day?

MA. If you graduate with good marks perhaps your father'll let you have one for graduation.

CAROLINE (*whining*). Oh, pa! do we have to wait while that whole funeral goes by?

Pa *takes off his hat.*

Ma *cranes forward with absorbed curiosity.*

MA. Take off your hat, Arthur. Look at your father.—Why, Elmer, I do believe that's a lodge-brother of yours. See the banner? I suppose this is the Elizabeth branch.

Elmer *nods.* Ma *sighs*: *Tchk—tchk—tchk. They all lean forward and watch the funeral in silence, growing momentarily more solemnized. After a pause,* Ma *continues almost dreamily*:

Well, we haven't forgotten the one that went on, have we? We haven't forgotten our good Harold. He gave his life for his country, we mustn't forget that. (*She passes her finger from the corner of her eye across her cheek. There is another pause.*) Well, we'll all hold up the traffic for a few minutes some day.

THE CHILDREN (*very uncomfortable*). Ma!

MA (*without self-pity*). Well, I'm "ready," children. I hope everybody in this car is "ready." (*She puts her hand on* Pa's *shoulder.*) And I pray to go first, Elmer. Yes. (Pa *touches her hand.*)

THE CHILDREN. Ma, everybody's looking at you. Everybody's laughing at you.

MA. Oh, hold your tongues! I don't care what a lot of silly people in Elizabeth, New Jersey, think of me.—Now we can go on. That's the last.

There is another lurch and the car goes on.

CAROLINE. "*Fit-Rite Suspenders. The Working Man's Choice.*" Pa, why do they spell Rite that way?

ELMER. So that it'll make you stop and ask about it, Missy.

CAROLINE. Papa, you're teasing me.—Ma, why do they say "*Three Hundred Rooms Three Hundred Baths*"?

ARTHUR. "*Mueller's Spaghetti: The Family's Favorite Dish.*" Ma, why don't you ever have spaghetti?

MA. Go along, you'd never eat it.

ARTHUR. Ma, I like it now.

CAROLINE (*with gesture*). Yum-yum. It looks wonderful up there. Ma, make some when we get home?

MA (*dryly*). "The management is always happy to receive suggestions. We aim to please."

The whole family finds this exquisitely funny. The children scream with laughter. Even Elmer *smiles.* Ma *remains modest.*

ELMER. Well, I guess no one's complaining, Kate. Everybody knows you're a good cook.

MA. I don't know whether I'm a good cook or not, but I know I've had practice. At least I've cooked three meals a day for twenty-five years.

ARTHUR. Aw, ma, you went out to eat once in a while.

MA. Yes. That made it a leap year.

This joke is no less successful than its predecessor. When the laughter dies down, Caroline *turns around in an ecstasy of well-being and kneeling on the cushions says:*

CAROLINE. Ma, I love going out in the country like this. Let's do it often, ma.

MA. Goodness, smell that air will you! It's got the whole ocean in it.—Elmer, drive careful over that bridge. This must be New Brunswick we're coming to.

ARTHUR (*jealous of his mother's successes*). Ma, when is the next comfort station?

MA (*unruffled*). You don't want one. You just said that to be awful.

CAROLINE (*shrilly*). Yes, he did, ma. He's terrible. He says that kind of thing right out in school and I want to sink through the floor, ma. He's terrible.

MA. Oh, don't get so excited about nothing, Miss Proper! I guess we're all yewman-beings in this car, at least as far as I know. And, Arthur, you try and be a gentleman.—Elmer, don't run over that collie dog. (*She follows the dog with her eyes.*) Looked kinda peaked to me. Needs a good honest bowl of leavings. Pretty dog, too. (*Her eyes fall on a billboard.*) That's a pretty advertisement for Chesterfield cigarettes, isn't it? Looks like Beulah, a little.

ARTHUR. Ma?

MA. Yes.

ARTHUR (*"route" rhymes with "out"*). Can't I take a paper route with the Newark *Daily Post?*

MA. No, you cannot. No, sir, I hear they make the paper boys get up at four-thirty in the morning. No son of mine is going to get up at four-thirty every morning, not if it's to make a million dollars. Your *Saturday Evening Post* route on Thursday mornings is enough.

ARTHUR. Aw, ma.

MA. No, sir. No son of mine is going to get up at four-thirty and miss the sleep God meant him to have.

ARTHUR (*sullenly*). Hhm! Ma's always talking about God. I guess she got a letter from him this morning.

Ma *rises, outraged.*

MA. Elmer, stop that automobile this minute. I don't go another step with anybody that says things like that. Arthur, you get out of this car. Elmer, you give him another dollar bill. He can go back to Newark, by himself. I don't want him.

ARTHUR. What did I say? There wasn't anything terrible about that.

ELMER. I didn't hear what he said, Kate.

MA. God has done a lot of things for me and I won't have him made fun of by anybody. Go away. Go away from me.

CAROLINE. Aw, ma—don't spoil the ride.

MA. No.

ELMER. We might as well go on, Kate, since we've got started. I'll talk to the boy tonight.

MA (*slowly conceding*). All right, if you say so, Elmer. But I won't sit beside him. Caroline, you come, and sit by me.

ARTHUR (*frightened*). Aw, ma, that wasn't so terrible.

MA. I don't want to talk about it. I hope your father washes your mouth out with soap and water.—Where'd we all be if I started talking about God like that, I'd like to know! We'd be in the speak-easies and night-clubs and places like that, that's where we'd be.—All right, Elmer, you can go on now.

CAROLINE. What did he say, ma? I didn't hear what he said.

MA. I don't want to talk about it.

They drive on in silence for a moment, the shocked silence after a scandal.

ELMER. I'm going to stop and give the car a little water, I guess.

MA. All right, Elmer. You know best.

ELMER (*to a garage hand*). Could I have a little water in the radiator—to make sure?

THE STAGE MANAGER (*in this scene alone he lays aside his script and enters into a role seriously*). You sure can. (*He punches the tires.*) Air all right? Do you need any oil or gas?

ELMER. No, I think not. I just got fixed up in Newark.

MA. We're on the right road for Camden, are we?

THE STAGE MANAGER. Yes, keep straight ahead. You can't miss it. You'll be in Trenton in a few minutes.

He carefully pours some water into the hood.

Camden's a great town, lady, believe me.

MA. My daughter likes it fine,—my married daughter.

THE STAGE MANAGER. Ye'? It's a great burg all right. I guess I think so because I was born near there.

MA. Well, well. Your folks still live there?

THE STAGE MANAGER. No, my old man sold the farm and they built a factory on it. So the folks moved to Philadelphia.

MA. My married daughter Beulah lives there because her husband works in the telephone company.—Stop pokin' me, Caroline!—We're all going down to see her for a few days.

THE STAGE MANAGER. Ye'?

MA. She's been sick, you see, and I just felt I had to go and see her. My husband and my boy are going to stay at the Y.M.C.A. I hear they've got a dormitory on the top floor that's real clean and comfortable. Had you ever been there?

THE STAGE MANAGER. No. I'm Knights of Columbus myself.

MA. Oh.

THE STAGE MANAGER. I used to play basketball at the Y though. It looked all right to me.

He has been standing with one foot on the rung of Ma's *chair. They have taken a great fancy to one another. He reluctantly shakes himself out of it and pretends to examine the car again, whistling.*

Well, I guess you're all set now, lady. I hope you have a good trip; you can't miss it.

EVERYBODY. Thanks. Thanks a lot. Good luck to you.

Jolts and lurches.

MA (*with a sigh*). The world's full of nice people.—That's what I call a nice young man.

CAROLINE (*earnestly*). Ma, you oughtn't to tell'm all everything about yourself.

MA. Well, Caroline, you do your way and I'll do mine.—He looked kinda thin to me. I'd like to feed him up for a few days. His mother lives in Philadelphia and I expect he eats at those dreadful Greek places.

CAROLINE. I'm hungry. Pa, there's a hot dog stand. K'n I have one?

ELMER. We'll all have one, eh, Kate? We had such an early lunch.

MA. Just as you think best, Elmer.

ELMER. Arthur, here's half a dollar.—Run over and see what they have. Not too much mustard either.

Arthur *descends from the car and goes off stage right.*

Ma *and* Caroline *get out and walk a bit.*

MA. What's that flower over there?—I'll take some of those to Beulah.

CAROLINE. It's just a weed, ma.

MA. I like it.—My, look at the sky, wouldya! I'm glad I was born in New Jersey. I've always said it was the best state in the Union. Every state has something no other state has got.

They stroll about humming.

Presently Arthur *returns with his hands full of imaginary hot dogs which he distributes. He is still very much cast down by the recent scandal. He finally approaches his mother and says falteringly:*

ARTHUR. Ma, I'm sorry. I'm sorry for what I said.

He bursts into tears and puts his forehead against her elbow.

MA. There. There. We all say wicked things at times. I know you didn't mean it like it sounded.

He weeps still more violently than before.

Why, now, now! I forgive you, Arthur, and tonight before

you go to bed you . . . (*She whispers.*) You're a good boy at heart, Arthur, and we all know it.

Caroline *starts to cry too.*

Ma *is suddenly joyously alive and happy.*

Sakes alive, it's too nice a day for us all to be cryin'. Come now, get in. You go up in front with your father, Caroline. Ma wants to sit with her beau. I never saw such children. Your hot dogs are all getting wet. Now chew them fine, everybody.—All right, Elmer, forward march.—Caroline, whatever are you doing?

CAROLINE. I'm spitting out the leather, ma.

MA. Then say: Excuse me.

CAROLINE. Excuse me, please.

MA. What's this place? Arthur, did you see the post office?

ARTHUR. It said Lawrenceville.

MA. Hhm. School. Kinda nice. I wonder what that big yellow house set back was.—Now it's beginning to be Trenton.

CAROLINE. Papa, it was near here that George Washington crossed the Delaware. It was near Trenton, mamma. He was first in war and first in peace, and first in the hearts of his countrymen.

MA (*surveying the passing world, serene and didactic*). Well, the thing I liked about him best was that he never told a lie.

The children are duly cast down.

There is a pause.

There's a sunset for you. There's nothing like a good sunset.

ARTHUR. There's an Ohio license in front of us. Ma, have you ever been to Ohio?

MA. No.

A dreamy silence descends upon them.

Caroline *sits closer to her father.*

Ma *puts her arm around* Arthur.

ARTHUR. Ma, what a lotta people there are in the world, ma. There must be thousands and thousands in the United States. Ma, how many are there?

MA. I don't know. Ask your father.

ARTHUR. Pa, how many are there?

ELMER. There are a hundred and twenty-six million, Kate.

MA (*giving a pressure about* Arthur's *shoulder*). And they all like to drive out in the evening with their children beside'm.

Another pause.

Why doesn't somebody sing something? Arthur, you're always singing something; what's the matter with you?

ARTHUR. All right. What'll we sing? (*He sketches:*)
"In the Blue-Ridge Mountains of Virginia,
On the trail of the lonesome pine . . ."
No, I don't like that any more. Let's do:
"I been workin' on de railroad
All de liblong day.
I been workin' on de railroad
Just to pass de time away."

Caroline *joins in at once.*
Finally even Ma *is singing.*
Even Pa *is singing.*
Ma *suddenly jumps up with a wild cry:*

MA. Elmer, that signpost said Camden, I saw it.

ELMER. All right, Kate, if you're sure.

Much shifting of gears, backing and jolting.

MA. Yes, there it is, Camden—five miles. Dear old Beulah.—Now, children, you be good and quiet during dinner. She's just got out of bed after a big sorta operation, and we must all move around kinda quiet. First you drop me and Caroline at the door and just say hello, and then you men-folk go over to the Y.M.C.A. and come back for dinner in about an hour.

CAROLINE (*shutting her eyes and pressing her fists passionately against her nose*). I see the first star. Everybody make a wish.
Star light, star bright,
First star I seen tonight.
I wish I may, I wish I might
Have the wish I wish tonight.
(*then solemnly*) Pins. Mamma, you say "needles."

She interlocks little fingers with her mother.

MA. Needles.

CAROLINE. Shakespeare. Ma, you say "Longfellow."

MA. Longfellow.

CAROLINE. Now it's a secret and I can't tell it to anybody. Ma, you make a wish.

MA (*with almost grim humor*). No, I can make wishes without waiting for no star. And I can tell my wishes right out loud too. Do you want to hear them?

CAROLINE (*resignedly*). No, ma, we know'm already. We've heard'm. (*She hangs her head affectedly on her left shoulder and says with unmalicious mimicry:*) You want me to be a good girl and you want Arthur to be honest-in-word-and-deed.

MA (*Majestically*). Yes. So mind yourself.

ELMER. Caroline, take out that letter from Beulah in my coat pocket by you and read aloud the places I marked with red pencil.

CAROLINE (*working*). *"A few blocks after you pass the two big oil tanks on your left . . ."*

EVERYBODY (*pointing backward*). There they are!

CAROLINE. *". . . you come to a corner where there's an A and P store on the left and a firehouse kitty-corner to it . . ."*

They all jubilantly identify these landmarks.

". . . turn right, go two blocks, and our house is Weyerhauser St. Number 471."

MA. It's an even nicer street than they used to live in. And right handy to an A and P.

CAROLINE (*whispering*). Ma, it's better than our street. It's richer than our street.—Ma, isn't Beulah richer than we are?

MA (*looking at her with a firm and glassy eye*). Mind yourself, missy. I don't want to hear anybody talking about rich or not rich when I'm around. If people aren't nice I don't care how rich they are. I live in the best street in the world because my husband and children live there.

She glares impressively at Caroline *a moment to let this lesson sink in, then looks up, sees* Beulah, *and waves.*

There's Beulah standing on the steps lookin' for us.

Beulah *has appeared and is waving.*

They all call out: Hello Beulah—Hello.

Presently they are all getting out of the car. Beulah *kisses her father long and affectionately.*

BEULAH. Hello, papa. Good old papa. You look tired, pa.—Hello, mamma.—Lookit how Arthur and Caroline are growing!

MA. They are bursting all their clothes!—Yes, your pa needs a rest. Thank Heaven, his vacation has come just now. We'll feed him up and let him sleep late. Pa has a present for you, Loolie. He would go and buy it.

BEULAH. Why, pa, you're terrible to go and buy anything for me. Isn't he terrible?

MA. Well, it's a secret. You can open it at dinner.

ELMER. Where's Horace, Loolie?

BEULAH. He was kep' over a little at the office. He'll be here any minute. He's crazy to see you all.

MA. All right. You men go over to the Y and come back in about an hour.

BEULAH (*as her father returns to the wheel, stands out in the street beside him*). Go straight along, pa, you can't miss it. It just stares at yuh. (*She puts her arm around his neck and rubs *her nose against his temple.*) Crazy old pa, goin' buyin' things! It's me that ought to be buyin' things for you, pa.

ELMER. Oh, no! There's only one Loolie in the world.

BEULAH (*whispering, as her eyes fill with tears*). Are you glad I'm still alive, pa?

She kisses him abruptly and goes back to the house steps. The Stage Manager *removes the automobile with the help of* Elmer *and* Arthur *who go off waving their good-bys.*

Well, come on upstairs, ma, and take off your things. Caroline, there's a surprise for you in the back yard.

CAROLINE. Rabbits?

BEULAH. No.

Caroline *runs off stage.*

Beulah *and* Ma *gradually go upstairs.*

There are two new puppies. You be thinking over whether you can keep one in Newark.

MA. I guess we can. It's a nice house, Beulah. You just got a *lovely* home.

BEULAH. When I got back from the hospital, Horace had moved everything into it, and there wasn't anything for me to do.

MA. It's lovely.

The Stage Manager *pushes out a bed from the left. Its foot is toward the right.* Beulah *sits on it, testing the springs.*

BEULAH. I think you'll find the bed comfortable, ma.

MA (*taking off her hat*). Oh, I could sleep on a heapa shoes, Loolie! I don't have no trouble sleepin'. (*She sits down beside her.*) Now let me look at my girl. Well, well, when I last saw you, you didn't know me. You kep' sayin' *When's mamma comin'? When's mamma comin'?* But the doctor sent me away.

BEULAH (*Puts her head on her mother's shoulder and weeps*). It was awful, mamma. It was awful. She didn't even live a few minutes, mamma. It was awful.

MA (*looking far away*). God thought best, dear. God thought best. We don't understand why. We just go on, honey, doin' our business.

Then almost abruptly—passing the back of her hand across her cheek.

Well, now, what are we giving the men to eat tonight?

BEULAH. There's a chicken in the oven.

MA. What time didya put it in?

BEULAH (*restraining her*). Aw, ma, don't go yet. I like to sit here with you this way. You always get the fidgets when we try and pet yuh, mamma.

MA (*ruefully, laughing*). Yes, it's kinda foolish. I'm just an old Newark bag-a-bones. (*She glances at the backs of her hands.*)

BEULAH (*indignantly*). Why, ma, you're good-lookin'! We always said you were good-lookin'.—And besides, you're the best ma we could ever have.

MA (*uncomfortable*). Well, I hope you like me. There's nothing like being liked by your family.—Now I'm going downstairs to look at the chicken. You stretch out here for a minute and shut your eyes.—Have you got everything laid in for breakfast before the shops close?

BEULAH. Oh, you know! Ham and eggs.

They both laugh.

MA. I declare I never could understand what men see in ham and eggs. I think they're horrible.—What time did you put the chicken in?

BEULAH. Five o'clock.

MA. Well, now, you shut your eyes for ten minutes.

Beulah *stretches out and shuts her eyes.*

Ma *descends the stairs absent-mindedly singing*:

"There were ninety and nine that safely lay
In the shelter of the fold,
But one was out on the hills away,
Far off from the gates of gold. . . ."

And the curtain falls.

Discussion of "The Happy Journey to Trenton and Camden"

A play such as "The Happy Journey"—which seems so uniquely American—is not what one might expect from a playright whose early education took place in a German school in Hong Kong and in an English mission school in Chefoo, China. Although he spent part of his youth in the United States, in his early twenties Thornton Wilder (1897-) was again abroad at the American academy in Rome. His early novels, such as *The Cabala, The Bridge of San Luis Rey* and *The Woman of Andros* all have settings and points of view which reflect this cosmopolitan background. With the publication of *The Long Christmas*

Dinner and Other Plays in 1931 ("The Happy Journey" is one of these) Wilder moves from the exotic to the ordinary and focuses on the revelation which the unexceptional can provide.

His success as a novelist, for *The Bridge of San Luis Rey* brought him the first of three Pulitzer Prizes and was an immediate best-seller, did not convince him that the novel was the best form suited to his talents. Indeed, he has insisted that "the theatre offers to an imaginative narration its highest possibilities." In support of this contention, Wilder suggests that the dramatic form offers the following advantages: On the stage it is always *now*, while in a novel there must be an intervening story-teller who is reporting the past in the present. A play, therefore, is what takes place. A novel is what one person tells us took place. This gives the drama a temporal vitality which the novel cannot match.

The second way in which the theatre is superior is that it is fundamentally *pretense* and therefore must live by conventions. Such conventions are agreed upon make-believe which provide participation by the spectator and which raise the action from the specific to the general. If we are presented with a chair on stage which we are told is to stand for a boat, we must use our imaginations if we are to follow the action which the playright is trying to provide. We thus become collaborators in creating the drama unfolding before us. In addition, the very fact that the chair doesn't really resemble a boat very accurately frees this symbol from representing just one boat. It is this generalized truth that the stage tries to tell, and it is the element of pretense which reinforces it. The novel is usually confined to a particular action—what happened "once upon a time."

Reading "The Happy Journey" instead of performing or seeing it may qualify the advantages mentioned above, but it does not entirely eliminate them. Note, for instance, the opening stage directions. There is no real scenery and only a few stage props. The stage manager takes all the minor parts, and we are explicitly told that he is to give no distinguishing characterization to them. Such an opening demands that we supply the "missing" background, and in so doing we become part of the creative act of the play.

The details of this profoundly simple play are real enough, yet note how conventional most of them are. The make of car, the father's job, the passing comments are all typical as well as particular. The very familiarity of the characters and situations calls forth a strong emotional response. We needn't have been acquainted with anyone exactly like the Kirbys, but they somehow seem to exemplify all the ordinary families we have ever known. The danger in such representation is that it may turn into caricature. How Wilder manages to keep his dramatic family in perfect match with the common image of the American lower middle class without resorting to satire or mere reporting is the genius of this play.

The growing sense of warmth, generated primarily by simplicity of dialogue, reaches a climax when the family arrives at the home of their married daughter. The stage at this point is so barren of ornament that all we have left are embodiments of love, understanding, courage, hope, security—in sum, happiness. And it is the mother who has turned this mixture into a compound. Although a number of her less attractive characteristics are casually displayed in this short piece, Mrs. Kirby is an appealingly human person. She handles youthful rebellion promptly and decisively, yet shows immediately that "increase" of love which the *Doctrine and Covenants* suggests should follow reproof. Her humor may be heavy-handed, and her conversation verges on the garrulous; yet she never stops trying to share her own zest for living with friends, family and even chance acquaintances.

L'Allegro

John Milton

Hence, loathed Melancholy,
Of Cerberus[1] and blackest Midnight born
In Stygian[2] cave forlorn,
'Mongst horrid shapes and shrieks and sights unholy!
Find out some uncouth[3] cell,
Where brooding darkness spreads his jealous wings,
And the night-raven sings;
There under ebon[4] shades and low-browed rocks,
As ragged as thy locks,
In dark Cimmerian[5] desert ever dwell.
But come, thou Goddess fair and free,
In heaven yclept[6] Euphrosyne,[7]
And by men heart-easing Mirth;
Whom lovely Venus, at a birth,
With two sister Graces more,
To ivy-crowned Bacchus bore;
Or whether (as some sager sing)
The frolic wind that breathes the spring,
Zephyr,[8] with Aurora[9] playing,
As he met her once a-Maying,
There on beds of violets blue
And fresh-blown roses washed in dew,
Filled her with thee, a daughter fair,
So buxom,[10] blithe, and debonair.
Haste thee, nymph, and bring with thee
Jest, and youthful Jollity,
Quips and cranks[11] and wanton wiles,

[1]the three-headed dog that guarded the entrance to Hades.
[2]of the infernal regions; the Styx was one of the rivers of Hades.
[3]unknown, strange.
[4]black.
[5]See *Odyssey,* xi, 14; a land of perpetual darkness and mist.
[6]called.
[7]Mirth, one of the three Graces.
[8]the west wind.
[9]the dawn.
[10]lively.
[11]conceits, clever turns of speech.

Nods and becks and wreathed smiles,
Such as hang on Hebe's[12] cheek,
And love to live in dimple sleek;
Sport that wrinkled Care derides,
And Laughter holding both his sides.
Come, and trip it as you go,
On the light fantastic toe;
And in thy right hand lead with thee
The mountain nymph, sweet Liberty;
And if I give thee honour due,
Mirth, admit me of thy crew,
To live with her, and live with thee,
In unreproved[13] pleasures free:
To hear the lark begin his flight,
And singing, startle the dull night,
From his watch-tower in the skies,
Till the dappled dawn doth rise;
Then to come in spite of sorrow,
And at my window bid good-morrow,
Through the sweet-briar or the vine,
Or the twisted eglantine;
While the cock, with lively din,
Scatters the rear of darkness thin,
And to the stack, or the barn-door,
Stoutly struts his dames before:
Oft listening how the hounds and horn
Cheerly rouse the slumbering morn,
From the side of some hoar hill,
Through the high wood echoing shrill:
Sometime walking not unseen,
By hedge-row elms, on hillocks green,
Right against the eastern gate
Where the great sun begins his state,[14]
Robed in flames and amber light,
The clouds in thousand liveries dight;[15]
While the ploughman, near at hand,
Whistles o'er the furrowed land,
And the milkmaid singeth blithe,
And the mower whets his scythe,

---

[12]the cup-bearer of the gods.
[13]blameless.
[14]triumphal progress.
[15]adorned.

And every shepherd tells his tale
Under the hawthorn in the dale.
Straight mine eye hath caught new pleasures
Whilst the landskip round it measures:
Russet lawns[16] and fallows[17] grey,
Where the nibbling flocks do stray;
Mountains on whose barren breast
The labouring clouds do often rest;
Meadows trim with daisies pied,
Shallow brooks and rivers wide;
Towers and battlements it sees
Bosomed high in tufted trees,
Where perhaps some beauty lies,
The cynosure[18] of neighbouring eyes.
Hard by, a cottage chimney smokes
From betwixt two aged oaks,
Where Corydon[19] and Thyrsis met
Are of their savoury dinner set
Of herbs and other country messes,
Which the neat-handed Phillis dresses;
And then in haste her bower she leaves,
With Thestylis to bind the sheaves;
Or, if the earlier season lead,
To the tanned haycock in the mead.
Sometimes, with secure[20] delight,
The upland hamlets will invite,
When the merry bells ring round,
And the jocund rebecks[21] sound
To many a youth and many a maid
Dancing in the chequered shade;
And young and old come forth to play
On a sunshine holiday,
Till the livelong daylight fail;
Then to the spice nut-brown ale,
With stories told of many a feat,
How faery Mab[22] the junkets eat.

---

[16]open fields.
[17]untilled or unsowed land.
[18]center of attraction.
[19]This and the names that follow are common in pastoral poetry; cf. Matthew Arnold's *Thyrsis*.
[20]carefree.
[21]fiddles.
[22]a fairy traditionally both tormentor and patron of servant maids.

She was pinched and pulled, she said;
And he, by friar's lantern[23] led,
Tells how the drudging goblin[24] sweat
To earn his cream-bowl duly set,
When in one night, ere glimpse of morn,
His shadowy flail hath threshed the corn
That ten day-labourers could not end;
Then lies him down, the lubber[25] fiend,
And, stretched out all the chimney's length,
Basks at the fire his hairy strength,
And crop-full out of doors he flings,
Ere the first cock his matin[26] rings.
Thus done the tales, to bed they creep,
By whispering winds soon lulled asleep.
Towered cities please us then,
And the busy hum of men,
Where throngs of knights and barons bold,
In weeds[27] of peace high triumphs hold,
With store of ladies, whose bright eyes
Rain influence[28] and judge the prize
Of wit or arms, while both contend
To win her grace whom all commend.
There let Hymen[29] oft appear
In saffron robe, with taper clear,
And pomp and feast and revelry,
With mask and antique pageantry;
Such sights as youthful poets dream
On summer eves by haunted stream.
Then to the well-trod stage anon,
If Jonson's[30] learned sock[31] be on,
Or sweetest Shakespear, Fancy's child,
Warble his native wood-notes wild.
And ever, against eating cares,
Lap me in soft Lydian[32] airs,

---

[23]the will o' the wisp.
[24]Robin Goodfellow.
[25]clumsy.
[26]morning song.
[27]garments.
[28]like the stars.
[29]god of marriage.
[30]Ben Jonson (1572-1637), author of *Volpone, Sejanus, The Alchemist,* etc.
[31]the light shoe worn by actors in ancient classical comedy.
[32]a sweet and delicate variety of Greek music.

Married to immortal verse,
Such as the meeting soul may pierce.
In notes with many a winding bout[33]
Of linked sweetness long drawn out,
With wanton heed and giddy cunning,
The melting voice through mazes running,
Untwisting all the chains that tie
The hidden soul of harmony;
That Orpheus'[34] self may heave his head
From golden slumber on a bed
Of heaped Elysian flowers, and hear
Such strains as would have won the ear
Of Pluto to have quite set free
His half-regained Eurydice.
These delights if thou canst give,
Mirth, with thee I mean to live.

Discussion of "L'Allegro"

John Milton (1608-1674) was born in London, the son of John and Sarah Milton. His father, a scrivener, had made a comfortable future in his business of drawing up business contracts, and was a musician and composer as well. The mother, of whom little is known, destined her son for the church and devoted herself to his religious training.

Encouraged by his father, young John began writing verse in imitation of classical models at an early age and soon gave up his early intention to enter the ministry in favor of a career in letters. His schooling at Cambridge reinforced his desire for literary eminence, and extensive travel abroad gave him a breadth of experience not common to his contemporaries.

Although the works which put him in the front rank among English poets—*Paradise Lost, Paradise Regained,*

[33]turn, involution.

[34]Orpheus obtained the release of his wife Eurydice from the lower regions by his music, but against Pluto's command he looked back at her when they were nearly out, and she vanished.

and *Samson Agonistes*—show Milton at his majestic best, the shorter—and earlier—poems demonstrate a skill which promises the great achievements to come. *L'Allegro,* for instance, is now thought to have been written as early as Milton's residence at Cambridge. With its companion piece, *Il Penseroso,* this exercise in mood creation has been one of the most popular poems in the English language.

Reasons for this esteem are not difficult to find. The happily modulated lines in which Milton describes a day in the life of a cheerful man (this is a reasonable translation of the Italian title) use appropriate mythological and pastoral imagery to build up a mood of contentment. The poem is full of light and movement. From the mock serious dismissal of "loathed Melancholy" in the opening lines to the serene resolution of its close, this work is a carefully controlled development. There is a prevailing sense of dignity in Milton's description of agricultural labor but it is never ponderous. The lighthearted tone remains crisp and authentic.

The metrical pattern is interesting. After a ten-line introduction made up of alternate trimeters (three feet) and pentameters (five feet) rhyming *abbacddee,* the remainder is in octosyllabic couplets. The balance of these lines helps us to understand that human experience has balancing, complementary sides. The aim of life is not uninterrupted gaiety. But we should be capable of responding fully to the gifts of each day. From the bright invitation of the morning lark, through simple but satisfying labor to the relaxation of evening music there is as much happiness as man is willing to claim in the daily routine of his life.

The Flight of Betsey Lane

Sarah Orne Jewett

One windy morning in May, three old women sat together near an open window in the shed chamber of Byfleet Poor-house. The wind was from the northwest, but their window faced the southeast, and they were only visited by an occasional pleasant waft of fresh air. They were close together, knee to knee, picking over a bushel of beans, and commanding a view of the dandelion-starred, green yard below, and of the winding, sandy road that led to the village, two miles away. Some captive bees were scolding among the cobwebs of the rafters overhead, or thumping against the upper panes of glass; two calves were bawling from the barnyard, where some of the men were at work loading a dump-cart and shouting as if everyone were deaf. There was a cheerful feeling of activity, and even an air of comfort, about the Byfleet Poor-house. Almost everyone was possessed of a most interesting past, though there was less to be said about the future. The inmates were by no means distressed or unhappy; many of them retired to this shelter only for the winter season, and would go out presently, some to begin such work as they could still do, others to live in their own small houses; old age had impoverished most of them by limiting their power of endurance; but far from lamenting the fact that they were town charges, they rather liked the change and excitement of a winter residence on the poor-farm. There was a sharp-faced, hard-worked young widow with seven children, who was an exception to the general level of society, because she deplored the change in her fortunes. The older women regarded her with suspicion, and were apt to talk about her in moments like this, when they happened to sit together at their work.

The three bean-pickers were dressed alike in stout brown ginghams, checked by a white line, and all wore great faded aprons of blue drilling, with sufficient pockets convenient to the right hand. Miss Peggy Bond was a very small, belligerent-looking person, who wore a huge pair of steel-bowed spectacles, holding her sharp chin well up in air, as if to supplement an inadequate nose. She was more than half blind, but the spectacles seemed to face upward instead of square ahead, as if their wearer were always on the sharp lookout for birds. Miss Bond had suffered much personal damage from time to time, because she never took heed where she planted her feet, and so was always tripping and stubbing her bruised way through the world. She had fallen down hatchways and cellarways, and stepped composedly into deep ditches and pasture brooks; but she was proud of stating that she was upsighted, and so was her father before her. At the poor-house, where an unusual malady was considered a distinction, upsightedness was looked upon as a most honorable infirmity. Plain rheumatism, such as afflicted Aunt Lavina Dow, whose twisted hands found even this light work difficult and tiresome,—plain rheumatism was something of every-day occurrence, and nobody cared to hear about it. Poor Peggy was a meek and friendly soul, who never put herself forward; she was just like other folks, as she always loved to say, but Mrs. Lavina Dow was a different sort of person altogether, of great dignity and, occasionally, almost aggressive behavior. The time had been when she could do a good day's work with anybody: but for many years now she had not left the town-farm, being too badly crippled to work; she had no relations or friends to visit, but from an innate love of authority she could not submit to being one of those who are forgotten by the world. Mrs. Dow was the hostess and social lawgiver here, where she remembered every inmate and every item of interest for nearly forty years, besides an immense amount of town history and biography for three or four generations back.

She was the dear friend of the third woman, Betsey Lane; together they led thought and opinion—chiefly opinion—and held sway, not only over Byfleet Poor-farm, but also the selectmen and all others in authority. Betsey Lane had spent most of her life as aid-in-general to the respected household of old General Thornton. She had been much trusted and valued, and, at the breaking up of that once large and flourishing family, she had been left in good circumstances, what with legacies and her own comfortable savings; but by sad misfortune and lavish generosity everything had been scattered, and after much illness, which ended in a stiffened arm and more uncertainty, the good soul had sensibly decided that it was easier for the whole town to support her than for a part of it. She had always hoped to see something of the world before she died; she came of an adventurous, seafaring stock, but had never made a longer journey than to the towns of Danby and Northville, thirty miles away.

They were all old women; but Betsey Lane, who was sixty-nine, and looked much older, was the youngest. Peggy Bond was far on in the seventies, and Mrs. Dow was at least ten years older. She made a great secret of her years; and as she sometimes spoke of events prior to the Revolution with the assertion of having been an eye-witness, she naturally wore an air of vast antiquity. Her tales were an inexpressible delight to Betsey Lane, who felt younger by twenty years because her friend and comrade was so unconscious of chronological limitations.

The bushel basket of cranberry beans was within easy reach, and each of the pickers had filled her lap from it again and again. The shed chamber was not an unpleasant place in which to sit at work, with its traces of seed corn hanging from the brown cross-beams, its spare churns, and dusty loom, and rickety wool-wheels, and a few bits of old furniture. In one far corner was a wide board of dismal use and suggestion, and close beside it an old cradle. There was a battered chest of drawers where the keeper of the poor-house kept his garden-seeds, with the withered remains of three seed cucumbers ornamenting the top. Nothing beautiful could be discovered, nothing interesting, but there was something usable and homely about the place. It was the favorite and untroubled bower of the bean-pickers, to which they might retreat unmolested from the public apartments of this rustic institution.

Betsey Lane blew away the chaff from her handful of beans. The spring breeze blew the chaff back again, and sifted it over her face and shoulders. She rubbed it out of her eyes impatiently, and happened to notice old Peggy holding her own handful high, as if it were an oblation, and turning her queer, up-tilted head this way and that, to look at the beans sharply, as if she were first cousin to a hen.

"There, Miss Bond, 'tis kind of botherin' work for you, ain't it?" Betsey inquired compassionately.

"I feel to enjoy it, anything that I can do my own way so," responded Peggy. "I like to do my part. Ain't that old Mis' Fales comin' up the road? It sounds like her step."

The others looked, but they were not farsighted, and for a moment Peggy had the advantage. Mrs. Fales was not a favorite.

"I hope she ain't comin' here to put up this spring. I guess she won't now, it's gettin' so late," said Betsey Lane. "She likes to go rovin' soon as the roads is settled."

" 'Tis Mis' Fales!" said Peggy Bond, listening with solemn anxiety. "There, do let's pray her by!"

"I guess she's headin' for her cousin's folks up Beech Hill way," said Betsey presently. "If she'd left her daughter's this mornin', she'd have got just about as far as this. I kind o' wish she had stepped in just to pass the time o' day, long's she wa'n't going to make no stop."

There was a silence as to further speech in the shed chamber; and even the calves were quiet in the barnyard. The men had all gone away to the field where corn-planting was going on. The beans clicked steadily into the wooden measure at the picker's feet. Betsey Lane began to sing a hymn, and the others joined in as best they might, like autumnal crickets; their voices were sharp and cracked, with now and then a few low notes of plaintive tone. Betsey herself could sing pretty well, but the others could only make a kind of accompaniment. Their voices ceased altogether at the higher notes.

"Oh my! I wish I had the means to go to the Centennial," mourned Betsey Lane, stopping so suddenly that the others had to go on croaking and shrilling without her for a moment before they could stop. "It seems to me as if I can't die happy 'less I do," she added; "I ain't never seen nothin' of the world, an' here I be."

"What if you was as old as I be?" suggested Mrs. Dow pompously. "You've got time enough yet, Betsey; don't you go an' despair. I knowed of a woman that went clean around the world four times when she was past eighty, and enjoyed herself real well. Her folks followed the sea; she had three sons an' a daughter married,—all shipmasters, and she'd been with her own husband when they was young. She was left a widder early, and fetched up her family herself,—a real stirrin', smart woman. After they'd got married off, an' settled, an' was doing well, she come to be lonesome; and first she tried to stick it out alone, but she wa'n't one that could; an' she got a notion she hadn't nothin' before her but her last sickness, and she wa'n't a person that enjoyed havin' other folks do for her. So one on her boys—I guess 't was the oldest—said he was going to take her to sea; there was ample room, an' he was sailin' a good time o' year for the Cape o' Good Hope an' way up to some o' them tea-ports in the Chiny Seas. She was all high to go, but it made a sight o' talk at her age; an' the minister made it a subject o' prayer the last Sunday, and all the folks took a last leave; but she said to some she'd fetch 'em home something real pritty, and so did. An' then they come home t' other way, round the Horn, an' she done so well, an' was such a sight o' company, the other child'n was jealous, an' she promised she'd go a v'y'ge long o' each of 'em. She was as sprightly a person as ever I see; an' could speak well o' what she'd seen."

"Did she die to sea?" asked Peggy, with interest.

"No, she died to home between v'y'ges, or she'd gone to sea again. I was to her funeral. She liked her son George's ship the best; 'twas the one she was going on to Callao. They said the men aboard all called her 'gran' ma'am,' an' she kep' 'em mended up, an' would go below and tend to 'em if they was sick. She might 'a' been alive an' enjoyin' of herself a good many years but for the kick of a cow; 't was a new cow out of a drove, a dreadful unruly beast."

Mrs. Dow stopped for breath, and reached down for a new supply of beans; her empty apron was gray with soft chaff. Betsey Lane, still pondering on the Centennial, began to sing another verse of her hymn, and again the old women joined her. At this moment some strangers came driving round into the yard from the front of the house. The turf was soft, and our friends did not hear the horses' steps. Their voices cracked and quavered; it was a funny little concert, and a lady in an open carriage just below listened with sympathy and amusement.

II.

"Betsey! Betsey! Miss Lane!" a voice called eagerly at the foot of the stairs that led up from the shed. "Betsey! There's a lady here wants to see you right away."

Betsey was dazed with excitement, like a country child who knows the rare pleasure of being called out of school. "Lor', I ain't fit to go down, be I?" she faltered, looking anxiously at her friends; but Peggy was gazing even nearer to the zenith than usual, in her excited effort to see down into the yard, and Mrs. Dow only nodded somewhat jealously, and said that she guessed 'twas nobody would do her any harm. She rose ponderously, while Betsey hesitated, being, as they would have said, all of a twitter. "It is a lady, certain," Mrs. Dow assured her; " 'tain't often there's a lady comes here."

"While there was any of Mis' Gen'ral Thornton's folks left, I wa'n't without visits from the gentry," said Betsey Lane, turning back proudly at the head of the stairs, with a touch of old-world pride and sense of high station. Then she disappeared, and closed the door behind her at the stairfoot with a decision quite unwelcome to the friends above.

"She needn't 'a' been so dreadful 'fraid anybody was goin' to listen. I guess we've got folks to ride an' see us, or had once, if we hain't now," said Miss Peggy Bond, plaintively.

"I expect 'twas only the wind shoved it to," said Aunt Lavina. "Betsey is one that gits flustered easier than some. I wish 'twas somebody to take her off an' give her a kind of a good time; she's young to settle down 'long of old folks like us. Betsey's got a notion o' rovin' such as ain't my natur', but I should like to see her satisfied. She'd been a very understandin' person, if she had the advantages that some does."

"Tis so," said Peggy Bond, tilting her chin high. "I suppose you can't hear nothin' they're saying? I feel my hearin' ain't up to whar it was. I can hear things close to me well as ever; but there, hearin' ain't everything; 'tain't as if we lived where there was more goin' on to hear. Seems to me them folks is stoppin' a good while."

"They surely be," agreed Lavina Dow.

"I expect it's somethin' particular. There ain't none of the Thornton folks left, except one o' the gran'darters, an' I've often heard Betsey remark that she should never see her more, for she lives to London. Strange how folks feels contented in them strayaway places off to the ends of the airth."

The flies and bees were buzzing against the hot window-panes; the handfuls of beans were clicking into the brown wooden measure. A bird came and perched on the window-sill, and then flitted away toward the blue sky. Below, in the yard, Betsey Lane stood talking with the lady. She had put her blue drilling apron over head, and her face was shining with delight.

"Lor', dear," she said, for at least the third time, "I remember ye when I first see ye; an awful pretty baby you was, an' they all said you looked just like the old gen'ral. Be you goin' back to foreign parts right away?"

"Yes, I'm going back; you know that all my children are there. I wish I could take you with me for a visit," said the charming young guest. "I'm going to carry over some of the pictures and furniture from the old house; I didn't care half so much for them when I was younger as I do now. Perhaps next summer we shall all come over for a while. I should like to see my girls and boys playing under the pines."

"I wish you re'lly was livin' to the old place," said Betsey Lane. Her imagination was not swift; she needed time to think over all that was being told her, and she could not fancy the two strange houses across the sea. The old Thornton house was to her mind the most delightful and elegant in the world.

"Is there anything I can do for you?" asked Mrs. Strafford kindly,—"anything that I can do for you myself, before I go away? I shall be writing to you, and sending some pictures of the children, and you must let me know how you are getting on."

"Yes, there is one thing, darlin'. If you could stop in the village an' pick me out a pritty, little, small lookin'-glass, that I can keep for my own an' have to remember you by. "Tain't that I want to set me above the rest o' the folks, but I was always used to havin' my own when I was to your grandma's. There's very nice folks here, some on 'em, and I'm better off than if I was able to keep house;

but sence you ask me, that's the only thing I feel cropin' about. What be you goin' right back for? ain't you goin' to see the great fair to Pheladelphy, that everybody talks about?"

"No," said Mrs. Strafford, laughing at this eager and almost convicting question. "No; I'm going back next week. If I were, I believe that I should take you with me. Good-by, dear old Betsey; you make me feel as if I were a little girl again; you look just the same."

For full five minutes the old woman stood out in the sunshine, dazed with delight, and majestic with a sense of her own consequence. She held something tight in her hand, without thinking what it might be; but just as the friendly mistress of the poor-farm came out to hear the news, she tucked the roll of money into the bosom of her brown gingham dress. " 'Twas my dear Mis' Katy Strafford," she turned to say proudly. "She come way over from London; she's been sick; they thought the voyage would do her good. She said most the first thing she had on her mind was to come an' find me, and see how I was, an' if I was comfortable; and now she's goin' right back. She's got two splendid houses; an' said how she wished I was there to look after things,—and remembered I was always her gran'ma's right hand. Oh, it does so carry me back, to see her! Seems if all the rest on 'em must be there together to the old house. There, I must go right up an' tell Mis' Dow an' Peggy."

"Dinner's all ready; I was just goin' to blow the horn for the men-folks," said the keeper's wife. "They'll be right down. I expect you've got along smart with them beans,—all three of you together;" but Betsey's mind roved so high and so far at that moment that no achievements of bean-picking could lure it back.

III.

The long table in the great kitchen soon gathered its company of waifs and strays,—creatures of improvidence and misfortune, and the irreparable victims of old age. The dinner was satisfactory, and there was not much delay for conversation. Peggy Bond and Mrs. Dow and Betsey Lane always sat together at one end, with an air of putting the rest of the company below the salt. Betsey was still flushed with excitement; in fact, she could not eat as much as usual, and she looked up from time to time expectantly, as if she were likely to be asked to speak of her guest; but everybody was hungry, and even Mrs. Dow broke in upon some attempted confidences by asking inopportunely for a second potato. There were nearly twenty at the table, counting the keeper and his wife and two children, noisy little persons who had come from school with the small flock belonging to the poor widow, who sat just opposite our friends. She finished her dinner before any one else, and pushed her chair back; she always helped with the housework,—a thin, sorry, bad-tempered-looking poor soul, whom grief had sharpened instead of softening. "I expect you feel too fine to set with common folks," she said enviously to Betsy.

"Here I be a-settin'," responded Betsey calmly. "I don' know's I behave more unbecomin' than usual." Betsey prided herself upon her good and proper manners; but the rest of the company, who would have liked to hear the bit of morning news, were now defrauded of that pleasure. The wrong note had been struck; there was a silence after the clatter of knives and plates, and one by one the cheerful town charges disappeared. The bean-picking had been finished, and there was a call for any of the women who felt like planting corn; so Peggy Bond, who could follow the line of hills pretty fairly, and Betsey herself, who was still equal to anybody at that work, and Mrs. Dow, all went out to the field together. Aunt Lavina labored slowly up the yard, carrying a light splint-bottomed kitchen chair and her knitting-work, and sat near the stone wall on a gentle rise, where she could see the pond and the green country, and exchange a word with her friends as they came and went up and down the rows. Betsey vouchsafed a word now and then about Mrs. Strafford, but you would have thought that she had been suddenly elevated to Mrs. Strafford's own cares and the responsibilities attending them and had little in common with her old associates. Mrs. Dow and Peggy knew well that these high-feeling times never lasted long, and so they waited with as much patience as they could muster. They were by no means without that true tact which is only another word for unselfish sympathy.

The strip of corn land ran along the side of a great field; at the upper end of it was a field-corner thicket of young maples and walnut saplings, the children of a great nut-tree that marked the boundary. Once, when Betsey Lane found herself alone near this shelter at the end of her row, the other planters having lagged behind beyond the rising ground, she looked stealthily about, and then put her hand inside her gown, and for the first time took out the money that Mrs. Strafford had given her. She turned it over and over with an astonished look: there were new bank-bills for a hundred dollars. Betsey gave a funny little shrug of her shoulders, came out of the bushes, and took a step or two on the narrow edge of turf, as if she were going to dance; then she hastily tucked away her treasure, and stepped discreetly down into the soft harrowed and hoed land,

and began to drop corn again, five kernels to a hill. She had seen the top of Peggy Bond's head over the knoll, and now Peggy herself came entirely into view, gazing upward to the skies, and stumbling more or less, but counting the corn by touch and twisting her head about anxiously to gain advantage over her uncertain vision. Betsey made a friendly, inarticulate little sound as they passed; she was thinking that somebody said once that Peggy's eyesight might be remedied if she could go to Boston to the hospital; but that was so remote and impossible an undertaking that no one had ever taken the first step. Betsey Lane's brown old face suddenly worked with excitement, but in a moment more she regained her usual firm expression, and spoke carelessly to Peggy as she turned and came alongside.

The high spring wind of the morning had quite fallen; it was a lovely May afternoon. The woods about the field to the northward were full of birds; and the young leaves scarcely hid the solemn shapes of a company of crows that patiently attended the corn-planting. Two of the men had finished their hoeing, and were busy with the construction of a scarecrow; they knelt in the furrows, chuckling, and looking over some forlorn, discarded garments. It was a time-honored custom to make a scarecrow resemble one of the poorhouse family; and this year they intended to have Mrs. Lavina Dow protect the field in effigy; last year it was the counterfeit of Betsey Lane who stood on guard, with an easily recognized quilted hood and the remains of a valued shawl that one of the calves had found airing on a fence and chewed to pieces. Behind the men was the foundation for this rustic attempt at statuary,—an upright stake and bar in the form of a cross. This stood on the highest part of the field; and as the men knelt near it, and the quaint figures of the corn-planters went and came, the scene gave a curious suggestion of foreign life. It was not like New England; the presence of the rude cross appealed strangely to the imagination.

IV.

Life flowed so smoothly, for the most part, at the Byfleet Poor-farm, that nobody knew what to make, later in the summer, of a strange disappearance. All the elder inmates were familiar with illness and death, and the poor pomp of a town-pauper's funeral. The comings and goings and the various misfortunes of those who composed this strange family, related only through its disasters, hardly served for the excitement and talk of a single day. Now that the June days were at their longest, the old people were sure to wake earlier than ever; but one morning, to the astonishment of everyone, Betsey Lane's bed was empty; the sheets and blankets, which were her own, and guarded with jealous care, were carefully folded and placed on a chair not too near the window, and Betsey had flown. Nobody had heard her go down the creaking stairs. The kitchen door was unlocked, and the old watch-dog lay on the step outside in the early sunshine, wagging his tail and looking wise, as if he were left on guard and meant to keep the fugitive's secret.

"Never knowed her to do nothin' afore 'thout talking it over a fortnight, and paradin' off when we could all see her," ventured a spiteful voice. "Guess we can wait till night to hear 'bout it."

Mrs. Dow looked sorrowful and shook her head. "Betsey had an aunt on her mother's side that went and drownded of herself; she was a pritty-appearing woman as ever you see."

"Perhaps she's gone to spend the day with Decker's folks," suggested Peggy Bond. "She always takes an extra early start; she was speakin' lately o' going up their way;" but Mrs. Dow shook her head with a most melancholy look. "I'm impressed that something's befell her," she insisted. "I heard her a-groaning' in her sleep. I was wakeful the forepart o' the night,—'tis very unusual with me, too."

" 'T wa'nt like Betsey not to leave us any word,' said the other old friend, with more resentment than melancholy. They sat together almost in silence that morning in the shed chamber. Mrs. Dow was sorting and cutting rags, and Peggy braided them into long ropes, to be made into mats at a later date. If they had only known where Betsey Lane had gone, they might have talked about it until dinner-time at noon; but failing this new subject, they could take no interest in any of their old ones. Out in the field the corn was well up, and the men were hoeing. It was a hot morning in the shed chamber, and the woolen rags were dusty and hot to handle.

V.

Byfleet people knew each other well, and when this mysteriously absent person did not return to the town-farm at the end of a week, public interest became much excited; and presently it was ascertained that Betsey Lane was neither making a visit to her friends the Deckers on Birch Hill, nor to any nearer acquaintances; in fact, she had disappeared altogether from her wonted haunts. Nobody remembered to have seen her pass, hers had been such an early flitting; and when somebody thought of her having gone away by train, he was laughed at for forgetting that the earliest morning train from

South Byfleet, the nearest station, did not start until long after eight o'clock; and if Betsey had designed to be one of the passengers, she would have started along the road at seven, and been seen and known of all women. There was not a kitchen in that part of Byfleet that did not have windows toward the road. Conversation rarely left the level of the neighborhood gossip: to see Betsey Lane, in her best clothes, at that hour in the morning, would have been the signal for much exercise of imagination; but as day after day went by without news, the curiosity of those who knew her best turned slowly into fear, and at last Peggy Bond again gave utterance to the belief that Betsey had either gone out in the early morning and put an end to her life, or that she had gone to the Centennial. Some of the people at table were moved to loud laughter,—it was at supper-time on a Sunday night,—but others listened with great interest.

"She never'd put on her good clothes to drownd herself," said the widow. "She might have thought 't was good as takin' 'em with her, though. Old folks has wandered off an' got lost in the woods afore now."

Mrs. Dow and Peggy resented this impertinent remark, but deigned to take no notice of the speaker. "She wouldn't have wore her best clothes to the Centennial would she?" mildly inquired Peggy, bobbing her head toward the ceiling. " 'T would be a shame to spoil your best things in such a place. An' I don't know of her havin' any money; there's the end o' that."

"You're bad as old Mis' Bland, that used to live neighbor to our folks," said one of the old men. "She was dreadful precise; an' she so begretched to wear a good alapaca dress that was left to her, that it hung in a press forty year, an' baited the moths at last."

"I often seen Mis' Bland a-goin' in to meetin' when I was a young girl," said Peggy Bond approvingly. "She was a good-appearin' woman, an' she left property."

"Wish she'd left it to me, then," said the poor soul opposite, glancing at her pathetic row of children: but it was not good manners at the farm to deplore one's situation, and Mrs. Dow and Peggy only frowned.

"Where do you suppose Betsey can be?" said Mrs. Dow, for the twentieth time. "She didn't have no money. I know she ain't gone far, if it's so that she's yet alive. She's b'en real pinched all the spring."

"Perhaps that lady that come one day give her some," the keeper's wife suggested mildly.

"Then Betsey would have told me;" said Mrs. Dow, with injured dignity.

VI.

On the morning of her disappearance, Betsey rose even before the pewee and the English sparrow, and dressed herself quietly, though with trembling hands, and stole out of the kitchen door like a plunderless thief. The old dog licked her hand and looked at her anxiously; the tortoise-shell cat rubbed against her best gown, and trotted away up the yard, then she turned anxiously and came after the old woman, following faithfully until she had to be driven back. Betsey was used to long country excursions afoot. She dearly loved the early morning; and finding that there was no dew to trouble her, she began to follow pasture paths and short cuts across the fields, surprising here and there a flock of sleepy sheep, or a startled calf that rustled out from the bushes. The birds were pecking their breakfast from bush and turf; and hardly any of the wild inhabitants of that rural world were enough alarmed by her presence to do more than flutter away if they chanced to be in her path. She stepped along, light-footed and eager as a girl, dressed in her neat old straw bonnet and black gown, and carrying a few belongings in her best bundle-handkerchief, one that her only brother had brought home from the East Indies fifty years before. There was an old crow perched as sentinel on a small, dead pine-tree, where he could warn friends who were pulling up the sprouted corn in a field close by; but he only gave a contemptuous caw as the adventurer appeared, and she shook her bundle at him in revenge, and laughed to see him so clumsy as he tried to keep his footing on the twigs.

"Yes, I be," she assured him. "I'm a-goin' to Pheladelphy, to the Centennial, same's other folks. I' just as soon tell ye's not, old crow;" and Betsey laughed aloud in pleased content with herself and her daring, as she walked along. She had only two miles to go to the station at South Byfleet, and she felt for the money now and then, and found it safe enough. She took great pride in the success of her escape, and especially in the long concealment of her wealth. Not a night had passed since Mrs. Strafford's visit that she had not slept with the roll of money under her pillow by night, and buttoned safe inside her dress by day. She knew that everybody would offer advice and even commands about the spending or saving of it; and she brooked no interference.

The last mile of the foot-path to South Byfleet was along the railway track; and Betsey began to feel in haste, though it was still nearly two hours to train time. She looked anxiously forward and back along the rails every few minutes, for fear of being run over; and at last she caught sight of an engine that was apparently coming toward her, and took flight into the woods before she could gather courage to follow the path again. The freight train proved to be at a standstill, waiting at a turnout; and some of the men were straying about, eating their early breakfast comfortably in this time of leisure. As the old woman came up to them, she stopped too, for a moment of rest and conversation.

"Where be ye goin'?" she asked pleasantly; and they told her. It was to the town where she had to change cars and take the great through train; a point of geography which she had learned from evening talks between the men at the farm.

"What'll ye carry me there for?"

"We don't run no passenger cars," said one of the young fellows, laughing. "What makes you in such a hurry?"

"I'm startin' for Pheladelphy, an' it's a gre't ways to go."

"So 'tis; but you're consid'able early, if you're makin' for the eight-forty train. See here! you haven't got a needle an' thread 'long of you in that bundle, have you? If you'll sew me on a couple o' buttons, I'll give ye a free ride. I'm in a sight o' distress, an' none o' the fellows is provided with as much as a bent pin."

"You poor boy! I'll have you seen to, in half a minute. I'm troubled with a stiff arm, but I'll do the best I can."

The obliging Betsey seated herself stiffly on the slope of the embankment, and found her thread and needle with utmost haste. Two of the trainmen stood by and watched the careful stitches, and even offered her a place as spare brakeman, so that they might keep her near; and Betsey took the offer with considerable seriousness, only thinking it necessary to assure them that she was getting most too old to be out in all weathers. An express went by like an earthquake, and she was presently hoisted on board an empty box-car by two of her new and flattering acquaintances, and found herself before noon at the end of the first stage of her journey, without having spent a cent, and furnished with any amount of thrifty advice. One of the young men, being compassionate of her unprotected state as a traveler, advised her to find out the widow of an uncle of his in Philadelphia, saying despairingly that he couldn't tell her just how to find the house; but Miss Betsey Lane said that she had an English tongue in her head, and should be sure to find whatever she was looking for. This unexpected incident of the freight train was the reason why everybody about the South Byfleet station insisted that no such person had taken passage by the regular train that same morning, and why there were those who persuaded themselves that Miss Betsey Lane was probably lying at the bottom of the poor-farm pond.

VII.

"Land sakes!" said Miss Betsey Lane, as she watched a Turkish person parading by in his red fez, "I call the Centennial somethin' like the day o' judgment! I wish I was going to stop a month, but I dare say 'twould be the death o' my poor old bones."

She was leaning against the barrier of a patent pop-corn establishment, which had given her a sudden reminder of home, and of the winter nights when the sharp kerneled little red and yellow ears were brought out, and Old Uncle Eph Flanders sat by the kitchen stove, and solemnly filled a great wooden chopping-tray for the refreshment of the company. She had wondered and loitered and looked until her eyes and head had grown numb and unreceptive; but it is only unimaginative persons who can be really astonished. The imagination can always outrun the possible and actual sights and sounds of the world; and this plain old body from Byfleet rarely found anything rich and splendid enough to surprise her. She saw the wonders of the West and the splendors of the East with equal calmness and satisfaction; she had always known that there was an amazing world outside the boundaries of Byfleet. There was a piece of paper in her pocket on which was marked, in her clumsy handwriting, "If Betsey Lane should meet with accident, notify the selectmen of Byfleet;" but having made this slight provision for the future, she had thrown herself boldly into the sea of strangers, and then had made the joyful discovery that friends were to be found at every turn.

There was something delightfully companionable about Betsey; she had a way of suddenly looking up over her big spectacles with a reassuring and expectant smile, as if you were going to speak to her, and you generally did. She must have found out where hundreds of people came from, and whom they had left at home, and what they thought of the great show, as she sat on a bench to rest, or leaned over the railings where free luncheons were afforded by the makers of hot waffles and molasses candy and fried potatoes; and there was not a night when she did not return to her lodgings with a pocket crammed with samples of spool cotton and nobody knows what. She had already collected small presents for almost everybody she knew at home, and she was such a pleasant, beaming old country body, so unmistakably appreciative and interested, that nobody ever thought of wishing that she would move on. Nearly all the busy people of the Exhibition called her either Aunty or Grandma at once, and made little pleasures for her as best they could. She was a delightful contrast to the indifferent, stupid crowd that drifted along, with eyes fixed at the same level, and seeing, even on that level, nothing for fifty feet at a time. "What be you making here, dear?" Betsey Lane would ask joyfully, and the most perfunctory guardian hastened to explain. She squandered money as she had never had the pleasure of doing before, and this hastened the day when she must return to Byfleet. She was always inquiring if there were any spectacle-sellers at hand, and received occasional directions; but it was a difficult place for her to find her way about in, and the very last day of her stay arrived before she found an exhibitor of the desired sort, an oculist and instrument-maker.

"I called to get some specs for a friend that's upsighted," she gravely informed the salesman, to his extreme amusement. "She's dreadful troubled, and jerks her head up like a hen a-drinkin'. She's got a blur a-growin' and spreadin', and sometimes she can see out to one side on 't, and more times she can't."

"Cataracts," said a middle-aged gentleman at her side; and Betsey Lane turned to regard him with approval and curiosity.

" 'Tis Miss Peggy Bond I was mentioning, of Byfleet Poor-farm," she explained. "I count on gettin' some glasses to relieve her trouble, if there's any to be found."

"Glasses won't do her any good," said the stranger. "Suppose you come and sit down on this bench, and tell me all about it. First, where is Byfleet?" and Betsy gave the directions at length.

"I thought so," said the surgeon. "How old is this friend of yours?"

Betsey cleared her throat decisively, and smoothed her gown over her knees as if it were an apron; then she turned to take a good look at her new acquaintance as they sat on the rustic bench together. "Who be you, sir, I should like to know?" she asked, in a friendly tone.

"My name's Dunster."

"I take it you're a doctor," continued Betsey, as if they had overtaken each other walking from Byfleet to South Byfleet on a summer morning.

"I'm a doctor; part of one at least," said he. "I know more or less about eyes; and I spend my summers down on the shore at the mouth of your river; some day I'll come up and look at this person. How old is she?"

"Peggy Bond is one that never tells her age; 'tain't come quite up to where she'll begin to brag of it, you see," explained Betsey reluctantly; "but I know her to be nigh to seventy-six, one way or t'other. Her and Mrs. Mary Ann Chick was same year's child'n, and Peggy knows I know it, an' two or three times when we've be'n in the buryin'-ground where Mary Ann lays an' has her dates right on her headstone, I couldn't bring Peggy to take no sort o' notice. I will say she makes, at times, a convenience of being upsighted. But there, I feel for her,—everybody does; it keeps her stubbin' and trippin' against everything, beakin' and gazin' up the way she has to."

"Yes, yes," said the doctor, whose eyes were twinkling. "I'll come and look after her, with your town doctor, this summer,—some time in the last of July or first of August."

"You'll find occupation," said Betsy, not without an air of patronage. "Most of us to the Byfleet Farm has got our ails, now I tell ye. You ain't got no bitters that'll take a dozen years right off an ol' lady's shoulders?"

The busy man smiled pleasantly, and shook his head as he went away. "Dunster," said Betsey to herself, soberly committing the new name to her sound memory. "Yes, I mustn't forget to speak of him to the doctor, as he directed. I do' know now as Peggy would vally herself quite so much accordin' to, if she had her eyes fixed same as other folks. I expect there wouldn't been a smarter woman in town, though, if she'd had a proper chance. Now I've done what I set to do for her, I do believe, an' 'twa'n't glasses, neither. I'll git her a pritty little shawl with that money I laid aside. Peggy Bond ain't got a pritty shawl. I always wanted to have a real good time, an' now I'm havin' it."

VIII.

Two or three days later, two pathetic figures might have been seen crossing the slopes of the poor-farm field, toward the low shores of Byfield pond. It was early in the morning, and the stubble of the lately mown grass was wet with rain and hindering to old feet. Peggy Bond was more blundering and liable to stray in the wrong direction than usual; it was one of the days when she could hardly see at all. Aunt Lavina Dow was unusually clumsy of movement, and stiff in the joints; she had not been so far from the house for three years. The morning breeze filled the gathers of her wide gingham skirt, and aggravated the size of her unwieldy figure. She supported herself with a stick, and trusted beside to the fragile support of Peggy's arm. They were talking together in whispers.

"Oh, my sakes!" exclaimed Peggy, moving her small head from side to side. "Hear you wheeze, Mis' Dow! This may be the death o' you; there, do go slow! You set here on the side-hill, an' le' me go try if I can see."

"It needs more eyesight than you've got," said Mrs. Dow, panting between the words. "Oh! to think how spry I was in my young days, an' here I be now, the full of a door, an' all my complaints so aggravated by my size. 'Tis hard! 'tis hard! but I'm a-doin' of all this for pore Betsey's sake. I know they've all laughed, but I look to see her ri' to the top o' the pond this day,—'tis just nine days since she departed; an' say what they may, I know she hove herself in. It run in her family; Betsey had an aunt that done just so, an' she ain't be'n like herself, a-broodin' an' hivin' away alone, an' nothin' to say to you an' me that was always sich good company all together. Somethin' sprung her mind, now I tell ye, Mis' Bond."

"I feel to hope we sha'n't find her, I must say," faltered Peggy. It was plain that Mrs. Dow was the captain of this doleful expedition. "I guess she ain't never thought o' drowndin' of herself, Mis' Dow; she's gone off a-visitin' way over to the other side o' South Byfleet; some thinks she's gone to the Centennial even now!"

"She hadn't no proper means, I tell ye," wheezed Mrs. Dow indignantly; "an' if you prefer that others should find her floatin' to the top this day, instid of us that's her best friends, you can step back to the house."

They walked on in aggrieved silence. Peggy Bond trembled with excitement, but her companion's firm grasp never wavered, and so they came to the narrow, gravelly margin and stood still. Peggy tried in vain to see the glittering water and the pondlilies that starred it; she knew that they must be there; once, years ago, she had caught fleeting glimpses of them, and she never forgot what she had once seen. The clear blue sky overhead, the dark pine-woods beyond the pond, were all clearly pictured in her mind. "Can't you see nothin'?" she faltered; "I believe I' wuss 'n upsighted this day. I'm going to be blind."

"No," said Lavina Dow solemnly; "no, there ain't nothin' whatever, Peggy. I hope to mercy she ain't"—

"Why, whoever'd expected to find you 'way out here!" exclaimed a brisk and cheerful voice. There stood Betsey Lane herself, close behind them, having just emerged from a thicket of alders that grew close by. She was following the short way homeward from the railroad.

"Why, what's the matter, Mis' Dow? You ain't overdoin', be ye? an Peggy's all of a flutter. What in the name o' natur' ails ye?"

"There ain't nothin' the matter, as I knows on," responded the leader of this fruitless expedition. "We only thought we'd take a stroll this pleasant mornin'," she added, with sublime self-possession. "Where've you be'n, Betsey Lane?"

"To Pheladelphy, ma'am," said Betsy, looking quite young and gay, and wearing a townish and unfamiliar air that upheld her words. "All ought to go that can; why, you feel's if you'd be'n all around the world. I guess I've got enough to think of and tell ye for the rest o' my days. I've always wanted to go somewheres. I wish you'd be'n there, I do so. I've talked with folks from Chiny an' the back o' Pennsylvany; and I see folks way from Australy that 'peared as well as anybody; an' I see how they made spool cotton, an' sights o' other things an' I spoke with a doctor that lives down to the beach in the summer, an' he offered to come up 'long in the first of August, an' see what he can do for Peggy's eyesight. There was di'monds there as big as pigeon's eggs; and I met with Mis' Abby Fletcher from South Byfleet depot; an' there was hogs there that weighed risin' thirteen hunderd"—

"I want to know," said Mrs. Lavina Dow and Peggy Bond, together.

"Well, 't was a great exper'ence for a person," added Lavina, turning ponderously, in spite of herself, to give a last wistful look at the smiling waters of the pond.

"I don't know how soon I be goin' to settle down," proclaimed the rustic sister of Sindbad. "What's for the good o' one's for the good of all. You just wait till we're setting together up in the old shed chamber! You know, my dear Mis' Katy Strafford give me a han'some present o' money that day she come to see me; and I'd be'n a-dreamin' by night an' day o' seein' that Centennial; and when I come to think on 't I felt sure somebody ought to go from this neighborhood, if 't was only for the good o' the rest; and I thought I'd better be the one. I wa'n't goin' to ask the selec'men neither. I've come back with one-thirty-five in money, and I see everything there, an' I fetched ye all a little somethin'; but I'm full o' dust now, an' pretty nigh beat out. I never see a place more friendly than Pheladelphy; but 't ain't natural to a Byfleet person to be always walkin' on a level. There, now, Peggy, you take my bundle-handkercher and the basket, and let Mis' Dow sag on to me. I'll git her along twice as easy."

With this the small elderly company set forth triumphant toward the poor-house, across the wide green field.

Discussion of "The Flight of Betsey Lane"

The reader who remembers "The Guests of Mrs. Timms" from volume two *Out of the Best Books* may well recognize the same delicacy of touch and tone in this story. At first glance, an account of three old ladies in a New England poorhouse a century ago, would not appear to be promising material for a successful short story, but the opening details are so convincing that we find ourselves caught up in this simple tale before we have time to become prejudiced against it.

Among Sarah Orne Jewett's gifts as a writer is the ability to see below stereotypes. In the long opening paragraph which sets background, we expect to find the inmates of this poor-house discouraged and resentful. For the most part they are quite the opposite. Miss Jewett's implication that lives can be so routine and drab that *any* change—even residence at the poor-farm—can be welcome, suddenly rings true.

If there are touches of sentimentality in this story (the appearance of the kindly eye doctor is a little too coincidental) most details display the matter-of-fact objectivity that is a hallmark of Miss Jewett's prose. Many modern authors find it difficult to write of the poor and downtrodden without idealizing, explaining, or exploiting them. Miss Jewett avoids all such quasi-literary approaches. She is not trying to account for the characters of her tale so much as to present them.

In the opening description of Peggy Bond, for instance, note how physical appearance, action, and attitude are all blended into a convincing picture:

> Miss Peggy Bond was a very small, belligerent-looking person, who wore a huge pair of steel-bowed spectacles, holding her sharp chin well up in the air, as if to supplement an inadequate nose. She was more than half-blind, but the spectacles seem to face upward instead of square ahead, as if their wearer were always on a sharp lookout for birds. Miss Bond had suffered much personal damage

from time to time, because she never took heed where she planted her feet, and so was always tripping and stubbing her bruised way through the world. She had fallen down hatchways and cellarways, and stepped composedly into deep ditches and pasture brooks; but she was proud of stating that she was up-sighted, and so was her father before her.

We not only see Miss Bond, we begin to understand her. When she further reveals herself as the story progresses, we are prepared for the hints of doggedness, pride, and independence which make her a three-dimensional, if only an incidental, figure in this story.

At the center of this account Betsey Lane is shown in some contrast to the ponderous Mrs. Dow and the luckless Peggy Bond. She is without the infirmities for which Peggy is usually compensating and she is still free of the years that have settled so heavily on Mrs. Dow. Yet what distinguishes Betsey Lane most is a still unquenched eagerness, a determination to make her lot as fulfilling as possible.

Such enthusiasm is often at the base of cheerfulness, especially cheerfulness that is achieved in the face of unusual difficulty. Betsey's almost childish wish for a "small lookin'-glass" of her own is requested with such frank eagerness, and her desire to attend "the great fair to Pheladelphy" is admitted with such candor that what might have seemed selfish becomes only charming. Her zest for life is communicated to all who meet her. Note how the trainmen start by merely being pleasant to an old woman but end with such concern that one of them tries to provide a place for her to stay while she is visiting the Centennial.

Miss Jewett manages to let us see her characters with a sharpness of detail that might seem harsh in less skillful hands. Her description of the three old women singing as they work is almost cruelly vivid:

Betsey Lane began to sing a hymn, and the others joined in as best they might, like autumnal crickets; their voices were sharp and cracked, with now and then a few low notes of plaintive tone. Betsey herself could sing pretty well, but the others could only make a kind of accompaniment. Their voices ceased all together at the higher notes. "Oh my! I wish I had the means to go to the Centennial," mourned Betsey Lane, stopping so suddenly that the others had to go on croaking and shrilling without her for a moment before they could stop.

The result of such detail is to keep the reader in the actual world. Here is no idealized poor-house or saintly old women. Their deficiencies are as real as their strengths and are as frankly shown. What Betsey lacks is never discounted, but neither is the creative power of her enthusiasm. When she finally arrives at the fair she is prepared to enjoy and assimilate it. She is not overwhelmed. As Miss Jewett shrewdly comments, "it is only unimaginative persons who can be really astonished." Betsey is determined to be friendly—and she finds friends everywhere. The sophisticated are charmed by her interest, and the indifferent warm to her appreciation. The result is wholly—and convincingly—positive. The final picture we have of the three old ladies, Mrs. Dow and Miss Bond having come out to find Betsey, is one of unforgettable triumph.

SECTION TWO

Honesty, a Measure of Life

by Bruce B. Clark

"The Holy Family"

By Andrea del Sarto (1486-1531), Italian (Rome, Galleria Nazionale)

Commentary by
Floyd E. Breinholt, Associate Professor of Art, Brigham Young University

If one will study the paintings of any sincere artist he will find that in a very real sense the paintings are portraits of the artist himself—not of his physical likeness but of an indefinable quality of his whole personality. The subjects he chooses, the way he uses the paint, the parts which are emphasized, the content he selects are all fused together and we see something of the artist. This is not done consciously if he is sincere, but it is inevitable and unavoidable. Just as a man's handwriting speaks of his character, so an artist's work mirrors his personality.

This is true in the work of Andrea del Sarto, known as "The Perfect Painter" by the Florentines of his day and whose character is so aptly described in Browning's Poem. Art historians seem to substantiate what Browning says about him. Worldly spendor and vivacity had come into the life of his time. He was impressionable and sensitive to his time and thus was able to reflect this culture in his work. Although not necessarily religious by nature, he painted religious subjects to please the court and has been referred to as a "religious court painter." He had great honor in his day. We sometimes tend to deify men because of their works—artists are still men with strengths and weaknesses. Andrea's strength was in his great talent and craftsmanship, his ability to say what he had to say. There are a sweetness and underlying note of pathos and tenderness that give his work a genuine character, although perhaps not the greatest.

Vasari, an artist, writer, and pupil of del Sarto's says, "Had this master possessed a somewhat bolder mind, had he been a more distinguished man, qualified by character as he was by artistic skill, he would have been without equal." Lack of force and conviction in his nature took ardor and animation out of his creative works.

Can you see Andrea del Sarto in his painting of "The Holy Family"? This is a good example of his work in which he uses the classical Renaissance style—soft, warm light, rich color, unified tonality, and the chiaroscuro (strong use of light and shade) for which he was noted. The model for the Madonna was no doubt his beautiful wife Lucrezia whom he idealized in many of his paintings. Do you also sense a certain character about the painting which is difficult to describe in words, but which is nevertheless just as real and is a reflection of the personality of the artist?

HONESTY, A MEASURE OF LIFE

The measure of life is not length, but honesty.

—John Lyly

Introductory Comments

In the Old Testament, in Chapter 6 of Proverbs, we read:

> These six things doth the Lord hate: yea, seven are an abomination unto him:
>
> A proud look, a lying tongue, and hands that shed innocent blood,
>
> An heart that deviseth wicked imaginations, feet that be swift in running to mischief,
>
> A false witness that speaketh lies, and he that soweth discord among brethren.
>
> (Verses 16-19)

Surely it is significant that two of the seven "abominations" explicitly refer to the evil of dishonesty—"a lying tongue" and "a false witness that speaketh lies." Three others seem also to involve forms of dishonesty—"an heart that deviseth wicked imaginations," "feet that be swift in running to mischief," and "he that soweth discord among brethren."

The Bible is filled with reminders from the Lord and His prophets that we should cultivate honesty and avoid dishonesty. Literature, also, is abundantly concerned with honesty as an ideal and dishonesty, in all its forms, as an evil. If we were just to list the great works of literature that in one way or another are concerned with honesty and dishonesty, we would fill a whole chapter of this book—such works as Shakespeare's *Othello* (drama), James Joyce's "Clay" and "The Dead" (short stories), Joseph Conrad's *Lord Jim* (novel), George Meredith's *Modern Love* (poem), Katherine Mansfield's "Miss Brill" (short story), Nathaniel Hawthorne's *The Scarlet Letter* (novel),

John Galsworthy's "The Apple Tree" (short story), Sir Walter Scott's *The Heart of Midlothian* (novel), Katherine Anne Porter's "Flowering Judas" and "Theft" (short stories), Thomas Hardy's *Tess of the d'Urbervilles* (novel), John Steinbeck's "The Chrysanthemums" (short story), and Fyodor Dostoyevsky's *Crime and Punishment* (novel). Such a list could be almost endless.

Through literature we have faith with Cervantes in *Don Quixote* that "honesty is the best policy," we painfully learn with Huck in Mark Twain's *Huckleberry Finn* that "you can't pray a lie," and we recognize with Alexander Pope in "An Essay on Man" that "an honest man's the noblest work of God," even though we may feel that Hamlet is too disillusioned when in his feigned madness he says to Polonius, "To be honest, as this world goes, is to be one man plucked out of ten thousand" (*Hamlet,* Act II, Scene 2). In any case we will likely agree with Stuart Chase in his famous essay "The Luxury of Integrity" written a few years ago that anyone who wishes to be scrupulously and undeviatingly honest must be willing to pay the price—which means adherence to principle, resistance to temptation, and refusal to compromise integrity at whatever cost and at all times.

Temptations to compromise honesty confront all of us daily. If we are to be fully honest we must be honest in all areas:

Honest with one's self.
Honest with one's family.
Honest with one's associates.
Honest with the Lord.

Honest in one's actions.
Honest in one's speech.
Honest in one's thoughts.

Perhaps the hardest of all is to be honest in one's thoughts and honest with one's self and with the Lord. Especially is this so because pride and selfishness distort our thoughts. Sometimes, like James Thomson in the following humorous lines, we even let pride exaggerate our sins:

> Once in a saintly passion
> I cried with desperate grief,
> "O Lord, my heart is black with guile,
> Of sinners I am chief."
> Then stooped my guardian angel
> And whispered from behind,
> "Vanity, my little man,
> You're nothing of the kind."

Probably the easiest way to approach the whole matter of honesty would simply be to discuss problems of honesty and dishonesty in people's everyday lives—business dealings, income tax computations, tithing, gossip among neighbors, school examinations, etc. This, however, would not be an approach through art; it would be through exposition or sermonizing instead. Another way would be to print several poems or stories directly illustrating the values of honesty. The difficulty here is that it is almost impossible to avoid being trite, stale, and obvious, and we want very much to be as fresh, stimulating, and provocative as possible.[1] Therefore, perhaps the best way is to explore problems of dishonesty as these in turn are explored in first-quality literary selections. Seeing these problems in the lives of literary figures can help us see—and thus solve—the problems in our own lives.

To do all of this we now print two poems and two short stories. The first is a short story, "The Waltz" by Dorothy Parker, showing the temptation that constantly

---

[1]For examples already printed in *Out of the Best Books* illustrating the values of honesty, see William Wordsworth's poem "Character of the Happy Warrior" (Volume 1, p. 67), John Galsworthy's short story "Quality" (Volume 1, p. 124), Robert Burns's poem "A Man's a Man for A' That" (Volume 1, p. 224), Wordsworth's poem "Michael" (Volume 1, p. 405), the excerpt from Carl Ewald's novel *My Little Boy* (Volume 2, p. 8), Leo Tolstoy's short story "Where Love Is, There God Is Also" (Volume 2, p. 270), Burns's poem "Epistle to a Young Friend" (Volume 2, p. 312), and the excerpt from Albert R. Lyman's novel *Man to Man* (Volume 2, p. 340).

confronts us to think one thing but say another. The second is a poem, "Richard Cory" by Edwin Arlington Robinson, dramatizing the need to be cautious in judging other people by appearances, because this is a form of dishonesty. The third is another poem, "Andrea del Sarto" by Robert Browning, portraying a man who is extensively dishonest both with himself and with everyone else, even God. And the fourth is another short story, "A Run of Gray" by Brian Kelly, emphasizing the need to face life honestly, recognizing that all living things, including especially people, are mixtures of good and bad.

The Waltz

by Dorothy Parker

Why, thank you so much. I'd adore to.

I don't want to dance with him. I don't want to dance with anybody. And even if I did, it wouldn't be him. He'd be well down among the last ten. I've seen the way he dances; it looks like something you do on St. Walpurgis Night. Just think, not a quarter of an hour ago, here I was sitting, feeling so sorry for the poor girl he was dancing with. And now *I'm* going to be the poor girl. Well, well. Isn't it a small world?

And a peach of a world, too. A true little corker. Its events are so fascinatingly unpredictable, are not they? Here I was, minding my own business, not doing a stitch of harm to any living soul. And then he comes into my life, all smiles and city manners, to sue me for the favor of one memorable mazurka. Why, he scarcely knows my name, let alone what it stands for. It stands for Despair, Bewilderment, Futility, Degradation, and Premeditated Murder, but little does he wot. I don't wot his name, either; I haven't any idea what it is. Jukes, would be my guess from the look in his eyes. How do you do, Mr. Jukes? And how is that dear little brother of yours, with the two heads?

Ah, now why did he have to come around me, with his low requests? Why can't he let me lead my own life? I ask so little—just to be left alone in my quiet corner of the table, to do my evening brooding over all my sorrows. And he must come, with his bows and his scrapes and his may-I-have-this-ones. And I had to go and tell him that I'd adore to dance with him. I cannot understand why I wasn't struck right down dead. Yes, and being struck dead would look like a day in the country, compared to struggling out a dance with this boy. But what could I do? Everyone else at the table had got up to dance, except him and me. There I was, trapped. Trapped like a trap in a trap.

What can you say, when a man asks you to dance with him? I most certainly will *not* dance with you, I'll see you in Hades first. Why, thank you, I'd like to awfully, but I'm having labor pains. Oh, yes, *do* let's dance together—it's so nice to meet a man who isn't a scaredy-cat about catching my beri-beri. No. There was nothing for me to do, but say I'd adore to. Well, we might as well get it over with. All right, Cannonball, let's run out on the field. You won the toss; you can lead.

Why, I think it's more of a waltz, really. Isn't it? We might just listen to the music a second. Shall we? Oh, yes, it's a waltz. Mind? Why, I'm simply thrilled. I'd love to waltz with you.

I'd love to waltz with you. I'd love to waltz with you. I'd love to have my tonsils out, I'd love to be in a midnight fire at sea. Well, it's too late now. We're getting under way. *Oh.* Oh, dear. Oh, dear, dear, dear. Oh, this is even worse than I thought it would be. I suppose that's the one dependable law of life—everything is always worse than you thought it was going to be. Oh, if I had had any real grasp of what this dance would be like, I'd have held out for sitting it out. Well, it will probably amount to the same thing in the end. We'll be sitting it out on the floor in a minute, if he keeps this up.

I'm so glad I brought it to his attention that this is a waltz they're playing. Heaven knows what might have happened, if he had thought it was something fast; we'd have blown the sides right out of the building. Why does he always want to be somewhere that he isn't? Why can't we stay in one place just long enough to get acclimated? It's this constant rush, rush, rush, that's the curse of American life. That's the reason that we're all of us so—*Ow!* For Pete's sake, don't *kick,* you idiot; this is only second down. Oh, my shin. My poor, poor shin, that I've had ever since I was a little girl!

Oh, no, no, no. Goodness, no. It didn't hurt the least little bit. And anyway it was my fault. Really it was. Truly. Well, you're just being sweet, to say that. It really was all my fault.

I wonder what I'd better do—kill him this instant, with my naked hands, or wait and let him drop in his traces. Maybe it's best not to make a scene. I guess I'll just lie low, and watch the pace get him. He can't keep this up indefinitely—he's only flesh and blood. Die he must, and die he shall, for what he did to me. I don't want to be of the over-sensitive type, but you can't tell me that kick was unpremeditated. Freud says there are no accidents. I've led no cloistered life, I've known dancing partners who have spoiled my slippers and torn my dress; but when it comes to kicking, I am Outraged Womanhood. When you kick me in the shin, *smile.*

Maybe he didn't do it maliciously. Maybe it's just his way of showing his high spirits. I suppose I ought to be glad that one of us is having such a good time. I suppose I ought to think myself lucky if he brings me back alive. Maybe it's captious to demand of a practically strange man that he leave your shins as he found them. After all, the poor boy's doing the best he can. Probably he grew up in the hill country, and never had no larnin'. I bet they had to throw him on his back to get shoes on him.

Yes, it's lovely, isn't it? It's simply lovely. It's the loveliest waltz. Isn't it? Oh, I think it's lovely, too.

Why, I'm getting positively drawn to the Triple Threat here. He's my hero. He has the heart of a lion, and the sinews of a buffalo. Look at him—never a thought of the consequences, never afraid of his face, hurling himself into every scrimmage, eyes shining, cheeks ablaze. And shall it be said that I hung back? No, a thousand times no. What's it to me if I have to spend the next couple of years in a plaster cast? Come on, Butch, right through them! Who wants to live forever?

Oh. Oh, dear. Oh, he's all right, thank goodness. For a while I thought they'd have to carry him off the field. Ah, I couldn't bear to have anything happen to him. I love him. I love him better than anybody in the world. Look at the spirit he gets into a dreary, comonplace waltz; how effete the other dancers seem, beside him. He is youth and vigor and courage, he is strength and gayety and—*Ow!* Get off my instep, you hulking peasant! What do you think I am, anyway—a gangplank? *Ow!*

No, of course it didn't hurt. Why, it didn't a bit. Honestly. And it was all my fault. You see, that little step of yours—well, it's perfectly lovely, but it's just a tiny bit tricky to follow at first. Oh, did you work it up yourself? You really did? Well, aren't you amazing! Oh, now I think I've got it. Oh, I think it's lovely. I was watching you do it when you were dancing before. It's awfully effective when you look at it.

It's awfully effective when you look at it. I bet I'm awfully effective when you look at me. My hair is hanging along my cheeks, my skirt is swaddled about me, I can feel the cold damp of my brow. I must look like something out of the Fall of the House of Usher. This sort of thing takes a fearful toll of a woman my age. And he worked up his little step himself, he with his degenerate cunning. And it was just a tiny bit tricky at first, but now I think I've got it. Two stumbles, slip, and a twenty-yard dash; yes, I've got it. I've got several other things, too, including a split shin and a bitter heart. I hate this creature I'm chained to. I hated him the moment I saw his leering, bestial face. And here I've been locked in his noxious embrace for the thirty-five years this waltz has lasted. Is that orchestra never going to stop playing? Or must this obscene travesty of a dance go on for a century?

Oh, they're going to play another encore. Oh, goody. Oh, that's lovely. Tired? I should say I'm not tired. I'd like to go on like this forever.

I should say I'm not tired. I'm dead, that's all I am. Dear, and in what a cause! And the music is never going to stop playing, and we're going on like this, Double-Time Charlie and I, throughout eternity. I suppose I won't care any more, after the first hundred thousand years. I suppose nothing will matter then, not heat nor pain nor broken heart nor cruel, aching weariness. Well. It can't come too soon for me.

I wonder why I didn't tell him I was tired. I wonder why I didn't suggest going back to the table. I could have said let's just listen to the music. Yes, and if he would, that would be the first bit of attention he has given it all evening. George Jean Nathan said that the lovely rhythms of the waltz should be listened to in stillness and not be accompanied by strange gyrations of the human body. I think that's what he said. I think it was George Jean Nathan. Anyhow, whatever he said and whoever he was and whatever he's doing now, he's better off than I am. That's safe. Anybody who isn't waltzing with this Mrs. O'Leary's cow I've got here is having a good time.

Still, if we were back at the table, I'd probably have to talk to him. Look at him—what could you say to a thing like that! Did you go to the circus this year, what's your favorite kind of ice cream, how do you spell cat? I guess I'm as well off here. As well off as if I were in a cement mixer in full action.

I'm past all feeling now. The only way I can tell when he steps on me is that I can hear the splintering of bones. And all the events of my life are passing before my eyes. There was the time I was in a hurricane in the West Indies, there was the day I got my head cut open in the taxi smash, there was the night the drunken lady threw a bronze ash-tray at her own true love and got me instead, there was that summer that the sailboat kept capsizing. Ah, what an easy, peaceful time was mine, until I fell in with Swifty, here. I didn't know what trouble was, before I got drawn into this *danse macabre*. I think my mind is beginning to wander. It almost seems to me as if the orchestra were stopping. It coudn't be, of course; it could never, never be. And yet in my ears there is a silence like the sound of angel voices. . . .

Oh, they've stopped, the mean things. They're not going to play any more. Oh, darn. Oh, do you think they would? Do you really think so, if you gave them fifty dollars? Oh, that would be lovely. And look, do tell them to play this same thing. I'd simply adore to go on waltzing.

Discussion of "The Waltz"

This story by the clever American writer Dorothy Parker (1893-1967) is included partly to provide a few minutes of humor, and partly because we can all benefit from the central problem it explores, because probably all of us are more like the woman in the story than we are ready to admit. Obviously the story is written primarily for fun, built around a contrast between the sugary sweet talk (in italics) and the exaggeratedly sarcastic thoughts of the woman. Granted, most people are not as extreme in their thoughts and speech as is this woman, and granted that the story is mostly comedy. Nevertheless, all of us at times are probably guilty of doing what this woman does, at least in milder form—that is, of saying one thing and thinking another.

Thoughts and Questions for Discussion:

1. How serious is the dishonesty of the woman in this story?

2. Should we speak our honest thoughts even though others will be offended by what we say? Does courteous small-talk involve dishonesty? Someone says "How are you?" and you answer "I am fine" even though you have a severe headache. Or someone says "How do you like my hat?" and you answer "I think it is very lovely" even though secretly you think it is unattractive and in bad taste. Should you say "My dear, I think you have used very poor judgment and wasted your money in buying that hat"? Where does courtesy end and dishonesty begin?

3. Are there times when it is best to be silent and other times when it is necessary to speak out? Discuss.

4. What should an honest, refined woman say when caught in a situation similar to that of the woman in this story? Would an honest, refined woman be caught in such a situation? That is, is it part of honesty and refinement to avoid the situation in which one will feel obliged to say what one does not think? Should one bluntly say what one thinks at all costs?

5. Finally, how does her language reveal that the woman in this story may be sophisticated but is not very honest or refined?

Richard Cory[1]

by Edwin Arlington Robinson

Whenever Richard Cory went down town,
We people on the pavement looked at him;
He was a gentleman from sole to crown,
Clean favored, and imperially slim.

And he was always quietly arrayed,
And he was always human when he talked;
But still he fluttered pulses when he said,
"Good-morning," and he glittered when he walked.

And he was rich—yes, richer than a king—
And admirably schooled in every grace:
In fine, we thought that he was everything
To make us wish that we were in his place.

So on we worked, and waited for the light,
And went without the meat, and cursed the bread;
And Richard Cory, one calm summer night,
Went home and put a bullet through his head.

Discussion of "Richard Cory"

In Volume 1 of *Out of the Best Books* we studied two poems—"Miniver Cheevy" and "Karma"—by the powerful American poet Edwin Arlington Robinson (1869-1935).[2] Now in Volume 3 we see Robinson again in his famous, excellent little poem "Richard Cory."

As will be evident to anyone who reads it, "Richard Cory" is a very adroit and interesting poem, especially made so by its closing two lines. We have printed it here, however, neither for its interest nor for its adroitness, but for its insight. To all who looked at him, Richard Cory seemed to have everything—wealth, health, culture, happiness, composure, even elegance. And yet, "one calm summer

[1]Reproduced by permission of Charles Scribner's Sons.
[2]See pp. 243-244 and 280.

night" he "went home and put a bullet through his head." Why? Probably everyone can remember a Richard Cory he has known—someone whose happy appearance covered a hidden anguish that ended in tragedy.

The point of the poem is, of course, that we cannot judge a person accurately by external appearances. Gradually as we get older and older, character may reflect in a person's face, but for the most part it is dangerous to look at a person and make snap judgments about his character and personality based on appearances. To do so is not only unfair but in a sense dishonest. We have judged on superficial, incomplete evidence—and is not this a kind of dishonesty?

Consider any group of people in a room—a school class, a Church congregation (such as a Relief Society group), or a public audience of any sort. Could you, looking at the group, even looking intently at each person one by one, tell the inner natures of each? In any such group there would be some happy, some sad; some optimistic by nature, some pessimistic; some strong in faith, some weaker; some with relatively clear consciences, some with troubled consciences; some with gay hearts, some with aching hearts; some with close-knit marriages and families, some with problem marriages or problem families; some with pleasant recollections of past years, some with recollections of past years that are filled with anguish. How much of all this can be known by looking at one another? Certainly not all. Perhaps very little. Some people expose their inner feelings by how they look; others hide their feelings.

The conclusion to all this is that we should be very hesitant to judge people by how they look, or to envy people for what they seem to have and we don't have. Sometimes people who are envied the most, like Richard Cory, have the most problems if we really knew—and who would then trade places? Instead of envy and jealousy, we should give understanding and friendship. There is no place for envy and jealousy in the world, but there is never enough genuine understanding, friendship, compassion, and help. Sometimes a smiling face conceals a crying, lonely, troubled heart.

Thoughts and questions for discussion: (1) Analyze "Richard Cory" closely and tell all that you can about Richard. Is it possible to know why he killed himself from the information given in the poem? Or is the point of the poem that he killed himself because of hidden personal problems not seen in his external appearance and manners? (2) To what extent do people reveal their inner natures in their outer appearances? (3) Is it true that neither books nor people should be judged by their covers? What are the dangers of judging people hastily or solely on appearances?

Introduction to "Andrea del Sarto"

In previous volumes we have several times explored poems by the great Robert Browning and have discussed the qualities of his writings and character.[1] Now we have an opportunity to study another of his brilliant dramatic monologues, "Andrea del Sarto."

Andrea d'Angelo di Francesca (1486-1531) was a Renaissance Italian painter called "del Sarto" because he was the son of a tailor (sarto). The perfect artistry of his frescoes in the Church of the Annunziato in Florence won him the title of "The Faultless Painter." In 1512 he married Lucrezia del Fede, a beautiful but unscrupulous woman, whose influence over him caused him to neglect his painting.

Browning's poem was written as an interpretation of a painting by Andrea del Sarto which hung in the Pitti Palace in Florence. One of Mrs. Browning's cousins had asked Browning to obtain a copy of the painting. Unable to obtain one, Browning composed this poem as a substitute.

As a young painter Andrea del Sarto did brilliant work, displaying not only obvious genius but also a buoyant creative joy. In his later work, however, the flawless craftsmanship remains but the zest and creative joy are gone. Many have felt that Andrea's unhappy marriage stifled his creative powers. The fire of his unhealthy love consumed his genius and left only the burnt ashes of his craftsmanship.

In his poem Browning endeavors to portray not only the qualities of Andrea del Sarto as a painter in his later years but also, and especially, his personality and character. Above all else we see the pathetic weaknesses of Andrea—his rationalizing as he alternately blames God, his wife,

---

[1]In Volume 1 of *Out of the Best Books,* see pp. 71-90, 234-242, and 459-468, which include, among other things, discussions of "A Grammarian's Funeral," "An Epistle of Karshish," "Johannes Agricola in Meditation," "Soliloquy of the Spanish Cloister," "Prospice," and "Rabbi Ben Ezra." In Volume 2 see pp. 46-49, 60-61, and 190-195, which tell of Browning's marriage to Elizabeth Barrett and include his poem "My Last Duchess."

and others for his failure; his vacillating self-pity and arrogance; his pride as a skilled craftsman mixed with his futile yearning to match Raphael, Michelangelo, and Leonardo da Vinci as great painters; his flashes of genuine recognition of weaknesses in himself as painter and man; and most of all his mixture of honesty and dishonesty.

We are here using the poem to portray a man and wife who are fundamentally dishonest. Andrea and Lucrezia are not only dishonest with each other, but Andrea is dishonest with King Francis I, with his other associates, with his parents, with God, and—most of all—with himself. Only occasionally, in some of the great lines of the poem, does Andrea examine himself honestly and admit his weaknesses. Even then he does not remain honest enough to overcome the weaknesses that he momentarily admits but slips back into the tragic rationalizing, resignation, and self-pity. It would be difficult to find another great poem so fully portraying dishonesty as this brilliant work by Browning.

Without further delay we now print the poem, with full footnotes to assist in its interpretation. As the poem is read, remember that it is a dramatic monologue. That is, we get one half of a conversation: we hear Andrea talking to his wife as she poses for a painting. Apparently she is talking also, but we hear only the words of Andrea.

Andrea del Sarto

Called "The Faultless Painter"

by Robert Browning

But do not let us quarrel any more,
No, my Lucrezia; bear with me for once.
Sit down and all shall happen as you wish.
You turn your face, but does it bring your heart?
I'll work then for your friend's friend,[1] never fear,
Treat his own subject after his own way,

---

[1]Apparently one of her admirers or lovers.

Fix his own time, accept too his own price.
And shut the money into this small hand
When next it takes mine. Will it? tenderly?
Oh, I'll content him—but tomorrow, Love! 10
I often am much wearier than you think,
This evening more than usual, and it seems
As if—forgive now—should you let me sit
Here by the window with your hand in mine
And look a half-hour forth on Fiesole,[2]
Both of one mind, as married people use,[3]
Quietly, quietly, the evening through,
I might get up tomorrow to my work
Cheerful and fresh as ever. Let us try.
Tomorrow how you shall be glad for this! 20
Your soft hand is a woman of itself,
And mine the man's bared breast she curls inside.
Don't count the time lost, neither; you must serve
For each of the five pictures we require—
It saves a model. So! keep looking so—
My serpentining beauty, rounds on rounds!—
How could you ever prick those perfect ears,
Even to put the pearl there! oh, so sweet—
My face, my moon, my everybody's moon,
Which everybody looks on and calls his,[4] 30
And, I suppose, is looked on by in turn,
While she looks—no one's: very dear, no less!
You smile? why, there's my picture ready made.
There's what we painters call our harmony!
A common grayness silvers everything—[5]
All in a twilight, you and I alike—
You, at the point of your first pride in me
(That's gone, you know)—but I, at every point;
My youth, my hope, my art, being all toned down
To yonder sober pleasant Fiesole. . . .[6] 40
And autumn grows, autumn in everything.[7]

---

[2]A suburb of Florence.

[3]That is, as married couples customarily do.

[4]Most of the time Andrea passively and wearily resigns himself to his wife's unfaithfulness, but occasionally he faces truth honestly, as here when he angrily says "my everybody's moon, which everybody looks on and calls his."

[5]Note how this line suggests the "common grayness" that is the mood of the poem. See also ll. 98-99.

[6]Lines 41-44 are here omitted.

[7]Note again how this line suggests the weary "autumn" and "twilight" mood of the poem.

Eh? the whole seems to fall into a shape
As if I saw alike my work and self
And all that I was born to be and do,
A twilight-piece. Love, we are in God's hand.
How strange now looks the life He makes us lead; 50
So free we seem, so fettered fast we are!
I feel He laid the fetter; let it lie![8]
This chamber, for example—turn your head—[9]
All that's behind us! You don't understand
Nor care to understand about my art,[10]
But you can hear at least when people speak; . . .[11]
I can do with my pencil what I know, 60
What I see, what at bottom of my heart
I wish for, if I ever wish so deep—
Do easily, too—when I say perfectly,
I do not boast, perhaps; yourself are judge,
Who listened to the Legate's[12] talk last week,
And just as much they used to say in France.
At any rate, 'tis easy, all of it!
No sketches first, no studies—that's long past—
I do what many dream of all their lives—
Dream? strive to do, and agonize to do, 70
And fail in doing. I could count twenty such
On twice your fingers, and not leave this town,
Who strive—you don't know how the others strive
To paint a little thing like that you smeared
Carelessly passing with your robes afloat—
Yet do much less, so much less, Someone says
(I know his name, no matter), so much less![13]
Well, less is more, Lucrezia; I am judged.
There burns a truer light of God in them,
In their vexed, beating, stuffed, and stopped-up brain, 80
Heart, or whate'er else, than goes on to prompt
This low-pulsed forthright craftsman's hand of mine.

---

[8]Note how in ll. 49-52 Andrea talks of fate and blames God for the conditions of his life rather than accepting the responsibility himself.

[9]Occasionally Browning inserts phrases such as "turn your head" to remind us that Andrea is painting a picture while his wife serves as a model.

[10]Now Andrea says that his wife's lack of understanding is the cause of his failure.

[11]Lines 57-59 are here omitted.

[12]The Legate was the representative of the Pope.

[13]Note how in ll. 60-77 Andrea boasts of his skill as a perfect craftsman. Then in the passage that follows (ll. 78-86 and beyond) Andrea in another flash of honesty recognizes himself for what he is—a skilled craftsman who has bartered his talent for cheap goals.

Their works drop groundward, but themselves, I know,
Reach many a time a heaven that's shut to me,
Enter and take their place there sure enough,
Though they come back and cannot tell the world.
My works are nearer heaven, but I sit here.
The sudden blood of these men! at a word—
Praise them, it boils, or blame them, it boils too.
I, painting from myself and to myself, 90
Know what I do, am unmoved by men's blame
Or their praise either. Somebody remarks
Morello's[14] outline there is wrongly traced,
His hue mistaken—what of that? or else,
Rightly traced and well ordered—what of that?
Speak as they please, what does the mountain care?[15]
Ah, but a man's reach should exceed his grasp,
Or what's a heaven for?[16] All is silver-gray,
Placid and perfect with my art—the worse![17]
I know both what I want and what might gain, 100
And yet how profitless to know, to sigh,
"Had I been two, another and myself,
Our head would have o'erlooked the world!" No doubt.
Yonder's a work now, of that famous youth,
The Urbinate,[18] who died five years ago.
('Tis copied, George Vasari[19] sent it me.)
Well, I can fancy how he did it all,
Pouring his soul, with kings and popes to see,
Reaching, that heaven might so replenish him,
Above and through his art—for it gives way; 110
That arm is wrongly put—and there again—
A fault to pardon in the drawing's lines,
Its body, so to speak; its soul is right,

---

[14]A high mountain peak north of Florence.

[15]After slipping into self-pity in the preceding lines, Andrea is now back to boasting of himself as a haughty "mountain."

[16]This is Browning's most famous statement (ll. 97-98) urging that we should set high goals and strive toward them even though we may not be able to reach them rather than set low goals. Success comes in striving towards high goals rather than in contented mediocrity, and heaven is for eternal progression—to complete the goals started in mortality.

[17]Again Andrea briefly faces himself with honesty, recognizing that as a painter he is a skilled craftsman rather than a great artist, and hating himself because he sees a sterile-gray perfection in his art rather than vivid life.

[18]Raphael Sanzio (1483-1520), one of the greatest of Italian painters. He was born in the city of Urbino.

[19]George Vasari (1512-1574), a pupil of Andrea del Sarto, and author of *The Lives of the Most Eminent Painters, Sculptors, and Architects.*

He means right—that, a child may understand.
Still, what an arm! and I could alter it.
But all the play, the insight, and the stretch—
Out of me, out of me! And wherefore out?[20]
Had you enjoined them on me, given me soul,
We might have risen to Rafael, I and you![21]
Nay, Love, you did give all I asked, I think— 120
More than I merit, yes, by many times.[22]
But had you—oh, with the same perfect brow,
And perfect eyes, and more than perfect mouth,
And the low voice my soul hears, as a bird
The fowler's pipe, and follows to the snare—
Had you, with these the same, but brought a mind!
Some women do so. Had the mouth there urged,
"God and the glory! never care for gain,
The present by the future, what is that?
Live for fame, side by side with Agnolo![23] 130
Rafael is waiting; up to God, all three!"
I might have done it for you. So it seems;[24]
Perhaps not. All is as God overrules.[25]
Beside, incentives come from the soul's self;
The rest avail not. Why do I need you?
What wife had Rafael, or has Agnolo?
In this world, who can do a thing, will not;
And who would do it, cannot, I perceive;
Yet the will's somewhat—somewhat, too, the power—

---

[20]In ll. 104-117 Andrea examines a painting by the great Raphael in which an arm seems imperfectly drawn. Andrea is annoyed by the imperfection and considers correcting it but hesitates, realizing that the soul of Raphael's painting is right even though the arm may be faulty. He fears that if he corrects the arm he may ruin the genius of the painting. He realizes that in his own perfect craftsmanship there is less genius than in the imperfections of Raphael.

[21]Once again Andrea blames his wife for his own failure, saying that if she had "given him soul" he might have been as great as Raphael.

[22]Now Andrea vacillates back into self-pity, saying that his wife gave him more than he merits.

[23]Michelangelo (1475-1564), great Italian renaissance painter, sculptor, architect, and poet.

[24]In ll. 122-132 Andrea continues to blame his wife for his own weaknesses, admitting his enslavement to her perfect features, which trap him like a bird in a snare (l. 124), but saying that if she had been intellectually stimulating and spiritually inspiring as some women are, urging him to paint for God and glory, not for money (l. 128), he might have risen to God in the genius of his painting as Raphael and Michelangelo did.

[25]In this line Andrea again shifts point of view, again blaming God, suggesting that God predestines us to be what we are.

And thus we half-men struggle.[26] At the end, 140
God, I conclude, compensates, punishes.
'Tis safer for me, if the award be strict,
That I am something underrated here,
Poor this long while, despised, to speak the truth.[27]
I dared not, do you know, leave home all day,
For fear of chancing on the Paris lords.
The best is when they pass and look aside;
But they speak sometimes; I must bear it all.[28] . . .[29]
Let my hands frame your face in your hair's gold,
You beautiful Lucrezia that are mine![30]
"Rafael did this, Andrea painted that;
The Roman's[31] is the better when you pray,
But still the other's Virgin was his wife"—[32]
Men will excuse me. I am glad to judge 180
Both pictures in your presence; clearer grows
My better fortune, I resolve to think.
For, do you know, Lucrezia, as God lives,
Said one day Agnolo, his very self,
To Rafael—I have known it all these years— . . .[33]
"Friend, there's a certain sorry little scrub
Goes up and down our Florence, none cares how, 190
Who, were he set to plan and execute
As you are, pricked on by your popes and kings,

---

[26]In ll. 134-140 Andrea, in another flash of insight, briefly again faces himself as he really is, admitting that incentives must come from "the soul's self" (l. 134), and that he is responsible for his own failure. In l. 140 he refers to himself honestly as a "half-man," possessing great skill but lacking the will to succeed.

[27]In ll. 140-144 Andrea once more slips back into self-pity, hoping that his "sufferings" and lack of recognition in this life will be compensated for by fame in the life hereafter.

[28]Here (ll. 145-148) Andrea says he is afraid of the "Paris lords." He has good reason to be afraid, for in ll. 149-174 (omitted in this printing) Andrea tells how he became a spoiled artist in the luxurious court of Francis I, king of France. However, when King Francis gave him money to buy some paintings, he instead fled France at his wife's beckoning and spent the money purchasing for her a costly house in Italy. Now the French authorities are after him for squandering the money.

[29]Lines 149-174 are here omitted.

[30]As the poem draws to an end we are given increasing evidence that Andrea is enslaved to his wife's beauty, no matter how shabbily she treats him. She, of course, is only partly his: she is his wife, but she is obviously unfaithful to him.

[31]Raphael's.

[32]Andrea acknowledges that Raphael's painting is more spiritual, but prides himself that his wife served as the model for his own painting of the Virgin.

[33]Lines 186-188 are here omitted.

Would bring the sweat into that brow of yours!"[34]
To Rafael's!—And indeed the arm is wrong.
I hardly dare—yet, only you to see,
Give the chalk here—quick, thus the line should go!
Aye, but the soul! he's Rafael! rub it out![35]
Still, all I care for, if he spoke the truth
(What he? why, who but Michel Agnolo?
Do you forget already words like those?), 200
If really there was such a chance, so lost—
Is, whether you're—not grateful—but more pleased.
Well, let me think so. And you smile indeed![36]
This hour has been an hour! Another smile?
If you would sit thus by me every night
I should work better, do you comprehend?
I mean that I should earn more, give you more.
See, it is settled dusk now; there's a star;
Morello's gone, the watch-lights show the wall,
The cue-owls[37] speak the name we call them by. 210
Come from the window, Love—come in, at last,
Inside the melancholy little house
We built to be so gay with. God is just.
King Francis may forgive me; oft at nights
When I look up from painting, eyes tired out,
The walls become illumined, brick from brick
Distinct, instead of mortar, fierce bright gold.
That gold of his I did cement them with!
Let us but love each other. Must you go?
That Cousin[38] here again? he waits outside? 220
Must see you—you, and not with me? Those loans?
More gaming debts to pay? you smiled for that?
Well, let smiles buy me! have you more to spend?
While hand and eye and something of a heart
Are left me, work's my ware, and what's it worth?

---

[34]The "sorry little scrub" referred to in l. 189 is, of course, Andrea himself. Note how self-pity and pride are intermixed in this observation that if he really set his mind to it he could make the great Raphael jealous.

[35]In ll. 194-197 Andrea finally corrects the imperfect arm that has been annoying him in the Raphael painting. Realizing, however, that he has ruined the "soul" of the painting by correcting its flaw, he erases the "correction."

[36]As the poem comes closer and closer to its end, Andrea becomes even more pitiable. Here (ll. 198-203) we realize that he is willing to please his wife at whatever cost, including especially the loss of his self-respect. As Lucrezia smiles (ll. 203 and 204) we get the uncomfortable feeling that she is contemptibly laughing at him as much as anything else.

[37]Small European owls.

[38]A euphemism for *lover*.

I'll pay my fancy. Only let me sit
The gray remainder of the evening out,
Idle, you call it, and muse perfectly
How I could paint, were I but back in France,
One picture, just one more—the Virgin's face, 230
Not yours this time! I want you at my side
To hear them—that is, Michel Agnolo—
Judge all I do and tell you of its worth.
Will you? Tomorrow, satisfy your friend.
I take the subjects for his corridor,
Finish the portrait out of hand—there, there,
And throw him in another thing or two
If he demurs; the whole should prove enough
To pay for this same Cousin's freak. Beside,
What's better and what's all I care about, 240
Get you the thirteen scudi[39] for the ruff!
Love, does that please you? Ah, but what does he,
The Cousin! what does he to please you more?[40]

I am grown peaceful as old age tonight.
I regret little, I would change still less.[41]
Since there my past life lies, why alter it?
The very wrong to Francis!—it is true
I took his coin, was tempted and complied,
And built this house and sinned, and all is said.
My father and my mother died of want.[42] 250
Well, had I riches of my own? you see
How one gets rich! Let each one bear his lot.
They were born poor, lived poor, and poor they died;[43]
And I have labored somewhat in my time
And not been paid profusely. Some good son

---

[39]Plural of *scudo*, an Italian coin worth about one dollar.

[40]Andrea's weak, pitiable, contemptible character becomes even clearer as we study ll. 204-243. He knows that his wife is unfaithful to him with her "cousin," knows even that the picture he is painting of her is apparently to be used to pay the gambling debts of her lover. Yet Andrea in his pathetic weakness is willing to plead with his wife to share her evenings with him, to buy him with her smiles. If only, he tells her, she will give him this one evening he will let her have her way in everything.

[41]There seems little question but that Browning intensely disliked and pitied Andrea. Especially Browning must have disliked Andrea's weak resignation and defeat, evidenced by ll. 244-245 and the passage that follows. It is one thing to make mistakes. It is another thing to make serious mistakes and not regret them, talking as Andrea in his vacillating weakness here talks.

[42]While Andrea was squandering money in luxury on his wife, he allowed his parents to live and die in poverty.

[43]Note that in his callous weakness Andrea even becomes cruel and cynical.

Paint my two hundred pictures—let him try![44]
No doubt, there's something strikes a balance. Yes,
You loved me quite enough, it seems tonight.
This must suffice me here. What would one have?
In heaven, perhaps, new chances, one more chance— 260
Four great walls in the New Jerusalem,
Meted on each side by the angel's reed,
For Leonard,[45] Rafael, Agnolo, and me
To cover—the three first without a wife,
While I have mine! So—still they overcome
Because there's still Lucrezia—as I choose.
Again the Cousin's whistle! Go, my Love.[46]

Thoughts and Questions for Discussion:

1. Point out all the evidences you can within the poem to show dishonesty in Andrea and his wife Lucrezia. Point out also moments of honesty.

2. How has this fundamental dishonesty corrupted their lives and ruined Andrea as a painter?

3. If possible, examine paintings by Andrea del Sarto. How successful is Browning in portraying the qualities of Andrea's later paintings? What differences do you see between Andrea's early and late paintings? Has Browning overemphasized the weaknesses in Andrea's life and paintings?

4. What would Andrea and Lucrezia as found in the poem need to do to rescue their marriage and rescue Andrea as a painter? Is it too late?

---

[44]Note the arrogance that mixes with other weaknesses in Andrea's pathetic nature.

[45]Leonardo da Vinci (1452-1519), another of the greatest of Italian painters. Andrea fancies himself (ll. 259-266) in the company of the great Leonardo da Vinci, Raphael, and Michelangelo, each painting murals on one of the four walls of the New Jerusalem—but the other three to be pitied, *and envied,* because they do not have his Lucrezia as a wife.

[46]This brilliant closing line emphasizes the pathetic contemptibleness of Andrea's weak character as he sends Lucrezia to her lover.

A Run of Gray

by Brian K. Kelly

The valley begins at the south end of Utah Lake. In the northeast corner of the valley stands an unusual mountain—unique because it stands alone and unattached.[1] In the southeast end of the valley both warm and cold springs rise, making the area around them a flat marsh pushed tight against the dry brush-covered hills.

The first white settlers that came to the valley to stay arrived in 1860. Before that, trappers and prospectors occasionally passed through.

Jasson Evans trapped in the valley during the winter of 1855. He named it Warm Springs, when he saw the clouds of steam that continually rose off the ponds in the south end of the valley. Jasson planned a canal from the springs out into the valley toward the lake.

Five years later he came, bringing others, to Warm Springs to stay. He built a one-room adobe house and helped to dig the canal. Cottonwood shoots were put in front of the house for shade. He planted a long row of poplar trees along the south side of the farm to soften the harsh winds from the desert.

* * * * * * * * *

I walked down the lane, caught in the spell of the past as memories of my childhood came in a torrent. I had thought of them before, but now, under the old cottonwoods they were more poignant. My childhood was close. Savouring each moment, I looked past the house down into the meadow, then back to the canal. Yes, it was all still here. The adobe house, the barn, the chicken coop. Everything looked the same except for the cottonwoods. They were crowded along the ditch bank now because of their bigness. Their trunks had turned from the chalky-green color of my youth to rough, scarred, gray supports for the tumbled foliage above them. The canal had fed them well. It had watered the whole valley. My mind wouldn't stay in the present; it kept drifting, going back, remembering my ninth spring in the valley.

The buds on the cottonwoods were beginning to show. It was early spring and the canal was still dry from the winter. Father told me that now I was nine, I was old enough to help clean the canal. The dry moss and old brown weeds had to be cut from the

---

[1]Editor's Note: Those familiar with the valley will recognize this as West Mountain—not Mt. Timpanogos (northeast of Utah Lake) or Mt. Nebo.

banks so the water could run smooth and easy when it was turned into the ditch.

That first day's work was hard. My arms and back were sore and aching. After work Dad said, "I've heard that back east they keep tame ducks to live on the ponds and slow streams. The ducks eat the moss and a lot of other water vegetation." The talk of tame ducks made my tired mind race. I'd never thought of tame ducks before but I knew that there were wild ones in the meadow behind the house. A few stayed near the open water holes during the winter instead of going south. If I could just find and tame some I wouldn't have to hack at these canal banks.

Every day while we worked on the ditch I watched the meadow. It was only a half-mile away and many times I could see ducks landing in the reeds. They would set their wings and glide out of sight behind a wall of rushes. The edge of the cow shed sighted with the corner fence post gave a sightline to the rushes where the ditch was cleaned. I was sure I could go straight to the rushes where I'd seen the ducks land. I didn't say anything to Dad or Mom about my idea. If it worked I wanted to surprise them.

Saturday after the second week of ditch cleaning was over I got up early and started chores by myself. By the time Dad got to the barn I had the heifer half milked. After chores and breakfast, I said that I wanted to go to the meadow to look for frogs. Dad didn't usually care for me doing useless things, but this morning he said it was okay. I guess he didn't have to question why a nine-year-old boy would be interested in frogs.

At first I didn't know what to look for. I followed the line from the side of the cow shed to the corner post, then straight towards the big clump of rushes I had picked out before. When I got to the rushes, I couldn't see anything except tangles of reeds lying every-way in the water. On one tangle of rushes I did see a white and tan pile of fluff that was dry and out of the water. It looked like some animal had killed a bird there. I searched back and forth between the several springs in the meadow until noon and still I didn't see a nest. On the way back to the house I saw another pile of down. This one was on dry ground, nestled in the salt grass. I put my hand on the fluff and underneath the softness felt something hard. Warily reaching in the softness I brushed some of the down away and counted nine eggs. They were bigger than chicken eggs and olive-green in color. Whipping off my shirt I tied knots in the sleeves and neck. Then one by one I placed the eggs carefully in it. On the way back to the house I waded out to the first pile of fluff I had seen. In this nest there were ten eggs.

It was hard to walk even. Nineteen eggs in the shirt made it heavy and it kept swinging back and forth, but I made it home without a mishap. Dad was surprised when I told him about the eggs. Together we fixed two nesting boxes with fresh straw and put them in the corner of the coop. We placed ten eggs in one nest and nine in the other one. We weren't sure whether we could get a hen to sit on the strange eggs, but we left a pan of wheat on the floor and went to the house. After supper Dad went back to the coop with a lantern. Sure enough two hens had adopted the nests.

I kept a close watch on the nests during the next three weeks. I didn't need to worry because the hens seemed to treat the eggs like their own. Every day or two they would slide back and forth on them and roll them with their beaks. Dad said that eggs had to be turned every day or so if they were going to hatch. Both Dad and I were afraid that the hens would get tired of sitting on the eggs. Duck eggs take a week longer to hatch than chicken eggs do.

The eggs started to hatch on the 28th day after I found them in the meadow. The hens didn't seem to know the difference. They treated the little yellow flat-billed balls of fluff like they were baby chicks. It was amusing to watch the hens scratching in the dirt around the coop for the ducks and them not even paying attention. The ducklings wouldn't gather under the hens' wings like chicks do. The most comical thing was when the ducks first took to water. The hens were trying to lead their new charges along the bank of the canal in search of food. Soon as the little ducks got near the water they scrambled down the bank and slid into the canal. The hens were frantic, they ran back and forth trying to call the ducklings back. The little ducks lived in the water a lot of the time from then on. Dad and I both kept a tab on them so they wouldn't travel too far up or down the canal. A hawk tried for the ducklings one day but they escaped by diving. This made us feel good; we knew we didn't have to worry about the ducks as long as the water was kept over a foot deep.

The following Sunday was Conference Sunday. This meant we had to make a five-mile trip to the Stake Center. A fun time coming and going, but the long talks at conference were hard to sit through. Kids played and most of the older people ended up sleeping in the afternoon.

All I got out of conference that day was that there is a natural and an unnatural man. I never noticed the difference before; I just figured that a man was good whether he had brown tobacco stains along the side of his wagon or not. I did like the part about children being pure and naturally good. I couldn't see how a natural child was good and a natural man was bad, but by this time I quit trying to figure it out and leaned against Dad and fell asleep.

On the way home from conference I asked Dad why God made some things to be good when they're natural and some naturally bad. "Well son," Dad answered, "a lot of it depends on the point of view. Before the pioneers settled out here the Indians waited every year for the coming of the grasshoppers. To them the grasshoppers were good. They thought God sent the grasshoppers to them for their food supply. When I was a boy in Salt Lake that first summer after we came west, we were depending on our meager crops to carry us through the coming winter. The crops were growing and we hoped for a good harvest. Then one day the sky became black with grasshoppers. They moved down from the hills towards the crops eating every green thing in their path. No one knew what to do. We tried to drown them in ditches, we burned them, and still they kept coming. The sky was black with them. Every morning your uncle and I would get up at dawn and walk back and forth through the grain holding a thirty foot rope between us. The rope would flip the stalks of wheat so that the grasshoppers would fall off before they could eat the heads of grain. Finally, when many people were ready to give up and began cursing the leaders, the Lord sent the seagulls to help us. For weeks they filled the sky, eating the grasshoppers until the crops were saved. Son, those gulls were naturally good for us. God sent them to help us. Now there were some good men who grumbled against the leaders. So they were sort of naturally good and bad at the same time. This is what free agency means. Everyone has to choose and we are not all good or all bad as some people think." Smiling wryly he added, "I guess most everyone has his natural times."

The conversation was interrupted as we drove down the lane to the farm. Gulls were circling and diving along the canal. We weren't alarmed until we got close enough to see that the canal was almost dry.

I scrambled over the side of the wagon and ran up the ditch to where the gulls were diving, just in time to scare a gull out of the bottom of the canal. Its mouth was open wide with a ball of yellow fluff in it. The white throat worked in and out as the yellow and then orange feet passed out of sight into the pulsing maw. It swallowed the duckling alive and whole, just like I had seen them eat mice. Dad came walking along in the muddy ditch with his head down searching along the banks for the ducks. Together we found three. Three out of nineteen. "I guess only these are left, son," Dad said. With my chest throbbing and eyes burning I ran to the haystack where no one could see me and cried.

I didn't see Dad until it was time to do chores. I started milking before he explained about the ducks. I was grateful for the delay. Somehow it was easier to listen with the cow's body between us. To lean my forehead against the warm flank gave me a sort of comfort. Also, the mechanical action of milking helped to ease my hurt. Dad said, "The reason the canal was dry was because Brother Wright had the whole stream turned on his farm. He opened all his headgates so he could let the water run on all of his fields. He said that it was wrong to change the water on Sunday. If he had used his share he would have had to change the water every three hours."

For me the blame wasn't on Brother Wright as much as the gulls. I didn't want to know reasons why; I wanted more direct action. I had to find a way to release the awful hurt inside of me.

When I awoke the next morning I knew exactly what I wanted to do. Somehow I would get even with those seagulls. After chores I headed for the point in the distance where the lone mountain meets the lake. This is where the gulls seemed to come from and disappear to. I didn't notice the sunny spring day. My ferocious conviction was driving me on a mission of destruction.

When I got to the foothills along the lake I couldn't help running. Caught in the combined force of gravity and my hate, I ran and stomped, in an erratic pattern, back and forth along the ledges and rocks above the water. A cloud of shrieking gulls circled and swooped over me. I didn't notice them, running back and forth along the bank stomping and kicking at the gull nests in my path. I didn't notice the shrill cries of the gulls. I didn't shy when they swooped at me. I was caught up in my frenzied death act.

The buff-green, brown-speckled eggs were easy to see along the ledges and among the rocks. Stupid birds, I could smash their whole nest with one kick. The eggs, usually in threes, were lying all along among the rocks, sometimes bunched around a few sticks and bits of debris but mostly alone and bare on the ground. The fact that they didn't build a nest made me want to destroy them all the more. They didn't seem fit to live. I was running more jerkily now but still seldom missed squashing a baby gull or mashing a speckled egg. A sickle-shaped horde of gulls shrieked and cried as they beat up and down in the air above the slashed path along the hillside. The more nests I destroyed, the thicker the cloud of gulls above me got. I wasn't conscious of fatigue, but I stumbled more and hated less. Suddenly as I lashed at a nest knee-high above me, I fell on the rocks. I struggled to get up but I couldn't. The pent-up hate and anger was leaving in its place an impotency. I didn't even care about getting up. I just lay and cried. Heart-broken convulsive sobs racked my body.

I didn't know how long I lay like this, but when I got up, the pieces of speckled shell and globs of yolk-mixed blood had hardened on me. Even the soft, pale hair on my arms was clotted with the mess. Slowly I made my way back up the foothill away from the water and the gull nests until I topped the slight crest of the hill where I had begun my run. In front of me the whole valley was visible. I could see the glinting ribbon of the canal that would lead me home. Turning my back on this, I faced toward the lake. The gulls were still above their ravaged nests. I didn't hate anything now. The mess on me had dried hard. This along with the vision of the frantic gulls in the distance made the empty feeling inside of me change to an ache of nausea. I began to be sick. Retching, I vomited, heaving up my hurt and nausea.

Standing, but weak and unsure on my feet, I stumbled down the hill towards the canal and home. Cutting the canal about four miles from home, I plunged in and waded in the waist-high cool water. I walked, leaning into the slight current, letting the dried egg and blood soak off. The cool water made me conscious of my senses —the bright sun, breeze from the hills, my tired muscles.

Two miles from home I came out of the water, clean of the mess. The egg and blood was being carried back to the lake.

The sun was down when I got home. Dad had already finished the chores, but he didn't say anything about it. Mother did make me change clothes before supper. She had cooked the big meal at noon, but there was bread and milk and honey left for supper. She didn't say anything when I passed the honey by and ate bread and milk and onions along with Dad. The bread and milk tasted pleasant with the fresh crispness of the onions except when Dad and Mom looked at me; then the whole mouthful went flat. In desperation I had to excuse myself and go to bed. I couldn't look them in the eye. I was alone and miserable.

Next morning started the same as others. Dad shook me so we could milk and do chores together. Somehow this morning I had to do my best. I milked the heifer so fast there was a solid-looking layer of foam covering the milk. This made it easy to flip out the occasional fly or speck of manure. On the way back to the house a few seagulls flew over and Dad saw me intently watching them. He spoke quietly beside me. "Son, they can't be blamed for killing your ducks, and they do eat a lot of mice and insects." I couldn't hold it any longer and began to tell him where I had been yesterday.

I tried to make it not sound so bad by telling how the gulls don't even build a nest. They just lay their eggs on the bare ground. They don't leave a cover of down over their eggs like the ducks do. Dad interrupted and began one of his sermon answers, "The gulls did what they did because of their nature. They are a special creation put here for a special purpose like you and me. It wasn't right to destroy those baby gulls. The seagulls killed your ducks so they could live, same as the Indians were pushed out of this valley. Those Indians got their food here and yet God sent us. I can't answer why. All I know is that we must do what we have to do. I guess compared to a duck a gull doesn't build a very good nest, but they do live and raise their young the same way. I've already told why the gulls are special to me. This summer I'd like you to watch them as they hatch and grow. Learn about them. When they are little they are about as ugly as you were when you were born. But they change. Look up at them now and see how they circle and glide, notice the set of their wings. I guess that next to a sailing ship, or the first time I saw your mother dancing, a gull in flight is the most graceful motion I've ever seen.

"Watch their color, besides the beauty of their shape. They get whiter and whiter as they grow older. They start a motley brown and gray color and every year come closer to pure white."

That summer I began to watch the gulls as they changed from ugly chicks to brown, then gray fledglings, then on to a purer shade of white each year. That summer I began to watch men age also. Many times since I have envied the white gulls.

Discussion of "A Run of Gray"

A year ago in Volume 2 of *Out of the Best Books* we included several selections by L.D.S. authors, partly to illustrate the excellent creative work being done by members of the Church. Now in Volume 3 we again want to include several such selections. As the first of these, we have a short story, "A Run of Gray" by Brian Kelly, winner of first place in the 1966 Vera Hinckley Mayhew Short Story Contest at Brigham Young University.[1]

[1]The story was previously published by the BYU Press in the Spring 1966 issue of the *Wye Magazine* and later appeared (abridged) in the May 1967 issue of *The Improvement Era*.

The young author, Brian Kermit Kelly, was born just twenty-seven years ago on 18 November 1940. He spent most of his youth in Santaquin, Utah, before moving to Provo, Utah, at the age of thirteen. Schooling was interrupted for a two-year Church mission to New Zealand in 1961-63. Then he graduated from Brigham Young University in the summer of 1966 with a major in Advertising and Public Relations. In May 1966 he married Petrea Gillespie. They are now living in Richland, Washington, where Brian is working as a public relations man and technical writer for Battelle-Northwest Laboratories, a worldwide research corporation. He indicates that creative writing is still his "real love" and says he hopes to continue writing in the years ahead, as surely a young man with his talent should.

Although written by a relatively inexperienced young author, "A Run of Gray" is an excellent story. It is vividly realistic in detail, skilled in language, and significant in meaning. It is also a very interesting story, appealing both to young and mature readers.

The story is not flawless. The simplicity of its sentence structure becomes a little monotonous, and it is ineffectively repetitious in a spot or two. Also, sometimes its words are not as dramatically intense and symbolically rich as they might be. These, however, are minor weaknesses in a story that is amazingly strong and meaningful for a beginning writer. Descriptively it is especially good, having vivid, realistic details reminding one of the stories of John Steinbeck: the poplar and cottonwood trees planted everywhere by early pioneers, the contrast between duck eggs and seagull eggs, and between duck nests and seagull nests, the ducks and gulls themselves, a boy milking cows with his head resting in the cow's warm flank as the heavy foam forms on the surface of the milk in the pail, the problems of hatching duck eggs with regular barnyard hens, the behavior of restless boys at Stake Conference, etc. Obviously the author knows what it is to be a boy on a farm.

The story goes beyond just descriptive excellence, however. Its dramatic conflict is equally vivid, especially the account of the gulls devouring the fluffy ducklings, the boy smashing the gull eggs and baby gulls in his fury, and the subsequent scene with the boy washing in the canal. This is first-quality narration, and woven into the whole story is a rich background of Mormon history, including the famous incident of the seagulls and the crickets. The result is a story that is well handled descriptively, narratively, dramatically, and historically. And central to all of this is its tightly integrated meaning, which lifts it from being merely a good boys' story to being a mature story for thoughtful adults.

The theme of the story is suggested from the beginning—in the very title, in fact: "A Run of Gray." It starts to take clear shape especially when the boy, while listening to a sermon, becomes puzzled about the difference between a natural and an unnatural man. Finally the meaning becomes fully clear when the boy realizes through painful experience that all living things are both good and bad, depending upon point of view and situation—the grasshoppers, the seagulls, Indians, Brother Wright, mankind, everybody and everything. This is a great and essential lesson for the boy to learn, and for everyone to learn in the process of growing up. Particularly is it important to learn that, since all our lives embrace tendencies towards both good and evil, it is vital that we develop attitudes that will strengthen the good within us; for, as experience teaches, attitude is a powerful determiner of human behavior.

Thoughts and Questions for Discussion:

1. Point out specific descriptive details that make this story realistically accurate.

2. Explain the title "A Run of Gray." In what ways are the grasshoppers, the seagulls, Brother Wright, and

men in general gray rather than black or white? Why is it important for us to see this about ourselves and about each other?

3. In the last paragraph the narrator says that after watching men and gulls age he has often envied the gulls, which (as the father says) grow "whiter and whiter" as they grow older. What are the implications of these comments? What can people do to resist and surmount the darkening pressures of life? What attitudes will help?

4. We have included this story in the section of the book concerned with honesty. In examining ourselves, other people, and the world around us it is important to be as honest as possible. What truths about people and life in general does the boy learn in the process of growing up in this story?

Notes on Two Other Short Stories

We had intended to add a third short story in this section, either "Miss Brill" by Katherine Mansfield, or "Counterparts" by James Joyce. Unfortunately, because of copyright regulations and other problems, these stories could not be included. Both stories, however, are significantly concerned with some aspects of honesty not covered by the other selections. Therefore, a few comments on them seem desirable.

"Miss Brill," as many readers familiar with the story will remember, brilliantly portrays a lonely woman who is basically dishonest with herself. She has withdrawn from family, friends, and responsibilities—withdrawn, that is, to a life of emptiness and trivial routine. This is not to imply, of course, that a woman without a family necessarily leads a lonely, empty life, and certainly not that such a woman is dishonest. All women may live abundantly and achieve happiness richly if they give of their talents freely in friendship and responsibility, and all women surely may be honest. But if a woman—married or unmarried, with or without children—never gives of herself in creativity or service to others, she is likely to be lonely and unhappy, and the temptation will be ever present to escape in dishonest pretense. Such a woman is Miss Brill. Apparently she has a job as a teacher, or tutor, but teaching, which could have provided her a full, rewarding life, obviously means little to her because she lives to escape from it to spend her Sunday afternoons at the park. And what Sunday afternoons they are! "Oh, how fascinating it was! How she enjoyed it! How she loved sitting here, watching it all!" Whom is she fooling? Certainly not the reader, nor the people around her, who generally are totally unaware of her. She is fooling only herself, of course, as she tries to escape from the dull, drab monotony of her pathetic, lonely life. She has no family, no friends, no responsibilities that are meaningful to her, no meaningful function of any kind.

Her life is so centered within herself and so empty, lonely, and superficial that whether she finds or does not find an almond in the slice of honey cake she buys once a week on the way home from the park makes all the difference between a successful day and sharp disappointment. As a result, she becomes a pathetic, dishonest day-dreamer, trying pitiably to pretend that life has meaning for her. (Question for discussion: For most women, life's fulfillment comes through marriage and children; but sometimes, for various reasons, a woman does not have a family, or her family has grown up and moved away. How can such a woman—and all women—avoid being like Miss Brill?)

"Counterparts" by James Joyce portrays a man who attempts to escape the frustrations of his own weak, dishonest life by drowning his weakness in drink and bullying those who are weaker than he is. Beyond just depicting the evils of drunkenness, the story shows how a man, confronted on all sides by personal frustrations in his office job and his relations with other people, takes these frustrations out at the end of the day on his own family, mistreating those he should love. (Thoughts for discussion: (1) Farrington, the central character in the story, although a large fattish man, is portrayed as basically a coward and weakling, both physically and morally—that is, he is a bully. Are bullies generally cowards, cowering to those with more strength and bullying those with less strength? (2) At the end of the story, after a day of increasing frustrations, Farrington, for seemingly trivial reasons, gets angry and whips his little son. Obviously the real reason is that Farrington is angry at the world and releases his anger by punishing the little boy. Is this a widespread human reaction, and a form of dishonesty—to take one's frustrations out on the members of one's family, and to hurt those we love? Do people tend to be harshest in human relations towards those we should treat with greatest tenderness—husbands and wives, parents and children? (3) The story centers around a man and his frustrations, but does the lesson apply equally to women? Do women sometimes express their frustrations by nagging their husbands and being sharp with their children? (4) Farrington is willing to admit some of his sins but is reluctant to admit his weaknesses, even to himself. Is this also a human tendency—to be more willing to admit one's sins than to admit one's weaknesses?)

SECTION THREE

Patience and Forbearance

by Robert K. Thomas

PATIENCE AND FORBEARANCE

"In your patience possess ye your souls."
—*New Testament*

Introductory Comments

It is appropriate that a section concerning patience should follow material discussing cheerfulness and honesty, for patience often carries needlessly bleak connotations and, occasionally, is surrounded by illusions.

Perhaps because the root of the word suggests suffering, we have become conditioned to equating patience with pain. The stereotype of the patient man is Job. Afflicted with boils, derided by many of his associates, he sits among ashes in tormented, passive resignation to the apparent will of God. If this is our view, we probably do both the Lord and Job an injustice. The first two chapters of the Book of Job may suggest such a picture, but beginning with chapter three we have thirty-nine chapters which should deepen our understanding of Job's special difficulty and the general problem of patience.

It is worth noting that Job seems to make little effort to probe his situation for the first few days but, after a week of unmitigated suffering, he wants to know *why*. He is not resigned to his state, and in dialogue with the three friends who come to comfort him he tries his best to understand what has happened. It is the so-called comforters who exhort him to simply accept. Lest we assume that this is what the Lord wants in this case, we need to remember His explicit statement to the comforters in the final chapter:

> My wrath is kindled against thee, and against thy two friends, for ye have not spoken of me the thing that is right, as my servant Job hath.
> 42:7

The fact that, at the end, Job doesn't really know *why* anymore than he did at the beginning should not lead us to assume that his efforts are in vain. In his desire to know the meaning of his suffering he learns much about himself that he hadn't really understood in the days of his health and ease. He finds out that he must control his pride—especially that self-righteousness that had colored a large part of his philanthropy in earlier days. He must also control his tendency to seek answers he is not prepared to receive. In the Lord's telling phrase, such a person "darkeneth counsel by words without knowledge."

In some degree, Job's plight is a very common one. We do not understand why some things happen, and we often try to rationalize our circumstances by assuming one or another of the two reactions which are explicitly condemned in the Book of Job: we assume that whatever happens is the Lord's will and simply endure resignedly, or we insist upon overly simple answers. The truly patient man—Job at the end of his book—exhibits forbearance; that is, the ability to recognize his ignorance and to control his present actions in light of faith in future knowledge. After the Lord has spoken to him from the whirlwind, Job does not insist upon immediate answers which resolve everything. If we would emulate such patience we should be willing to wait and work, confident that answers exist but also aware that we may need to prepare ourselves to receive them.

This preparation may not involve great physical effort. John Milton's Sonnet 19—later entitled "On His Blindness"—concludes with the celebrated assertion: "They also serve who only stand and wait." It should be noted, however, that the implied injunction here is not really passive. Rather, each one should be prepared to do what he can. The whole mood of this poem would be altered if the word "sit" were exchanged for "stand" in the final line.

In Betsey Barton's *And Now to Live Again* we see

a very courageous young woman persist and grow. Confined to a wheelchair from her youth as the result of an automobile accident, Miss Barton lets us see her beginning despondency and final triumph. When she finally sets down an account of her private Gethsemane she has been able to transmute pain and despair into insight and understanding. In so doing she details the process by which we may all turn from the apparently hopeless to the clearly hopeful.

In the simple poems of Wang Wei and the classic aphorisms of Marcus Aurelius we encounter philosophies of patience which, at first glance, are attractive and persuasive. It is only when we think about the implications of these works that we are disturbed. For the basic thought underlying Wang Wei's gentle lines is one of negation, and the Stoic position of Marcus Aurelius tries to solve difficulties by asserting that they have no real existence.

The selection which concludes our discussion of patience and forbearance is Walt Whitman's "A Noiseless, Patient Spider." Here we are introduced to persistent effort that is both significant and successful. Note what an affirmation of life there is in this poem. It helps us understand that basic to patience is faith in goals that are both worthwhile and achieveable.

Sonnet 19 "On His Blindness"

by John Milton

When I consider how my light is spent,
Ere half my days, in this dark world and wide,
And that one talent[1] which is death to hide,
Lodged with me useless, though my soul more bent
To serve therewith my maker, and present
My true account, lest he returning chide,
'Doth God exact day-labor, light denied,'
I fondly[2] ask; But patience to prevent
That murmur, soon replies, 'God doth not need
Either man's work or his own gifts, who best
Bear his mild yoke, they serve him best, his state
Is kingly. Thousands[3] at his bidding speed
And post[4] o'er land and ocean without rest:
They also serve who only stand and wait.'

Discussion of "Sonnet 19"

The sonnet form was first used in Italy in the twelfth century. From there it spread to France, Spain and England, becoming particularly important in Great Britain during Elizabethan times. With the printing of Shakespeare's *Sonnets* in 1609, however, the great wave of English sonnet writing began to subside. So sudden and complete was this shift away from sonnet writing that by 1630—when John Milton turned to the sonnet form in English—he was almost alone in his interest.

Although he left a total of only twenty-three sonnets (five in Italian, the remainder in English), Milton had an extraordinary influence upon the development of this form in English. When there was a revival of interest in lyric

---

[1]cf. Matthew 25:14-30
[2]foolishly
[3]of angelic beings
[4]travel with speed, as on post horses

poetry near the end of the eighteenth century, it was to the Miltonic sonnet that poets turned. The Italian or Petrarchan sonnet, so-called because it was brought to its fullest development by Francesco Petrarch (1304-74), is a fourteen line poem in which there is usually a clear pause after the first eight lines and a rather precise rhyme scheme in the final six lines.

As you will note in "Sonnet 19," there is no pause at all after the first eight lines; in fact line eight is an explicitly "run-on" line. The effect of such an approach is to free the sonnet from one of its mechanical restrictions and thus make it appropriate for informal, highly personal statements. While sonnets were traditionally love poems, theme and form had become so stylized by Elizabethan times, that convention often tyrannized content. The Miltonic sonnet rescued this form from poetic pedantry.

Although there has been some discussion by critics concerning the precise date of this poem, it is generally agreed that it was probably written between 1652 and 1655 while Milton was Secretary for Foreign Tongues to the Council of State. Apparently he was totally blind by 1652, although the exact cause of his blindness has never been discovered. There is no question but that Milton was overwhelmed by his loss, and his usual self-confidence appears to have been dealt a crushing blow. But there is little justification in citing this poem as one of total abnegation. There is promise of some recovery in this poem, for Milton has made peace with his fate. He is saying that his own deeds and genius are of less value than personal integrity. He is prepared to receive counsel at the Lord's hand.

The result is dynamic. Waiting is not an end in itself but the prelude to something he has yet to envision. Few poems are more successful than this in establishing a fresh look at patience. The problem is not whether one can endure calamity; the real test is whether one can persist and grow.

And Now to Live Again

by Betsey Barton

There are, it seems to me, two tragic facts in human existence: We do not appreciate what we have until we lose it. And we only advance through suffering.

A man must indeed lose his life to find it—to appreciate what he has lost more fully. And we are awakened and sensitized to the beauty and preciousness of life, to the mysterious and implacable rules by which it was planned for us by a guiding spirit, only through suffering.

I would have denied both these facts not so long ago. I would have said that one man can learn by another's experience. I would have said that suffering did not lead to anything but despair and death. My circle of suffering has completed its full turn, however. And I see now that the reason the advance of the human race seems so painfully slow, the reason it seems to be of so little use to study history, is because we cannot learn by example: we must learn by direct experience.

Each generation must go through the same struggles and pitfalls as the one before. No generation can blame another. We can only wait our turn at the helm of the world-ship and pass on our inadequate charts to the quicker eyes and hands of those who follow. Wisdom and vision are granted to few, and the few that gain these do so, I have come to believe, in the degree that they are sensitive, in the degree that they suffer.

It is for this reason that the salvaging of the life of one who has been badly hurt is so important. Here is the raw stuff of wisdom and of vision. Too often it is allowed to dwindle into bitterness and failure because of ignorance. Yet if the salvage work is successful, it is like assisting at a birth, a rebirth. There are labor pains and dark, dangerous hours. Death may sometimes be very close. Madness may approach like a haunting specter. One life has been lost and left behind; a new one is beginning. It will need patience and intelligence and courage to see the new life born whole, to see it mature and realize its full possibilities. Nothing will come quickly here. This is a growth, like all of living, and its fulfilment takes months and years.

The growth must be guided by skilled workers and good advice, by understanding, and by love. And when the job is completed, the person who was denied, the person who lost and fell behind in the race with others, will, like the tortoise, come out ahead. For he will have grown in vision. He will know the value of what he has lost and of what he has dared to regain. And, through his new and wiser eyes, he will see that although he lost one life, he has won a new life that in many delicate and tender ways is a far better one.

Had I read this years ago when first I lost the use of my legs I would have thrown down the book in disgust. I was not ready then for any such philosophical phrases. There seemed to be no existing compensation for a boy who has lost a leg, for a child who is born a spastic, for the man who has tuberculosis, or for a girl who cannot move her hand. Yet it has been pressed in upon me that the power which created us, provided for this, too: for faith in the face of despair, for courage in the face of loss, and for tenderness in the face of hopelessness. We are never, we cannot be, left alone. We are taken care of, if we allow ourselves to be, and the law of compensation is a fact. He who loses his life, can find it, in the fullest and most complete sense of the word "find."

This finding does not come about easily or quickly. It demands education: compensation is an acquired taste. It means, at first, a compromise, a substitute for the real, better thing. So I do not like the name rehabilitation. It is meaningless to me. I prefer to call this a reeducation; it is an education for a new life.

If you have a son, or a husband, or a friend, who has suddenly joined the ranks of the invalid, you are privileged. Through them you can watch this process of rebirth take place. You can assist it, or hinder it; you can gain insight into your own education. Just as the study of the insane helps us to understand our own behavior more clearly, because we see ourselves and our behavior dramatized and distorted, so will the study of and participation in the reeducation of a person who has been suddenly hurt, help you to understand yourself. For here, in exaggerated and visible form, is bared the fretwork of human character in the making under pressure. Hidden resources will be tapped. People who seemed weak before may suddenly appear strong. The heroic, stubborn will to survive raises its impressive head. And some who long for death will not die because of this instinct, which is stronger than ourselves, and that pulls us through sickness and shock long after our conscious striving has ceased.

Thus as you watch these forces at work on one you love, do not shrink from them, but try to enter into them through the power of your imagination. Know this man's fears as your fears, slightly exaggerated. See his hopes as your hopes, made more plain. And remember always that he is not different from you, he is not *other* because his outer shell is torn or shattered. He can become part of your education and growth just as you can become part of his. He can make you see through new eyes. You can give him strength through your greater fund of energy. So you can share and draw upon the experience of each other.

2

The dread effects of disaster and disease are a constant in all of human life. But now, more than ever, there are families, and wives and friends who will be receiving the wounded they love back into their circle: the dear people who went from them whole and healthy and who are returned not as they went away, but stricken and hurt. They may be soldiers smashed in battle, they may be children struck by disease, or men and women impaired somehow by accident. Whatever the disaster that has shattered them, their families and friends will stand waiting to receive them—yearning, anxious, wondering; hoping and praying that their acts and feelings toward the ones they love are those that will help them, heal them, and comfort them in their terrible distress.

The anguish of the families must be very great. The agony my parents suffered over my accidents was sharper than my own. I know this now. For the spirit that created us steps in again here and at first the shock is so great it anesthetizes. We who have recently suffered the blow of disaster do not feel it or understand its consequences. We are saved from apprehension by the force of the thing that struck us down, but those who stand beside us are not so well preserved. They can assess the strength of the blow and look ahead to its consequences, and they suffer more for us than we do ourselves because there is nothing they can do at first to alleviate our hurt.

When I look back I see my parents waiting helplessly in the anterooms of hospitals time and again while I was wheeled by them on a stretcher, a still, white, unconscious figure, going up into the mysteries of the dreaded places to remain for long hours while the doctors did necessary things to me in the name of healing. Those times were not hard for me. I was carefully taken care of, preserved from pain. But the suffering of my parents while they waited for the elevators doors to open and for the long stretcher to emerge was very great. They knew what the operations entailed. They knew what was at stake.

How could I know these things, or how it was for them? So bound, so caught within the immediate urgencies of my anesthesia. And when the anesthetic wore off and I was healed and taken home, I remember now how the way was smoothed for me, how everything was made cheerful and beautiful about me, and I did not see it.

I could not look beyond the periphery of my own concerns, my own instant and new concerns. The whole resource of my being was mustered to meet the pain, or the new situation, or the harsh exercise. And I could not look very far into the hearts of those who loved me and who suffered more each time my fever rose. I rarely thought of them. I was myself the only thing, the only sufferer. And so it will be with those who are coming back now, to their families, hurt and torn. These will be the only sufferers, in their eyes, too.

The things that were done for me, endlessly—they come back now. They come tumbling through the years that have gone and buried them over. I remember a little yellow canary my father bought that he placed in the hospital window, to help while the hours away. The canary was a stout fellow and he sat there in the only shaft of sunlight that struck the room through the canyon of the tall buildings outside. He stood on his perch and shouted his heart out for me. And I did not notice.

Some one thought to give me some pet fish. Exotic and tiny they were, silver and vermillion with wide fan tails. They swam beside the bed there in their high, complicated tank. They swam and ate and mated and died. They flirted with me and invited me to look. And I did not notice.

All the things. The special pillows that were brought. The ideas for meals to tempt my shrunken appetite. The books and friends and things arranged. All these come tumbling back now. I had not thought of them for years. But I accepted them all, I think, and sighed and turned away.

How can we be gentle enough to these, the fallen? How can we start to win them back to some belief? How can we, while they lie or sit or stand in our homes, so different? So much the same; so still and weak.

I try to remember how it was with me, so I can tell you now. But nothing comes except time. Time, and days passing. And time again and days passing. Time in which the wounds healed, and the muscles once more held me when I tried to sit up. And time passing once more before the deep scars in the mind began to knit and draw together, before the bitterness receded and the negative, detached feeling lifted. For before I could get well, I had to be taught to care again.

When each new thing was brought to me then and anxious, pleading voices asked me to try, to make an effort, I turned aside. What's the use? I said. And I turned back to the book I was reading, or the puzzle I was working. And we let it go again for a while; we let it go at that.

—But love suffers for the one it adores. It suffers and tries and comes back again. It comes back to win, to coax, to plead. To ask: try now, please, make an effort.

—And love here must have a greater love for the hurt one than that of the immediate attachment. It must be wise, it must look ahead. For here is a beaten thing. Something in it has died. And we do not want to suffocate it with too much offered it yet, as the small, tender plant is killed by the noonday sun. Yet we must try to reach out again and again, as they did with me so long ago, try to reach out and create appetites where there is no appetite for anything. Create the appetite for doing a little more, for wanting a little more strength, a little more activity. Create it and then feed it. And never give food that is too strong meat for the weak-tea capacity, but create the hunger, and give it food in accord with the smallness of its need.

I remember first, the only thing I wanted to do as I lay in bed was to learn to typewrite. I was flat on my back and could not be moved, but this was my only desire, and they made a wooden frame for the machine to hold it. I had a paper with the keys written on it and I memorized them and then set out to type, for I could not see the tops of the keys.

Little things like this at first. Little things, with more to be added later, as the strength of structure grows, as the shock is weakened and finally erased altogether.

Slowly. Slowly. We are weak. We have been hurt. We are irritable, angry, sullen, bitter; there is no hope. Yet the one who loves us enough and who has informed himself about our hurt, about the disease of the one whom he loves, can recognize his appetites, and can help the beloved to feed himself.

3

—Disaster doesn't prepare us. Or if it would prepare, we do not heed the warnings. The soldier in battle sees his comrades fall and is still convinced that he will be safe, until the constant fire and the long time without adequate food and sleep wears his resistance to the ragged edge, and he begins to suspect that every shell has his name written on it. Our friends are hit by a drunken driver, or their child is struck by infantile paralysis—but these things do not happen to us. We are safe, somehow caught in the miraculous fallacy of the human race, the assurance that we are guarded, that it is all right to cross the street carelessly where many have been killed because we are secure, we have a lucky star.

When disaster comes, then, depriving us of an arm, or a leg, or twisting the muscles into uselessness, the reaction must be hard. No matter how much we have been exposed to danger, we were not ready; we did not believe; we were not prepared. We took for granted the security, the safety, the sameness. Took it for granted, watched its upkeep carelessly, let the caterpillar eat at the leaf.

In one second the car twists off the slippery road into a ditch, in one second the pilot in the B-26 crashes and is covered in flaming gasoline, in an instant paralysis may travel over the body, and in a moment of time the already overtaxed nervous system may snap at some final incident, collapsing into deep neurosis.

The cut is there. The face is burned, the body broken, the muscles have already begun to wither—the harsh tread of disaster has left its mark. The flesh feels it; the muscles and nerves show the dreadful scars. But the heart and mind do not see it yet. They do not look. They cover their faces and turn away, since the body must protect itself against such terrible pain. The mind and heart do not pry or fret or question at first when disaster strikes. They do not dare.

The swift plunge from one life to another, the exchange of one costume for another in the dressing-room of Time—this was too quick. It cannot help but fill the victim with dismay, especially if he was used to a normal healthy life before. I do not know for those born into a different, abnormal body. I can only look, as you can, and enter into their lives through the penetrating key of imagination. But I know this: the swift exchange of a once normal body for an impaired, abnormal one, is very hard.

The memories are there, you see. The memories of laughter and of running in the wind, of climbing hill-tops, of walking through the dim and smoky afternoon of a New England fall. Of scrunching to the waves' edge upon the beach's stretch—memories of ease, of light, swift motion, of speed, of grace, of perfect coordination. And the memories cannot be denied at first. They crowd and cluster in each cell of earth and air, of fire and water, that compose the body shell. They crowd and cluster and jostle and mock. They are loud, these memories, blatant.

The boy who could never run, the man who has never been able to move without a spastic quivering, the girl who has never danced—these can know and hear the voices of the memories crowding the wounded soldier's mind, only by inference. They cannot, perhaps, listen to the wretched voices themselves.

So, here, first of all, lies the beginning of rebirth. And it must come through a leave-taking, a purging, almost a denial of the other life, the one before. The boy with a leg now gone can revisit the winding road up which he hiked to the pool at the foot of the waterfall to fish. Of course he can. But not yet, not yet. The memories of the other life must be shut out. The steel door of repression snaps shut on them and stays shut fast. When it opens over the years and old memories are allowed to escape into the conscious, like the evils from Pandora's box, they will have lost their sting a little. They may no longer jostle or bustle and shout. They may be a little faded, quieter. Not so shrill.

The memories have their use, however. They can be used as a bridge into the new life. There need be nothing wasted or lost in all of our experience. There is an economy within the body-mind that can be valuable, that can be turned into coin of the realm—if we run into the right economist. The memories can act as the bridge to recovery in this way:

The nurse takes the withered leg of the child who has just had infantile paralysis in her hand and puts it through the motions of bending and straightening. She says to the child as she does it: "Remember how it was when you could do this for yourself. Use those memories in the muscles there. Remember that."

Dr. Earl Carlson, who was born a spastic and who has overcome his disease to a great extent, adds evidence on this. In his book he writes of a young baseball player who had been ill with sleeping sickness. He came to Carlson for help and stood inertly upon the lawn of his house, unable to think straight, unable to move. Someone picked up a baseball and shouted and threw the ball straight at the young man. And, suddenly, his right arm shot out and caught the ball and his body swung into the graceful, easy pose of the pitcher as he sped the ball back to the man who had thrown it, then he stood still, once more inert. But the memories were there and they responded.

The man who was good at games, who was athletic, can use those memories to help him learn to handle his artificial leg, to get his balance, and to walk with coordination. And the girl who had been a pianist was seen to lose herself in the rapture of the music that came from her speeding fingers upon the piano, although she was unable, when she was away from the piano, to control them enough to feed herself.

The memories are the precious bridge, as well as the dreadful torture. The right economist can weed out the memories, using those that will reeducate muscles and nerves to the coordination they once had, discarding those memories that are no longer applicable to our new life. The memories are images, images of what we could do and of what we were going to do. Some of those images must be scrapped, the impossible ones—like learning to skate, or to ride a horse—and other, more compatible images, substituted in their place.

Because of this precious bridge of memory—this bridge that fades and recedes so fast when disaster strikes—the timing of the rescue work is of prime importance. If the wounds have healed and the fever is normal, if the scars are healed and the bones are whole, then substitution of the new images should begin immediately.

Rescue cannot come too quickly, or start too early. If it is not brought to the victim of disaster soon, if he is allowed to lie in bed for a long time doing nothing, there will be a seroius psychic lesion which may result in total paralysis of the will. The previous bridge, the memory of normal and coordinated motion, fades. The mind retreats and hides. It withdraws from the painful points of contact with reality—the wounded, or injured parts, and takes refuge in dreaming, or escapes into fantasy. The link is lost, the chain is broken between one life and the next. What Sister Kenny calls mental alienation sets in. The mind wanders off, and becomes strange to the parts it must habitate, to the parts with which it must cooperate in healing.

I have seen the fatal results of rescue work begun late. I have felt them in myself. For a year after my accident I was allowed to lie in bed doing nothing. I was given no exercise, no proper diet. I lost weight rapidly. I became so thin I had to lie on a rubber mattress so my bones wouldn't stick through the thin covering of flesh and make sores. No one told me I could do anything for myself. The nurse massaged my legs at night, while I read a book. The only movements I made for almost a year in bed were rolling motions when I was turned from side to side.

In recent months I have been able to visit some of the people who sit in back bedrooms around the city because rescue work was not brought to them. I have seen them there in chairs, or in bed, hopelessly despairing, negative, suicidal, believing there was never to be any relief from their situation. A young girl in the Bronx, after breaking her neck in a high dive, was sent home from the hospital and allowed to lie for five years in bed, without knowing that she could get up in a wheel-chair, that she could dress and feed herself, that with proper exercise, she could learn to open her paralyzed fingers and turn the pages of the book her starved mind longed to read. A boy of nine had infantile paralysis and was taken to the hospital, where he lived as a favorite of the nurses and doctors for nineteen years in a wheel-chair. He was gay, witty and clever. Everybody liked him. But the last time I saw him he was a happy man because he had learned to walk at last on braces and crutches and is now working as a jeweler.

The instances could be multiplied many times. You probably know of some one in your neighborhood who needs help now and who is not getting it. The longer they are allowed to lie in bed or to sit in wheel-chairs doing nothing, the further away from hope they grow. The paralysis creeps up into the heart and into the mind. There is no courage. The will is gone. When rescue finally comes it takes years to win the mind and heart back into useful work, back into a useful attitude. The break was complete, the wires are down, the poles no longer stand. The memories have faded, receded, been denied. They must be won back and reestablished; they must be restored all over again.

When disaster strikes, rescue should not only come right away, but it should in some measure be successful. For if repeated efforts fail, this also leads to heartbreak, to a belief that there is no real aid in existence, and finally again to paralysis of the will. How much truth we can stand about our condition must be left to the judgment of the worker. But I believe that in the long run honesty works out better than any attempt to sugarcoat the truth. The truth should be told, but the door must be left open on recovery. We should not ever be told that our case is hopeless. We know so little about the powers of healing. We are not even sure how long it takes nerves to regenerate. We are just beginning to discover the livingness of the tissue of the body and to find that, if this livingness can be maintained, nerves and muscles and eyes and organs can be transplanted from one body to another. Medicine is just beginning; we are in the midst of rapid progress. A doctor cannot now look a patient in the face and say, "Your case is hopeless." There is always the chance that he will recover, and there is always grace.

But just as we must be left with some hope, so must we not be given to hope falsely. There were too many men, in the beginning of my pilgrimage, who looked me in the eye and said, "I will make you well." There can be no greater falsehood than this for no person can make another well. I knew so little then, I believed these men. They enlisted all my confidence and trust. And when there was no progress under their care, the heartbreak came again, and the will died its second or third, or fourth death.

Thus rescue should come immediately, as it is doing at the battlefronts, to be its most effective, to achieve the greatest possible recovery. And rescue must be successful in some measure, if the effort at rebirth, the transition from one life to another, is not to end still-born.

6

As we examine the living body-brain processes that have been jarred into disharmony by disaster, we begin to see something of the subtle and intricate business realignment must be. We begin to understand that if reeducation is to start it must begin by convincing us in mind and heart that if we are to recover what we have lost, we must first become ready to desire recovery by facing and accepting the fact of our hurt.

It takes time, but it will come, it must come—the ability to see and bear with what has happened, and now to move ahead. It will come always if we can start slowly enough with the few little things we are able to do, and begin to build on them. Not looking back; not looking ahead, but working steadily *now*. If we are faithful over these first few things, we will be rewarded. If we are faithful, we will become able, finally, to do much more. And if there are ninety-nine things missing and lost and only one present and found, let us try to remember the one that is present and take it and build upon it. For reeducation begins often in a tiny way, with little things, gently.

Sometimes the things it must begin with are very unpropitious. Sometimes it may seem that there is no use beginning at all. But the way in which I began was so small, with so little hope, that perhaps it will be of use to tell about it here.

I remember so well when I came to the man who helped me to face the fact of my hurt, and who helped me to help myself. I had been six weary years looking for the right kind of direction and here, suddenly, in an unexpected place, I found it, right next door.

There were ninety-nine things I could not do then, and two I could. I could breathe. "Breathe then," the strange man said. "Breathe like this."

And he showed me.

And he said, "There is one other thing you can do—move your abdominal muscles. So move them," he said, "like this."

And he showed me.

And then he said the things that made it all right for me to breathe and move my tummy muscles. Made it all right for me to start in and in this tiny way, go to work.

He said: "Don't believe me. Don't listen to what I say. Just do these simple things—these innocent things. Do them hard. And let them prove themselves."

I started in then. I desperately needed acts, not words. I needed deeds, not phrases about patience and courage and faith. I needed something I could *do*. And the only things I could do were these: to breathe and to exercise my tummy muscles. But upon these two exercises hung my health. With these two simple things as rungs, I started to climb the ladder of strength to win back my life.

As I did the exercises and felt myself getting strong and found through the breathing that my sluggish circulation was becoming quick and clean and clear, I began to have the qualities I had been expected to have: I began to have courage and patience and faith. Faith because the exercises worked. Faith without works doesn't come easily when we have been badly hurt. And courage because courage can only come from inner strength. And, finally, patience, because I began to see that if I did these things long enough and hard enough, they could not help but build up my health and increase my vitality.

Our mental attitude becomes better the minute we have been shown how to begin. The fever is down; the wounds are healed. Let us start with simple things: deep breathing and internal work. We can manage some exercises while we are lying here. We must be helped back to general strength with what remains to us, and our specific hurt, like those of the sick soldiers, will clear up more rapidly.

Once we have recognized that the total person needs reeducation, and not just a part, it is a simple step to see that no specific hurt can be treated and the rest of the body-mind left to go as it will. Too often in reeducation I have seen the mistake of treating the specific hurt and nothing else, and each time I have seen it, recovery has been long and delayed and tedious. We must begin to tone ourselves up from the inside out, starting with the place where we have our life: the torso. For this is the center of the body, this contains all the vital organs of digestion, assimilation, elimination, circulation.

14

Last winter the Air Force sent selected personnel through the Institute to study its methods of reeducation, in preparation for the wounded men who would be coming back from overseas.

One of these men, a sergeant, came down every afternoon to work with those of us who were exercising in the big room at the Institute which is equipped to prepare us for the situations we will meet in the world outside. There are life-size models in this room of bus steps, subway steps, and ordinary house steps. Two wooden models of street curbs stand at either end of the room, and a replica of a streetlight can be turned on to time the person who is trying to get across the street before the light changes. The room is as long as the ordinary New York avenue is wide.

There is a row of chairs standing against the wall in this room—chairs of all different kinds, from the heavy, overstuffed chair to the small folding metal chair which some misguided person invented to be used at social functions. There are mats on the floor where those who need muscle strength before they can attempt to walk lie in rows and exercise in rhythm together. And finally there are parallel bars, ladders, wooden gym bars set in the wall, some stretching machines for arm-strengthening, a rowing machine, an electric bicycle, and all the rest of the usual gym equipment.

The sergeant watched us each day, trying to attain some ease in walking, trying to learn to balance on legs which were unsteady or paralyzed, trying to overcome the cold fear of falling down. He saw people who had come to the class for the first time, clutched by this fear, frozen to their crutches, unable to move, begin to overcome the fear as they practised going up and down the room again and again, while strong helpers walked behind and in front of them, to catch them when they lost their balance and fell. He saw the assurance gained in walking begin to feed the starved minds and hearts of these people, as each day they improved a bit more, and their lessening fear allowed them to joke a bit now when they fell, and to talk to the others as they worked without the terrible tense whiteness in their faces as they concentrated on staying on their elusive feet.

The sergeant saw men and women who had been badly hurt in some crushing accident of life, begin to restore themselves slowly to hope, to the small hill where they could gain some perspective and once again look outside themselves, look around. He saw a colored man learn to use wooden legs after he had lost his own above the knee when they had been frozen on a long trip in the winter woods. He saw the natural rhythm of the colored people stand this man in good stead as he overcame his fear and began to hum a little boogie woogie to himself as he clicked out his wooden feet to sway along in the angular gait of those rare few who manage to walk on wooden legs that are unhinged at the knee.

The sergeant saw a man of sixty-eight learn to walk again after a double amputation, made necessary when the old man had become despondent and in an attempt at suicide had thrown himself under a train. The old man was called Pop affectionately by all of us, and we watched him as his attitude of wan indifference, the dead indifference of a man who had died and come back to life, changed to a caring, a desire to live. And finally, with his continued success in learning to walk, his mood burst into cheerful warm light.

I remember one day especially when the old man had managed to climb the model of the bus steps. He had done it alone, when no one was looking. And he stood now triumphantly looking about. He gave a kind of shout to call attention to himself. And he looked down at me and smiled and waved a crutch. "I'm on top of the world," he said.

The sergeant saw lame men learning lens-grinding in the vocational training section of the Institute, and girls and boys learning stenography and accounting. He saw paralytics learning commercial art and mechanical drawing, and one-armed men learning to weld. He visited the benches where men and women whose backs and legs were so deformed from infantile paralysis or from some injury that they had to have a sitting job, were learning to use their quick, capable hands in the careful art of making jewelry.

The sergeant saw all this, and he was surprised. Like most people, he had felt that there was little to be done for a person who had been drastically injured—they were the sad, wasted, broken parts of life that must be left to live out their days in institutions, or in the back bedrooms of their family home. He told me that these people, laboring so concentratedly to learn a trade, to walk, to take care of themselves, seemed to him not only wonderful but very happy. And he added:

"When I used to see a man on crutches in the street I felt sorry for him. I pitied him. He seemed to be having such a hard time dragging himself along. But now that I have been here and seen all you people working, I won't feel this way any more. When I see a man or a woman like that now I feel guilty if I pity them. I can only say to myself: 'Isn't it fine that that person has overcome his disability and is learning to get around so well.' "

The change in attitude, the switch from a negative, regretful feeling, to a positive, encouraging feeling in the sergeant to ward us came from his familiarity with the work and the effort that had gone behind the awkward gait of the man on crutches in the street. He did not see the broken or unfinished body. He did not see the stumbling walk. He saw only the perseverance, the courage, and the faith in this man that had made it necessary for him to relearn, somehow, to walk.

He saw the man. He saw his qualities, his moral character, as if etched before him on an X-ray plate. The magic rays had for the moment burned away the flesh and bone of the man and left only the shadowy but clear outline of his spirit on the negative, as the perceptive man, the wise, and the saintly would go into a roomful of normal people and see, perhaps, the X-ray plate of their moral character to be as twisted and as torn as the bodies of these called crippled. "Behind the realm of the seen lies the realm of the unseen, which is the realm of the real," the Buddha once said. And those of us who are sensitive and gentle will be quicker to see the character X-ray of the fallen and the diseased than to fasten our gaze upon any outward disfigurement.

For there is always this problem for all of us who do not look like the imperial, normal race outwardly, who move a little slower, a little more awkwardly, who do the same things in a different way. There is always the problem for us (which is really a kind of fear) that we will be taken for what we look like rather than for what we are.

In America, especially, perhaps, is it hard to dare people to look behind the appearance. We are much in love with appearance here. We spend a good deal of money on it. Cosmetics involve one of the biggest single sums of money spent in any one year by Americans. "People give thousands for appearance and not ten cents for reality," said Wilde. And, for us, he was right. Our vision does not go very deep or penetrate very far. We are planning now for a postwar world in which we hope the appearance of things will be much changed. The sky filled with air-autos, the landscape filled with streamlined homes full of new, shiny streamlined equipment: better iceboxes, better cooking ranges, better materials for clothes. We wait in excitement for the material postwar world. Yet we fear its moral character. We long for peace and dread it at the same time.

The unreal world we see has changed and is changing. But not the real world behind it. The world that contains our fears and hopes and faith. The world that ultimately decides our fate, as it erupts into mass sickness, mass waves of terror and brutality and fear and greed. We set much store upon appearance. If the fruit is the biggest and brightest it is, of course, the best.

There is this problem then for the abnormal, for those of us who look different. In meeting people for the first time we who live in abnormal bodies will be aware of the reaction we exact from those around us. But we can dictate the attitude of those we meet by our own inner attitude.

When I meet people I find myself speaking to them earnestly in all the ways that we do speak to each other without words. I have found that others who have been hurt in this way, consciously or unconsciously, do the same thing. We shake them by the hand firmly and look them in the eyes and smile. "I am fine, I am well, I am whole," we find ourselves insisting with our eyes and our hands and our smiles. "Look at *me,*" we ask. "Not at the other but at *me.*"

Katharine Hathaway comes to add her evidence upon this problem, the problem of appearance. She knew herself to be perfect inside herself, whole. She acted as though she were a charming and attractive and intelligent person. The only time her confidence was shaken was when she looked in the mirror. There the knives of appearance cut swiftly into her self-confidence, destroying it, ripping it to shreds. And after one look in the mirror it might take her many hours to reassemble the wholeness within herself again.

But she found, as I have found, and others like us, that we can exact the coin we wish from those we meet for the first time. We can exact it, but we must have some help from them. For Katharine found as she grew older that although she felt herself to be the beautiful and desirable companion she must have been, those around her insisted after a while upon her assuming the role of her appearance—that of the winsome gnome, the endearing jester, the little adorable clown.

Because the weight of opinion about her vibrated so heavily in the air, she found herself losing the moral and real X-ray photograph of herself, even in her own mind. She found herself accepting the role they were forcing upon her. She found herself becoming what they felt her to be, what they wanted her to be, to amuse them. And so, for a time, until she realized what was happening to her, she played their part.

We can dictate the attitude we would prefer to be shown toward us, but only to a degree. We must have some loving, perceptive cooperation from the outside, and go with and be loved by those who find, through their discerning eyes, that we are not our badly distorted bodies but the free and whole and courageous spirits marked by the shadows on our moral X-ray photographs.

19

What the pressure of accident or war or circumstance began—this search into the nature of life, this beginning of a freedom within ourselves—purposeful activity can deepen and enlarge. If we would attain complete freedom of spirit perhaps we must again learn to pray, and through prayer deliberately widen our experience and understanding of the spirit and the spirit's ways.

Most of us have forgotten how to pray. We have forgotten even what prayer originally was for, and we pray now only in moments of distress or agony or danger. Yet prayer has a long history and when properly used, has been used always for one purpose: to gain direct experience of the spirit. It is the way, the technique, for bringing the individual into closer touch with that which animates all things.

* * *

We are being forced to realize the amazing practicality of the religious point of view. We are beginning to see that any other view has been and must always be, impractical. For we are beginning to realize the unity of the body of mankind, that we can not be isolationist. We are beginning to realize the unity of all men, that we can not act independently, that all men are brothers, that to act as if anything else were true, is disastrous. We are beginning to see that if we save ourselves, we are not saving ourselves alone, but must, by our wider linkage with our fellows, help them also. And we are beginning, finally, to realize the unity within the mind-body and to find that the only practical treatment of it is to act as if it were a whole.

With our increasing understanding of the nature of all life, we can now perhaps begin to change our idea of the nature of prayer. For we see that if this is, in reality, a monistic universe which is pervaded by and guided by the spirit, then all of life is spiritual: this is a spiritual universe. If the dualism of matter and spirit, of material and immaterial, is dead, then so must the dualism of sacred and profane be dead. All of life is sacred.

* * *

The battles that are fought in the real world that lies within us—the world of our qualities—are as fierce and fiery and terrible as those fought on any battle-front. They involve minute armies and miniature batteries, but the conflict within each human soul is as mighty as any campaign on land or sea. And the winning or the losing of it by each of us, the outcome of this real war, is more significant than skies filled with clouds of bombers and seas choked with submarines. For the real war within us affects the unreal war of men and armies outside ourselves. It lies behind the unreal war: it is its cause and holds within it the seeds of antisepsis. The good man—the man who has won the real war within himself—can undo the evil of thousands precisely because his acts are selfless, are antiseptic, because they hold no germ of hatred or greed or fear in them. But the victories in the unreal wars are meaningless: they settle nothing; they sow the seeds of hatred and greed and bitterness for generations to come. Hatred and bitterness and fear caused by blood and alleviated only by exacting more and more and more blood.

If we would help heal the deep sickness which cuts into the body of mankind now, perhaps we must look, as all of us who are subject to disaster must look, within ourselves. At the real war that lies behind and within the unreal war and the winning of which by each of us is the only thing that will decide, ultimately, whether we are forever to have the unreal wars devastating our world, tearing all our constructive thoughts and hopes and dreams to shattered ruins about us.

* * *

Thus those of us who are thoughtful, and who have been badly hurt, may ultimately be cheered in another way than we had dreamed: by our growing awareness. And as we learn to care about the greater, more significant reality within ourselves, we come to see the groundlessness of most of our fears. And we find, as time goes on, that our best contribution toward what is called peace in the world is this active and constant striving for insight and inner peace through the reality within us.

Discussion of "And Now to Live Again"

The daughter of advertising executive Bruce Barton, Betsey Barton (1917-1962) was in her mid-teens when an automobile accident left her with a broken back and no hope of ever walking again. *And Now to Live Again* is the sensitive, skillful account of what she calls her "re-education."

One of the traditional functions of literature is to console man in his afflictions. Yet consolation can be no more than easing of pain, mere soothing in time of discomfort. Such effort may be necessary when misery is either fresh or intense, but it is not a long-range answer. There comes a day for us all when we must face positively the situation in which we find ourselves—no matter how disheartening or distasteful—or simply succumb to it. Miss

Barton's book is written for those who have survived the initial shock of disability and who are determined "to live again."

At the time this small work was written it had a special relevance to many who were undergoing the experience of welcoming home loved ones who had been maimed in World War II. Yet there is nothing dated about this book. It is as current as today's accident, tomorrow's loss. It speaks to all who not only want to make the best of a difficult situation but who want to do it with grace.

Not the least of Miss Barton's accomplishment is persuading her readers that expectation of recovery need not underlie patience. In fact, the full meaning of patience is lost on the person who finds in it only the discipline of waiting for his pain to cease. Miss Barton tactfully but firmly points out that the spectacular miracle is possible but that many are probably not going to recover the life they once had; instead, they must make a new one.

To establish such a life—often the more frightening because so little similar to earlier experience—can require a type of patience that goes far beyond mere endurance. To reach toward an end which is not clearly foreseen or to strive endlessly to acquire such simple skills as walking or dressing oneself requires a determination that refuses to count failures and yet is willing to settle for something less than perfection.

And Now to Live Again is not a romantic story of how one person succeeded in spite of a severe handicap. It is the realistic account of success *because* of difficulties. It took suffering to unveil hidden resources, to trigger appreciation of small gifts, and to understand the nature of unconditional love. In Miss Barton's case patience became the willingness to try.

The difficulty of her effort is not passed over lightly. She is particularly effective in describing the effect of memory upon one who has become an invalid:

> The memories are there you see. The memories of laughter and of running in the wind, of climbing hilltops, of walking through the dim and smoky afternoon of a New England fall. Of scrunching to the waves edge upon the beach—memories of light, swift motion, of speed, of grace, of perfect coordination. And the memories cannot be denied at first. They crowd and cluster in each cell of earth and air, of fire and water, that compose the body shell. They crowd and cluster and jostle and mock. They are loud, these memories, blatant.

Anyone who has undergone a confining illness will recognize something of his own experience in the above lines.

Miss Barton's life was not a long one, and it was apparently full of tragic accidents. Her death, at the age of 45, could be thought of as the final blow, for she fell into a swimming pool in her wheelchair and was drowned. Yet anyone who has read *And Now to Live Again* and has caught the spirit of this remarkable book will be able to accept this earthly ending to Miss Barton's story without resentment or resignation. The *why* of human affliction may never be understood in this world, but every man knows *how* to improve his situation to some degree. Patience is willingness to become what we can, not readiness to accept what we are.

Poems by Wang Wei (699-759)

Translated by Arthur Christy

There are many new houses in Nan-shu;
Old trees are gone but the willows remain.
One does not know who of the coming generation will visit here.
No matter—in the same way did the last generation conjecture.

The tall trees of the grove double the shadows which cover the four boundaries of the pavilion.
Thick green mosses upon the stones tell how long it is since visitors have come.
My friend is lying in the middle of the pavilion, lost in reverie;
I have no doubt that he is dreaming of another world.

At the little dock by the willow trees people are embarking on journeys—
I know that the boatman will bring you safe to your destination.
When the fresh colors of Spring return I will think of you,
Whether you travel South or North, my thoughts will follow you.

Daily man grows old without the hope of youth's return,
Though Springtime yearly fades to reappear again.
Therefore drink with tranquil hearts,
And grieve not for the falling petals of Spring flowers.

Discussion of the Poetry of Wang Wei

While English versions of Chinese poems have achieved faddish popularity from time to time, the problems of translating Chinese poetry are unusually formidable.

To begin with, the Chinese poet was intensely concerned with the "tones" of his language. He adhered strictly to long established rules governing stressed and unstressed syllables. The result was a stanza in which there was remarkable symmetry of sound. Verse patterns developed intricate and rigid forms. The simple blank verse we know so well today was apparently unknown in early Chinese poetry. Although every line did not rhyme, rhythm was carefully controlled.

There are no truly epic poems in Chinese. Brevity is expected and valued. If this gives much Chinese poetry a cryptic sound to Western ears, we need to become more sensitive to nuance and suggestion. While all good poetry requires active participation on the part of the reader, Oriental poetry is especially demanding in this regard. For, until recently, little attempt was made to use the language of common speech. Instead, the concentrated root-ideas of scholar's ideograph were used exclusively. The inflections and word order which provide direction in Western poetry are almost totally lacking. To illustrate the difficulty of translating such pictorial concepts, the following poem by Meng Hao-jan, a contemporary of Wang Wei, is shown in its literal and final translation:

Ch'un Hsiao

Spring Dawn

Ch'un *Spring*	mien *sleep*	put *not*	chueh *sense*	hsiao *dawn*
Ch'u *Place*	ch'u *place*	wen *hear*	ti *twitter*	hiao *bird*
Yeh *Night*	lai *come*	feng *wind*	yu *rain*	sheng *voice (sound)*
Hua *Flower*	lo *fall*	cheh *know*	to *much*	shao *few*

As rendered into English, the poetic sentiment of the original becomes as follows:

> Spring sleep—before I know it, dawn!
> Everywhere the singing of birds is heard.
> During the night come sounds of wind and rain;
> Who knows how many flowers have fallen.[1]

---

[1]Both poems are from *Images in Jade* by Arthur Christy. Permission to reprint them was given by E. P. Dutton and Co. Inc.

Besides being a major poet, Wang Wei (699-759) was a fine painter and musician. In addition he was known as a physician. Under the Emperor Hsuan Tsung he became what we would describe as an Assistant Secretary of State. As such, he became deeply involved in politics and was imprisoned for a time. When he was in his early thirties, his wife died, and he retired from government activity to devote himself to poetry and religion. As a young man, Wang Wei had become a proficient narrative poet, but the poems we remember him best for today are the short, intuitive lyrics which catch the essence of his Taoist-Buddhist devotion.

The limitations of the Taoist approach to life are aptly summed up in the following quotation:

> To Tao Tzu (the founder of Taoism) the problem of solving the ills of human life was to do nothing, to be carried along by the mighty current of the cosmos. The way, he said, to clear the world of its dirt and muddy aspect was identically the way we cleared a bucket of muddy water. Agitation, an attempt to be rid of the impurities merely prolonged their evil influence and presence. The thing to do was to do nothing. The sediment would settle to the bottom, the water would clear itself. So with man and his world. With a wise passivity the eternal Way could exert itself.[2]

Note, for instance, the long perspective of the opening poem. To see oneself as part of a continuing cycle may help set present difficulties in context, but it can also induce a what-difference-does-it-make attitude. The second poem is equally serene—and in this sense appealing—but the note of lassitude which exudes from this poem is finally a bit disquieting. For prolonged reverie, and the context does suggest this, can become an end in itself.

The third poem is wholly attractive. If bodies are bound to specific places, thoughts are unfettered and can accompany those we love while we must wait patiently for their physical return. The final four lines breathe such

---

[2] Arthur Christy, *Images in Jade*, New York, 1929, pp. 26-27.

tranquility that it almost seems like carping to question the mood that is engendered. Yet acceptance can be a sign of weakness as well as strength. For the whole magnificent doctrine of repentance can be compromised if we decide too quickly that neither people nor circumstances can change. When resignation has folded its hands gracefully and stopped trying, patience is still seeking answers and preparing to use them profitably.

Meditations of Marcus Aurelius

III, 16. If many qualities are held in common, there remains that which is peculiar to the good man. His distinction lies in being pleased and content with what happens, and with the thread that is spun for him. . . . And if all men refuse to believe that he lives a simple, modest, and contented life, he is neither angry with any of them, nor does he deviate from the way which leads to the end of life, to which a man ought to come pure, tranquil, ready to depart, and perfectly reconciled to his fate.

IV, 31. Love your occupation, poor though it may be, and be content with it. Then pass through the remainder of your life like one who has entrusted to the gods his body and soul, making thyself neither the tyrant nor the slave of any man.

IV, 33. The words which were formerly familiar are now antiquated; so also the names of those who were famed of old, are now in a manner antiquated: Camillus, Caeso, Volesus, Leonnatus, and a little after also Scipio and Cato, then Augustus, then also Hadrianus and Antoninus. For all things soon pass away and become a mere tale, and complete oblivion soon buries them. And I say this of those who have shone in a wondrous way. For the rest, as soon as they have breathed out their breath, they are gone, and no man speaks of them. And, to conclude the matter, what is even an eternal remembrance? A mere nothing. What, then, is that about which we ought to employ our serious pains? This one thing: thoughts just, and acts social, and words which never lie, and a disposition which gladly accepts all that happens, as necessary, as usual, as flowing from a principle and source of the same kind.

IV, 34. Willingly give thyself up to Clotho (one of the fates), allowing her to spin thy thread into whatever things she pleases.

V. 8. Just as we must understand when it is said, that Aesculapius prescribed to this man horse-exercise, or bathing in cold water, or going without shoes, so we must understand it when it is said, That the nature of the universe prescribed to this man disease or mutilation or loss of anything else of the kind. For in the first case prescribed means something like this; he prescribed this for this man as a thing adapted to procure health; and in the second case it means, that which happens to (or suits) every man is fixed in a manner for him suitably to his destiny. For this is what we mean when we say that things are suitable to us, as the workman say of squared stones in walls or the pyramids, that they are suitable, when they fit them to one another in some kind of connection. For there is altogether one fitness (harmony). And as the universe is made up out of all bodies to be such a body as it is, so out of all existing causes necessity (destiny) is made up to be such a cause as it is. And even those who are completely ignorant understand what I mean, for they say, It (necessity, destiny) brought this to such a person. This, then, was brought and this was prescribed to him. Let us then receive these things, as well as those which Aesculapius prescribes. Many, as a matter of course, even among his prescriptions, are disagreeable, but we accept them in the hope of health. Let the perfecting and accomplishment of the things, which the common nature judges to be good, be judged by thee to be of the same kind as thy health. And so accept everything which happens, even if it seems disagreeable, because it leads to this, to the health of the universe and to the prosperity and felicity of Zeus (the universe). For he would not have brought on any man what he has brought, if it were not useful for the whole. Neither does the nature of anything, whatever it may be, cause anything which is not suitable to that which is directed by it. For two reasons, then, it is right to be content with that which happens to thee; the one, because it was done for thee and prescribed for thee, and in a manner had reference to thee, originally from the most ancient causes spun with thy destiny; and the other, because even that which comes severally to every man is to the power which administers the universe a cause of felicity and perfection, nay even of its very continuance. For the integrity of the whole is mutilated, if thou cuttest off anything whatever from the conjunction and the continuity either of the parts or of the causes. And thou dost cut off, as far as it is in thy power, when thou art dissatisfied, and in a manner triest to put anything out of the way.

VI, 16. What then is worth being valued? To be received with clapping of hands? No. Neither must we value the clapping of tongues for the praise which comes from the many is a clapping of tongues. Suppose then that thou hast given up this worthless thing called fame, what remains that is worth valuing? This, in my opinion, to move thyself and to restrain thyself in conformity to thy proper constitution, to which end both all employments and arts lead. For every art aims at this, that the thing which has been made should be adapted to the work for which it has been made; and both the vine-planter who looks after the vine, and the horse-breaker, and he who trains the dog, seek this end. But the education and the teaching of youth aim at something. In this then is the value of the education and the teaching. And if this is well, thou wilt not seek anything else. Wilt thou not cease to value many other things too? Then thou wilt be neither free, nor sufficient for thy own happiness, nor without passion. For of necessity thou must be envious, jealous, and suspicious of those who can take away those things, and plot against those who have that which is valued by thee. Of necessity a man must be altogether in a state of perturbation who wants any of these things; and besides, he must often find fault with the gods. But to reverence and honor thy own mind will make thee content with thyself, and in harmony with society, and in agreement with the gods, that is, praising all that they give and have ordered.

VI, 49. Thou art not dissatisfied, I suppose, because thou weighest only so many litre and not three hundred. Be not dissatisfied then that thou must live only so many years and not more; for as thou art satisfied with the amount of substance which has been assigned to thee, so be content with the time.

VII, 27. Think not so much of what thou hast not as of what thou hast: but of the things which thou hast select the best, and then reflect how eagerly they would have been sought, if thou hadst them not. At the same time, however, take care that thou dost not through being so pleased with them accustom thyself to overvalue them, so as to be disturbed if ever thou shouldst not have them.

IX, 37. Enough of this wretched life and murmuring and apish tricks. Why art thou disturbed? What is there new in this? What unsettles thee? Is it the form of the thing? Look at it. Or is it the matter? Look at it. But besides these there is nothing. Toward the gods, then, now become at last more simple and better. It is the same whether we examine these things for a hundred years or three.

X, 1. Wilt thou, then, my soul, never be good and simple and one and naked, more manifest than the body which surrounds thee? Wilt thou never enjoy an affectionate and contented disposition? Wilt thou never be full and without a want of any kind, longing for nothing more, nor desiring anything, either animate or inanimate, for the enjoyment of pleasures? nor yet desiring time wherein thou shalt have longer enjoyment, or place, or pleasant climate, society of men with whom thou mayest live in harmony? but wilt thou be satisfied with thy present condition, and pleased with all that is about thee, and wilt thou convince thyself that thou hast everything and that it comes from the gods, that everything is well for thee, and will be well whatever shall please them, and whatever they shall give for the conservation of the perfect living being, the good and just and beautiful, which generates and holds together all things, and contains and embraces all things which are dissolved for the production of other like things? Wilt thou never be sure that thou shalt dwell in community with gods and men as neither to find fault with them at all, nor to be condemned by them?

X, 28. Imagine every man who is grieved at anything or discontented to be like a pig which is sacrificed and kicks and screams.

Like this pig also is he who on his bed in silence laments the bonds in which we are held. And consider that only to the rational animal is it given to follow voluntarily what happens; but simply to follow is a necessity imposed on all.

X, 35. The healthy eye ought to see all visible things and not to say, I wish for green things; for this is the condition of a diseased eye. And the healthy hearing and smelling ought to be ready to perceive all that can be heard and smelled. And the healthy stomach ought to be with respect to all food just as the mill with respect to all things which it is formed to grind. And accordingly the healthy understanding ought to be prepared for everything which happens; but that which says, Let my dear children live, and let all men praise whatever I may do, is an eye which seeks for green things, or teeth which seek for soft things.

Discussions of the "Meditations" of Marcus Aurelius

Marcus Aurelius Antoninus was born at Rome on the 26th of April, 121 A.D. As the adopted son of the Emperor Antoninus Pius, he was raised with the utmost care and given the best education available in his day. Very early in life—tradition says at the age of eleven—Marcus began wearing the philosophers' simple dress and adopting their mode of life.

When his adopted father became emperor in 138 A.D., young Marcus became associated with him in the administration of the state. At the death of Antoninus Pius in 161 A.D. Marcus Aurelius was urged to take the sole direction of the empire, but he insisted that the other adopted son of Pius be associated with him. Theirs was a generally troubled reign. In the years just prior to their accession little had been done to extend the empire, and the borders were being threatened in several places. In fact, Marcus Aurelius conducted a number of campaigns against invaders from the north himself.

Nor were his troubles confined to foreign wars. Plagues, famine and revolt by one of his most trusted officers all kept his reign in turmoil. But in the midst of overwhelming difficulty, Marcus Aurelius managed to retain a remarkable sweetness and forbearance. If Christians were persecuted while he was in power, it should not be forgotten that the persecution was political rather than religious. In refusing to acknowledge the Emperor as one of its deities, Christianity was regarded as a threat to the state, and was so treated.

In order to understand Marcus Aurelius—and thereby set his *Meditations* in some context—it is necessary to review briefly the basic doctrines of the Stoic philosophy with which he aligned himself. Founded by Zeno in Athens about 300 B.C., the Stoic school was imported to Rome in the first century before Christ. In answer to the basic question, how can an individual lead a happy life, the Stoic answers that a man is happy when he obeys reason, for reason leads to virtue and virtue is the only good. In practice, this doctrine stresses overcoming the world of passion and emotion. Since, the Stoics assert, each man is a fragment of the universal, divine force, he should strive to put himself in harmony with that force. In such a long view, external circumstance—health, wealth, a good name—are not significant.

In the *Meditations* we see Roman Stoicism at its best. Again and again it returns to the fundamental principle that the universe has been wisely ordered, that every man is a part of it and must conform to that order which he cannot change. It follows from such an assertion that men are related to one another; and, since each is part of the divine, deserves to be cherished. In practice, however, the cherishing was subordinate to self-discipline. Each man became so preoccupied with keeping the divinity within himself free from the corruption of the world that the best men became apathetic. The easiest way to keep unspotted was to do nothing.

Serenity purchased at such a price may be the unwitting ally of the most despicable wrongs. In the defensive question of Cain, "Am I my brother's keeper?" there is caught up the whole problem of solving the ills of the world by divesting ourselves of responsibility. Patience and forbearance may be lonely states, but they are not meaningfully achieved by isolation from the world.

A Noiseless, Patient Spider

by Walt Whitman

A noiseless, patient spider,
I mark'd, where, on a little promontory, it stood, isolated;
Mark'd how, to explore the vacant, vast surrounding,
It launch'd forth filament, filament, filament, out of itself;
Ever unreeling them—ever tirelessly speeding them.

And you, O my Soul, where you stand,
Surrounded, surrounded, in measureless oceans of space,
Ceaselessly musing, venturing, throwing,—seeking the spheres, to
connect them;
Till the bridge you will need, be form'd—till the ductile anchor hold;
Till the gossamer thread you fling, catch somewhere, O my Soul.

Discussion of "A Noiseless, Patient Spider"

When Walt Whitman (see Vol. II, pp. 284-5 for biographical detail) confided to a friend that "language interests me, I can never get it out of my mind," he was providing a basic key to his own writing. For Whitman's habit of reworking his poems—often several times over many years—enables us to see language *determining* thought as well as expressing it.

"A Noiseless, Patient Spider," for instance, exists in Whitman's notebooks in a remarkably different form from the one we have come to know in Whitman's major collection, *Leaves of Grass*. This early version is as follows:

The Soul, reaching, throwing out for love,
As the spider, from some little promontory, throwing out filament
after filament, tirelessly out of itself, that one at least may catch
and form a link, a bridge, a connection
O I saw one passing alone, saying hardly a word—yet full of love
I detected him, by certain signs
O eyes wishfully turning! O silent eyes!

For then I thought of you o'er the world
O latent oceans, fathomless oceans of love!
O waiting oceans of love! yearning and fervid; and of you sweet souls perhaps in future, delicious and long:
But Dead, unknown on the earth-ungiven, dark here, unspoken, never born:
You fathomless latent souls of love—you pent and unknown oceans of love!

By the time Whitman placed this poem in the "Whispers of Heavenly Death" section in the latter part of *Leaves of Grass* he had salvaged the one good image of this effort —the spider spinning the threads by which it hoped to establish links outside itself—and made it the shaping metaphor of the later version. The diffuse, rhetoric has been toned down, and the needlessly specific references have been eliminated.

The very size of the subject seems to overwhelm the earlier draft, and it wanders off in windy exclamations. Many of Whitman's most obvious faults are on embarrassing display. Note, for instance, the repeated attempt to gain emphasis by the use of exclamation marks; the adjectives which almost become a Whitman signature: delicious, latent, pent, fathomless; or the needless complexity of "earth-ungiven."

Contrast all this with the beautifully controlled, precisely shaped version we finally get. No longer is the thought a bit woolly and the diction merely repetitious. In the first draft, the spider is almost incidental, at best an illustration. In the second, it almost takes on personality— but not quite. It is now real enough to be seen and symbolic enough to be meaningful but not specific enough to narrow the poem. Descriptive words are used in developing sequence: "musing, venturing, throwing," and the perfect adjective, "ductile" replaces the jumble of qualifiers found in the notebook version.

Above all, the meaning is extended and enriched by

the focused expression. Instead of a vague yearning for human fulfillment there is now a spiritual dimension to this skilfully wrought poem. Man's relationship to divinity —both in life and death—is successfully probed. As the poem originally stands, it would have little use in our section on patience; as it now is, it becomes an appropriate conclusion. For the effort, persistence and aspiration which distinguish real patience from counterfeits such as resignation are here in evidence. Even the usual loneliness of patience is touched upon. The final line carries just the right tone. It is not *if* "the gossamer thread you fling catch somewhere," but "till." At this point, the little folk saying which insists that patience is always rewarded receives poetic affirmation.

SECTION FOUR

Obedience, the Mother of Success

by Bruce B. Clark

"To Them Of The Last Wagon"

By Lynn Fausett, American (Brigham Young University Library, Provo, Utah)

Commentary by
Floyd E. Breinholt, Associate Professor of Art, Brigham Young University

Some of the factors which help us enjoy and appreciate works of art are dependent upon our intuitive feelings, our cultural background, and our perceptive ability. Three factors which broaden our concepts and also lead to greater enjoyment of art are: first, a knowledge of what the artist is saying—the content or the message; second, an understanding of how he did it—his technique, his materials, and procedure; third, something about the artist himself—who he was. Let us look at these three—*what, how,* and *who* in relation to this painting.

Just as a portrait painter is obliged to reproduce in his painting a certain likeness to the sitter, so an artist who illustrates an event is bound somewhat by the event itself. Near the close of Utah's centennial year 1947, during his conference address, President J. Reuben Clark, Jr. said in words what the artist Lynn Fausett has created in paint—"So through the dust and dirt, dirt and dust, during the long hours, the longer days—that grew into weeks and then into months they crept along till, passing down through its portals, the valley welcomed them to rest and home."

As we so justly honor the leaders of the great trek west, so, too, those who followed—even to the last wagon—were equally worthy of praise because of their obedience to the directions of the Lord.

Look at the painting and read the first four verses of Edward L. Hart's poem "To Utah." The churchman, the poet, and the artist tell the same story each in his own way.

When Brother Fausett was asked to describe how this painting came to be, he submitted the following statement:

"The painting,'To Them of the Last Wagon,' was commissioned by President Clark's son-in-law, Ivor Sharp, for a gift on President Clark's eightieth birthday. The occasion was celebrated and the painting presented at a large dinner at Camp Williams, where many of President Clark's friends and associates were guests. The painting was presented by one of his granddaughters. I felt highly honored not only to be selected as the artist to paint this story but also to speak. I tried to explain how our artists give an added living reality to our history, beliefs, and testimonies, just as the old masters did to the Bible and early Christian story. I said that I was convinced that while criticizing the truth they projected, but still giving them artistic

Lynn Fausett

freedom, our Latter-day Saint artists could evolve an art tradition that could do for our Church what the old masters did for the early Christian Church, if only we would use them and give them opportunities."

Prior to painting a picture, an artist likely finds it necessary to do some careful research so that the subject matter shown will be authentic. These sketches, then, could be arranged and composed according to the sensitivity of the artist in harmony with his understanding of the elements and principles of design and his thorough knowledge of his craft.

Mr. Fausett generally uses what is often referred to as "the old master technique" of painting. On a toned panel, usually a warm brown, the darks are painted in a darker brown. When dry, white pigment is used to build up the lights and care is taken to scumble some over-all areas. At this stage, the painting appears as though one were viewing a monochrome picture through a white veil. It is allowed to dry, and then transparent colors in medium are glazed over it. The objects still maintain their form, but now have color. Successive glazes may be repeated over the same areas after preceding glazes dry. Dark details are then painted and, finally, highlights are placed in with opaque pigment. This kind of painting usually results in a smooth, glossy surface and the light, being reflected through the successive layers of glaze, gives a certain luminosity which cannot be attained in any other way. This luminous quality is often lost to a great degree in reproduction.

Lynn Fausett of Salt Lake City is a Westerner, a native of Price, Utah, where he became acquainted at first hand with the subject matter found in many of his paintings and murals. He went East to study at the Art Students League of New York and later became president of that institution. He did numerous murals in the East and the West. Among his best known are the ones in the Chrysler Building in New York and at the "This Is the Place" monument in Salt Lake City. Mrs. Fausett, perhaps his best critic, designs and finishes the beautiful frames which enhance his easel paintings.

OBEDIENCE, THE MOTHER OF SUCCESS

Obedience is the mother of success, the wife of safety.
—Aeschylus

Introductory Comments

All of us recognize that obedience is one of the great principles of human living for both life now and life eternally. First and foremost, we should be obedient to our Father in Heaven and to all of His commandments. To break these divine laws is to bring suffering in this life and thwart progress in the life hereafter. Second, we should be obedient to the laws of nature and the universe. To break these natural laws, such as the law of gravity by stepping off a roof-top or the law of nutrition by drinking poison, is to invite physical disaster. Third, we should be obedient to the laws of government. To break these laws of the people is to defy the happiness and security of society and violate the rights of others. Fourth, we should be obedient to the laws of marriage and the family, recognizing that we should place the needs and happiness of those we love ahead of our own desires and comforts. For love at its best is unselfish, not selfish. To break these laws of the family is to invite unhappiness and threaten the very foundation of civilization. President David O. McKay once said:

> Obedience is heaven's first law, and it is the law of the home. There can be no true happiness in the home without obedience—obedience obtained, not through physical force, but through the divine element of love.[1]

The scriptures and history, as well as literature, are filled with incidents illustrating the principle of obedience, not only the positiveness of obedience itself, but also the

---

[1]David O. McKay, *Pathways to Happiness* (Salt Lake City: Bookcraft, 1957), p. 118.

problems of disobedience. For example, the whole account of Adam and Eve in the Garden of Eden, or the obedience of Nephi (including even the slaying of Laban) contrasted with the disobedience of Laman and Lemuel in the Book of Mormon, or the anguished obedience of Abraham as he prepared to sacrifice his son Isaac, or the unquestioning obedience of the two thousand "sons of Helaman," also in the Book of Mormon.

As we review these and many other examples of obedience, we see that, if it is important to be obedient when one is a follower, it is even more important to be obedient when one is a leader. The follower needs to be obedient to those in authority over him, but the leader has the greater responsibility to be obedient to divine guidance, noble principle, and the ideal of love. For the good leader, *including the good mother or father,* earns authority through the leadership of love rather than the leadership of fear—that is, through qualities of understanding, personal integrity, high courage, sensitivity to divine inspiration, and respect for every individual human personality.

To illustrate some of the ideals of obedience, we first examine three poems—by John Henry Newman, Edward Hart, and Clinton Larson. Then to explore some problems of the wrong kinds of obedience or wrong ways of requiring obedience, we examine another poem, a short story, and a modern drama—by Tennyson, James Joyce, and Robert Bolt. Fittingly, the Bolt drama with which the section ends not only explores some problems of obedience but especially emphasizes the ideal of obedience to the whisperings of inner conscience.

Lead, Kindly Light

by John Henry Newman

Lead, Kindly Light, amid the encircling gloom.
Lead Thou me on!
The night is dark, and I am far from home—
Lead Thou me on!
Keep Thou my feet; I do not ask to see
The distant scene—one step enough for me.

I was not ever thus, nor prayed that Thou
Shouldst lead me on.
I loved to choose and see my path; but now
Lead Thou me on!
I loved the garish day, and, spite of fears,
Pride ruled my will; remember not past years.

So long Thy power hath blessed me, sure it still
Will lead me on,
O'er moor and fen, o'er crag and torrent, till
The night is gone;
And with the morn those angel faces smile
Which I have loved long since, and lost awhile.

Discussion of "Lead, Kindly Light"

John Henry Newman (1801-1890) was one of England's and the world's great religious, educational leaders of the nineteenth century.[1] Among many other things, he wrote several little poems that have become world-beloved hymns, sung in many churches. One of these is "Lead, Kindly Light,"[2] also often called "The Pillar of the Cloud."

---

[1]For fuller comments on Newman's life and writings, see pp. 196-199 of Volume 2 of *Out of the Best Books*, where "The Educated Gentleman" is printed and discussed.

[2]This hymn is printed in the LDS Hymnbook—arranged for congregational singing, No. 112, and arranged for women's voices, No. 366.

Although usually thought of as a hymn, this is also an excellent, beautiful little poem, rich in symbolism. Part of its subject is obedience—sensitive, faithful obedience to spiritual guidance. Studied carefully, the poem sets a lovely pattern for people to follow, led through mortal life by the beacon light of God's truth, which ultimately will reunite them not only with God but also with beloved family members and friends, from whom they have been temporarily separated.

Questions and thoughts for discussion: (1) What does the "kindly light" in line 1 symbolize? (2) What does Newman mean in line 3 when he says "the night is dark, and I am far from home"? What is the night? Where is home? (3) Note how in stanza 2 the poet reviews his past years, when his faith was weak, and when he lived in worldliness and pride, relying upon his worldly self rather than upon spiritual faith. (4) Note also how in stanza 3, after overcoming the worldliness of stanza 2, he relies on obedience to the spirit for both earthly and eternal guidance. What does "the morn" in the next-to-last line symbolize? And what is the implication of the last two words of the poem?

To Utah

by Edward L. Hart

I. Arrival

Nobody wanted this place:
Spaniards saw it and turned back;
Trappers endured the taste
Of salt in the wind for the fur pack
Or love of space.

When settlers planned
Westward treks it was California
They chose and cursed this land
For standing in the way with its thorns and
Hot sand.

The sun of a late July
Burns varnish onto summit rock.
Wagons and teams go by.
Escarpments[1] for a moment block
The scalding sky.

Teams trail in a line now,
Over the downward roll of the hill,
Brushed by cedar bough;
Then ages of Indian stone worlds spill
From an iron plow.

II. Laying out the City

A sextant captures a light train
Bounced from the moon to a Great Basin
Point where Brigham Young's cane
Marks the site for the temple mason.

Rays of base lines running through
South Temple and Main embrace
The cosmos in a grid beginning at a new
Meridian of time and space.

---

[1]Steep precipitous slopes of cliff.

III. The Gathering

They came by thousands at a slow clip,
All but those buried at Haun's Mill
Or Florence or some place that the lip
Of man had no name for yet to trip
The tongue of the young, who wanted still
To find home over the next hill
Or lush pastures past each desert strip.
They came over the mountains and around
The Horn[2] in ships and wagons, or dragged
Handcarts over stony and frozen ground,
Often opened and shoveled in a mound
Upon women and children or the man who lagged
In his shafts only on the day he sagged
In death on the crosspiece: Zion bound.

IV. Preparing for Fire

Leaving the City

You build a city and leave it, maybe
To burn. All morning wagons piled
Full have gone by to the south,
And now we leave our house with straw
Stacked in the doorway, ready for fire.
Where we go next, who knows?
Sonora,[3] maybe: It's a long way.

Instructing the Torchbearers

Then it's settled; you know the signal.
The city burns if only one soldier
Steps out of line or raises his hand
As a vandal or takes for his own use
One spoon or disturbs a stick of kindling.
Soldiers will not tie our hands
Here and hold us tamely for mobs
To rub in the dust again: never!
Joseph's body was propped by a pump
As a target for soldiers sent to protect him
From themselves. Before that happens

---

[2]The southern tip of South America, around which some sailed instead of crossing the plains.

[3]A state in northwest Mexico.

Here we'll level the city with fire
And leave them the ashes of our past.

General Albert Sidney Johnston Marches through
Salt Lake City

The naked bayonets of the Fifth
Infantry flash in the van of the Union
Army in morning sunshine. Baggage
Wagons and caissons still rumbling
At dusk through deserted streets send
Echoes rattling from locked and hollow
Houses to the valley walls while
Crickets shrill in cadence from the hills.

V. Expansion

Any of a hundred places: name it
And go there and try to claim it
From Indians and insects, rodents and drouth.
Try, for instance, going south
To Pipe Spring, in the northern strip
Of Arizona above the ripped
Rock at Grand Canyon and stay
For years, two hundred miles away
From a boy who'd ask your boy to play.

VI. Temple

Cradled in world-weighted darkness
The core cooled slowly, and granite grew
Into flecks of mica and pods of quartz
Around flowering feldspar and hornblende.
Weathering winds and rains cut off
Soft cover, and light glinted
From orthoclastic patterns as quarrying
Frost pried free a block at last
To stand capstone at the temple crest.

Discussion of "To Utah"

"To Utah" is, in my opinion, the best poem yet written on the westward movement of the Mormon pioneers and the colonization of Utah and adjacent areas. In artistry it is excellent, with a skilled control of those devices that combine to make exciting poetry—rhyme, alliteration, assonance, delayed rhythms, symbolism, varied metrical patterns, etc., and with just enough balance between simplicity and complexity to both communicate and challenge.

Note how much is woven into the poem. In Section I we have mostly description of the scorching Utah valleys wanted by no one except the Mormons—a scorned people in a scorned land. In Section II Salt Lake City is laid out, the central dream of a new empire, both earthly and spiritual, both temporal and eternal. Section III recalls the varied ways in which the pioneers arrived, with tragedy and joy intermixed in their journeyings, and with a vibrant faith anchored in obedience both to God and to their earthly leaders. Then comes the anguish of Section IV as the saints are threatened with destruction by a federal government that does not understand their faith or their customs; rather than yield they will destroy all that they have built and start anew in some other land. But note their courage, their strength, their determination to be loyal to their convictions and their leaders at whatever cost. Finally, the crisis over, in Sections V and VI the building of an inland empire continues—first the physical building, with Salt Lake City serving as the hub of a wheel of expansion from which the saints move outward in all directions along the spokes, obedient to the instructions of Brigham Young; then the spiritual building, symbolized in the erection out of granite of the great Temple. History, faith, courage—all are skillfully interwoven in this excellent lyric-dramatic poem. And the central theme is obedience—obedience to the Church leaders, obedience to conscience, and obedience to God.

The author, Dr. Edward L. Hart, one of our own L.D.S. writers, has been a Professor of English at Brigham Young University since 1952, having taught also at the University of Utah, the University of Washington, and the University of California at Berkeley. He was born in 1916 in Bloomington, Idaho. In 1939 he graduated with honors from the University of Utah, where he was both a Phi Beta Kappa scholar and a conference champion in the mile run. Later he earned an MA at the University of Michigan and, as a Rhodes scholar, attended Oxford University in England for several years, where he received a doctorate in 1950, after a war-time interruption of four years during which he served as an officer and Japanese-language translator in the U. S. Navy. Since then he has achieved distinction in three directions—as a teacher, as a publishing scholar, and as a poet. "To Utah," previously published in *The Improvement Era,* won special recognition at the Utah State Institute of Fine Arts in 1963. It has also been set to choral music by Robert Cundick, Salt Lake Tabernacle organist, and was performed for the first time at the University of Utah in 1965.

Excerpts from "The Mantle of the Prophet"[1]

by Clinton F. Larson

From Act II

(Scene: *Near Nauvoo, Illinois, approximately a month after the martyrdom of Joseph Smith.*)

BRIGHAM YOUNG (*Addressing Joseph's coffin*)

We are as straws together in a swirl of wind;
We pass over the land until the wind puts us down.
Joseph, the Twelve remain, and the ache
Of your vision is with us and must be fulfilled.
I have stumbled in your presence, wondering
    How to serve you and whom you served.
My hard hands have taken yours, inquiring.

(*Kneeling*)

How can I be of use? I have looked into your eyes
And have seen the far horizons of the West,
The wagons and the prairies white and golden
Under a summer day. I have seen the cleavage
Of land from the mountains. In the depths
Of my heart I wander there, where the gulls
Ride above a silver sea and the sky
Like a veil hangs over a great valley.
How can I know where this may be,
Except as I remember you in my stride
That brings me west? I have come from the East
To find you, and I have found you only here,
As you are carried in death, so I must find you
Beyond the river, along the trail
To Laramie, or if not there, westward still
Where the people may gather, where
The mountains decline with the sun.
I have seen the inland sea in the silence
Of your eyes. Where can you have gone but there?
You are gone, and I look around at the strange land;
You are gone, and I hear the wind answer me.
In the west the valley lies: the great blue peaks

---

[1]Clinton F. Larson, *The Mantle of the Prophet and Other Plays* (Salt Lake City: Deseret Book Company, 1966.)

Rise in the haze where the wagons go; where we go
The land is like the palm of God. Joseph,
I await the touch of your hand and your arm about me
To guide me there; where you call, I must go
As I have always gone.

From Act III

(Scene: *Conference of the Church on 8 August 1844, with Brigham Young addressing the assembled people.*)

BRIGHAM YOUNG

Until now, we have walked by sight and not by faith. We have had the Prophet in our midst. We have walked by sight and without much pleading to the Lord to know whether things were right.

We have had a prophet of the Lord to speak to us, but he has sealed his testimony with his blood, and now for the first time, we are called to walk by the abiding faith he gave us. The Church will not die.

(*In the voice of Joseph*)

I know your feelings, my people:
We saw him walk from our city, I in my heart
And you in your sight, and he was alone among us.
He gave us his vision, and under his hand I left you
To do as he bid me to do, to preach the testament of the new world:
But we did not know him as we do now.
I feel his presence and his loneliness;
He would go to Carthage for us, he would die for us,
And we did not want him to stay if he could do more.
"If my brethren do not value my life, neither do I" he cried.
And he went among his enemies, who wanted him.
Now the light comes in the sky of my vision,
The bird of God alights on the branch of Ephraim,
The ages cry in my marrow:
My heart shakes with the wonder of his knowing, the voice
Of the millenniums in the crystal of earth;
My hand trembles over them, and they ripple
Like the waters of Jordan and Zion
In the meridian day of the Lord:
I know the Testament and the voice

That runs like the wonder of heaven
Among the groves of Olivet.
It draws me with it, and abroad as my mission has been
Speaks his name. Joseph, your hand! Where can you be?

STEPHEN FORBES

Brother Clayton, look!
It is Joseph.
The mantle of the Prophet has fallen on him!

BRIGHAM YOUNG

Joseph, I feel your ghost, and you have delivered me
Over the veil into the velvet planes
And the white air that shatters into the rivers of stars
We listen to from the pavilions of heaven,
And all is new in the earth,
Where the petals fall like the leaves of another year.
Before me the people feel the breath of your being:
The Saints must leave Nauvoo,
And they weep in the fields for the harvests of grain;
They watch the light flowing from the grove, westward
To the cities of America in the havens of spring.
The Spirit thrives in them,
And I am left open to your people,
And they weep for the mission before us
And the scroll of the covenants you wrote upon:
The dust rises; the seasons disappear;
The people stir like the wings of returning memory
And the exile of forgotten ages: the bronzed hand
Breaks the seal, the lance of God
Springs from the taut bow;
Rushing, rushing, it rides in the waning afternoon;
Joseph, the swiftness is upon me;
The certain hour and the flight of what is to be
Arrow my days of wondering
And you are with me in the mission
You brought me to, that I cannot deny.
Saints of the latter days, come west with the Twelve
And fulfill the Kingdom of God in Zion!

Discussion of Excerpts from "The Mantle of the Prophet"

Another of our gifted L.D.S. writers—in fact, probably the foremost contemporary poet and poetic dramatist in the Church—is Clinton F. Larson, also a Professor of English at Brigham Young University. Now forty-eight years old, he received BA and MA degrees in English from the University of Utah in 1943 and 1947 and a PhD degree in English from Denver University in 1956. He has been a teacher at B.Y.U. since 1947, where he is also Chairman of the Creative Writing Program.

Not only very talented but also impressively energetic, Dr. Larson has written twenty-one full-length plays to date plus hundreds of poems and several dozen essays, short stories, and miscellaneous other works. Although they explore a great variety of subjects and themes, most of them are drawn from Mormon materials and are dedicated to the belief that Jesus is the Christ, the Redeemer of the world. Included among them are *The Lord of Experience* (a volume of poems) and the following plays: "The Brother of Jared," "Mary of Nazareth," "Third Nephi," "Saul of Tarsus," "The Redeemer," "Coriantumr," "Moroni," "Button, Button," and "Snow White and the Mirror." Many awards have come to Dr. Larson for his creative work, and his plays are now receiving wider and wider recognition.

"The Mantle of the Prophet" dramatizes the anguish of the saints following the martyrdom of Joseph Smith and their eventual rallying behind the great leadership of Brigham Young, President of the Council of the Twelve. The two brief scenes depicted here show, first, the heart-broken resolution of the sorrowing Brigham Young to follow as best he can the leadership of the martyred prophet and, second (later, during the Conference of the Church on 8 August 1844), the now strong, faith-filled determination of Brigham Young to lead the people westward. Both scenes are filled with the spirit of obedience, to follow the will of God and His earthly prophets. But in the first scene

Brigham Young is broken-heartedly obedient, still overwhelmed by the recent slaying of the beloved Prophet Joseph; and in the second scene the mantle of the prophet falls upon Brigham as, in Joseph's voice, he addresses the saints assembled in conference and a great strength comes over him, miraculously showing the grief-stricken, groping saints that he is now their prophet, to be honored and followed as they had honored and followed the Prophet Joseph. The relationship of all this to the theme of obedience and our responsibility to be obedient to spiritual guidance and to our Church leaders is dramatically clear.

Thoughts for further consideration: (1) Check Church history to read the account of the conference when Brigham Young seemed to talk miraculously in the voice of the martyred Prophet Joseph and the "mantle of the prophet" fell on him, showing the assembled saints that he was the new leader of the Church, appointed by God. Prior to this momentous incident many of the saints were floundering among themselves, wondering which direction to go and what their future would be. When they saw Brigham Young standing powerful before them and heard him speak, many felt as if it were the Prophet Joseph again speaking to them and they knew it was the Lord's will that they should follow Brigham and the Twelve. (2) Discuss how the strength of one great leader, such as Brigham Young on this occasion, can spread strength, courage, faith, and obedience to a whole people.

Dora

by Alfred, Lord Tennyson

With farmer Allan at the farm abode
William and Dora. William was his son,
And she his niece. He often looked at them,
And often thought, "I'll make them man and wife."
Now Dora felt her uncle's will in all, 5
And yearned toward William; but the youth, because
He had been always with her in the house,
Thought not of Dora.

Then there came a day
When Allan called his son, and said: "My son,
I married late, but I would wish to see 10
My grandchild on my knees before I die;
And I have set my heart upon a match.
Now therefore look to Dora; she is well
To look to; thrifty too beyond her age.
She is my brother's daughter; he and I 15
Had once hard words, and parted, and he died
In foreign lands; but for his sake I raised
His daughter Dora. Take her for your wife;
For I have wished this marriage, night and day,
For many years." But William answered short: 20
"I cannot marry Dora; by my life,
I will not marry Dora!" Then the old man
Was wroth, and doubled up his hands, and said:
"You will not, boy! you dare to answer thus!
But in my time a father's word was law, 25
And so it shall be now for me. Look to it;
Consider, William, take a month to think,
And let me have an answer to my wish,
Or, by the Lord that made me, you shall pack,
And never more darken my doors again." 30
But William answered madly, bit his lips,
And broke away. The more he looked at her
The less he liked her; and his ways were harsh;
But Dora bore them meekly. Then before
The month was out he left his father's house, 35
And hired himself to work within the fields;
And half in love, half spite, he wooed and wed
A laborer's daughter, Mary Morrison.

Then, when the bells were ringing, Allan called
His niece and said: "My girl, I love you well; 40
But if you speak with him that was my son,
Or change a word with her he calls his wife,
My home is none of yours. My will is law."
And Dora promised, being meek. She thought,
"It cannot be; my uncle's mind will change!" 45
And days went on, and there was born a boy
To William; then distresses came on him,
And day by day he passed his father's gate,
Heart-broken, and his father helped him not.
But Dora stored what little she could save, 50
And sent it them by stealth, nor did they know
Who sent it; till at last a fever seized
On William, and in harvest time he died.
Then Dora went to Mary. Mary sat
And looked with tears upon her boy, and thought 55
Hard things of Dora. Dora came and said:
"I have obeyed my uncle until now,
And I have sinned, for it was all through me
This evil came on William at the first,
But, Mary, for the sake of him that's gone, 60
And for your sake, the woman that he chose,
And for this orphan, I am come to you.
You know there has not been for these five years
So full a harvest. Let me take the boy,
And I will set him in my uncle's eye 65
Among the wheat, that when his heart is glad
Of the full harvest, he may see the boy,
And bless him for the sake of him that's gone."
And Dora took the child, and went her way
Across the wheat, and sat upon a mound 70
That was unsown, where many poppies grew.
Far off the farmer came into the field
And spied her not, for none of all his men
Dare tell him Dora waited with the child;
And Dora would have risen and gone to him, 75
But her heart failed her; and the reapers reaped,
And the sun fell, and all the land was dark.
But when the morrow came, she rose and took
The child once more, and sat upon the mound;
And made a little wreath of all the flowers 80
That grew about, and tied it round his hat

To make him pleasing in her uncle's eye.
Then when the farmer passed into the field
He spied her, and he left his men at work,
And came and said: "Where were you yesterday? 85
Whose child is that? What are you doing here?"
So Dora cast her eyes upon the ground,
And answered softly, "This is William's child!"
"And did I not," said Allan, "did I not
Forbid you, Dora?" Dora said again: 90
"Do with me as you will, but take the child,
And bless him for the sake of him that's gone!"
And Allan said: "I see it is a trick
Got up betwixt you and the woman there.
I must be taught my duty, and by you! 95
You knew my word was law, and yet you dared
To slight it. Well—for I will take the boy;
But go you hence, and never see me more."
So saying, he took the boy that cried aloud
And struggled hard. The wreath of flowers fell 100
At Dora's feet. She bowed upon her hands,
And the boy's cry came to her from the field
More and more distant. She bowed down her head,
Remembering the day when first she came,
And all the things that had been. She bowed down 105
And wept in secret; and the reapers reaped,
And the sun fell, and all the land was dark.
Then Dora went to Mary's house, and stood
Upon the threshold. Mary saw the boy
Was not with Dora. She broke out in praise 110
To God, that helped her in her widowhood.
And Dora said: "My uncle took the boy;
But, Mary, let me live and work with you.
He says that he will never see me more."
Then answered Mary: "This shall never be, 115
That thou shouldst take my trouble on thyself;
And, now I think, he shall not have the boy,
For he will teach him hardness, and to slight
His mother. Therefore thou and I will go,
And I will have my boy, and bring him home: 120
And I will beg of him to take thee back.
But if he will not take thee back again,
Then thou and I will live within one house,
And work for William's child, until he grows

Of age to help us."

So the women kissed 125
Each other, and set out, and reached the farm.
The door was off the latch; they peeped, and saw
The boy set up betwixt his grandsire's knees,
Who thrust him in the hollows of his arm,
And clapped him on the hands and on the cheeks, 130
Like one that loved him; and the lad stretched out
And babbled for the golden seal that hung
From Allan's watch and sparkled by the fire.
Then they came in; but when the boy beheld
His mother, he cried out to come to her; 135
And Allan set him down, and Mary said:
"O father!—if you let me call you so—
I never came a-begging for myself,
Or William, or this child; but now I come
For Dora; take her back, she loves you well. 140
O sir, when William died, he died at peace
With all men; for I asked him, and he said,
He could not ever rue his marrying me—
I had been a patient wife; but, sir, he said
That he was wrong to cross his father thus. 145
'God bless him!' he said, 'and may he never know
The troubles I have gone through!' Then he turned
His face and passed—unhappy that I am!
But now, sir, let me have my boy, for you
Will make him hard, and he will learn to slight 150
His father's memory; and take Dora back,
And let all this be as it was before."
So Mary said, and Dora hid her face
By Mary. There was silence in the room;
And all at once the old man burst in sobs: 155
"I have been to blame—to blame. I have killed my son.
I have killed him—but I loved him—my dear son.
May God forgive me!—I have been to blame.
Kiss me, my children."

Then they clung about
The old man's neck, and kissed him many times. 160
And all the man was broken with remorse;
And all his love came back a hundredfold;
And for three hours he sobbed o'er William's child
Thinking of William.

So those four abode
Within one house together, and as years
Went forward Mary took another mate;
But Dora lived unmarried till her death.

Discussion of "Dora"

Alfred, Lord Tennyson (1809-1892) was a poet undeniably great but with undeniable weaknesses and limitations. In hundreds of short poems and dozens of long ones he for more than half a century showed his lyric richness to the world, re-creating in modern language tales of the heroic past and legends of the even more distant mythological past, and endeavoring to compromise the conflicts in his age between science and religion. He was, especially in his masterpiece, *In Memoriam,* the spiritual guide and phrasemaker of nineteenth-century England. But with the passage of time Tennyson has seemed less and less the giant poet of his age, as Browning has emerged larger and larger above him. Even so, and in spite of a sentimental lushness that characterizes many of Tennyson's poems, he still stands, and probably will always stand, as one of the great lyric poets of the world.[1]

"Dora" is one of Tennyson's English idylls, a group of poems concerning simple village life. Tennyson once commented that because the poem tells of a "nobly simple" country girl, it "had to be told in the simplest possible poetic language, and therefore was one of the poems which gave most trouble." A short story in blank verse (unrhymed iambic pentameter), the poem is less musical, less decorative, less heroic-romantic, and more prosaic than most of Tennyson's poetry. It is included here principally for two reasons: (1) because its straightforward story will appeal

[1]For other poems by Tennyson in earlier volumes of *Out of the Best Books,* see "Flower in the Crannied Wall" on pp. 44-45 of Volume 1, "Tithonus" on pp. 474-477 of Volume 1, and a lyric from *The Princess* on p. 339 of Volume 2.

to many readers who are not attracted to more complicated poetry; (2) because through it we can explore some significant aspects of obedience.

To stimulate discussion of this poem, the best approach is probably not exposition but a few suggestions and questions:

1. Analyze Farmer Allan's personality and character, pointing out details showing that he is too harsh, too authoritarian, too dictatorial. Note, among other things, such comments as "My will is law" and "My word is law." Do people obey him through love or through fear?

2. Analyze Dora's personality and character. Is her unselfishness in all instances admirable? Is she too submissive?

3. Analyze William's rebelliousness. To what extent is Farmer Allan responsible for the rebelliousness and disobedience of his son? Obviously there is danger in parents being too permissive with their children. Is there also danger in being too strict?

4. Can love be compelled, as Farmer Allan tries to compel William to love Dora? Does compelling sometimes destroy natural affections and cause contrary reactions? Why does William marry Mary Morrison?

5. In line 56, why does Mary think "hard things of Dora"?

6. In line 58, why does Dora say she has sinned? Has she sinned?

7. Does the poem become somewhat sentimental and melodramatic at its end, weakening its impact?

8. Finally, what does the poem as a whole tell us, directly and by implication, about the wrong and right methods for parents to teach obedience in their children?

Clay

by James Joyce

The matron had given her leave to go out as soon as the women's tea was over and Maria looked forward to her evening out. The kitchen was spick and span: the cook said you could see yourself in the big copper boilers. The fire was nice and bright and on one of the side-tables were four very big barmbracks. These barmbracks seemed uncut; but if you went closer you would see that they had been cut into long thick even slices and were ready to be handed round at tea. Maria had cut them herself.

Maria was a very, very small person indeed but she had a very long nose and a very long chin. She talked a little through her nose, always soothingly: *"Yes, my dear,"* and *"No, my dear."* She was always sent for when the women quarreled over their tubs and always succeeded in making peace. One day the matron had said to her:

"Maria, you are a veritable peace-maker!"

And the sub-matron and two of the Board ladies had heard the compliment. And Ginger Mooney was always saying what she wouldn't do to the dummy who had charge of the irons if it wasn't for Maria. Everyone was so fond of Maria.

The women would have their tea at six o'clock and she would be able to get away before seven. From Ballsbridge to the Pillar, twenty minutes; from the Pillar to Drumcondra, twenty minutes; and twenty minutes to buy the things. She would be there before eight. She took out her purse with the silver clasps and read again the words *A Present from Belfast.* She was very fond of that purse because Joe had brought it to her five years before when he and Alphy had gone to Belfast on a Whit-Monday trip. In the purse were two half-crowns and some coppers. She would have five shillings clear after paying tram fare. What a nice evening they would have, all the children singing! Only she hoped that Joe wouldn't come in drunk. He was so different when he took any drink.

Often he had wanted her to go and live with them; but she would have felt herself in the way (though Joe's wife was ever so nice with her) and she had become accustomed to the life of the laundry. Joe was a good fellow. She had nursed him and Alphy too; and Joe used often say:

"Mamma is mamma but Maria is my proper mother."

After the break-up at home the boys had got her that position in the *Dublin by Lamplight* laundry, and she liked it. She used to have such a bad opinion of Protestants but now she thought they were very nice people, a little quiet and serious, but still very nice people to live with. Then she had her plants in the conservatory and she liked looking after them. She had lovely ferns and wax-plants and, whenever anyone came to visit her, she always gave the visitor one or two slips from her conservatory. There was one thing she didn't like and that was the tracts on the walls; but the matron was such a nice person to deal with, so genteel.

When the cook told her everything was ready she went into the women's room and began to pull the big bell. In a few minutes the women began to come in by twos and threes, wiping their steaming hands in their petticoats and pulling down the sleeves of their blouses over their red steaming arms. They settled down before their huge mugs which the cook and the dummy filled up with hot tea, already mixed with milk and sugar in huge tin cans. Maria superintended the distribution of the barmbrack and saw that every woman got her four slices. There was a great deal of laughing and joking during the meal. Lizzie Fleming said Maria was sure to get the ring and, though Fleming had said that for so many Hallow Eves, Maria had to laugh and say she didn't want any ring or man either; and when she laughed her grey-green eyes sparkled with disappointed shyness and the tip of her nose nearly met the tip of her chin. Then Ginger Mooney lifted up her mug of tea and proposed Maria's health while all the other women clattered with their mugs on the table, and said she was sorry she hadn't a sup of porter to drink it in. And Maria laughed again till the tip of her nose nearly met the tip of her chin and till her minute body nearly shook itself asunder because she knew that Mooney meant well though, of course, she had the notions of a common woman.

But wasn't Maria glad when the women had finished their tea and the cook and the dummy had begun to clear away the tea-things! She went into her little bedroom and, remembering that the next morning was a mass morning, changed the hand of the alarm from seven to six. Then she took off her working skirt and her house-boots and laid her best skirt out on the bed and her tiny dress-boots beside the foot of the bed. She changed her blouse too and, as she stood before the mirror, she thought of how she used to dress for mass on Sunday morning when she was a young girl; and she looked with quaint affection at the diminutive body which she had so often adorned. In spite of its years she found it a nice tidy little body.

When she got outside the streets were shining with rain and she was glad of her old brown waterproof. The tram was full and she had to sit on the little stool at the end of the car, facing all the people, with her toes barely touching the floor. She arranged in her mind all she was going to do and thought how much better it was to be independent and to have your own money in your pocket. She hoped they would have a nice evening. She was sure they would but she could not help thinking what a pity it was Alphy and Joe were not speaking. They were always falling out now but when they were boys together they used to be the best of friends: but such was life.

She got out of her tram at the Pillar and ferreted her way quickly among the crowds. She went into Downes's cake-shop but the shop was so full of people that it was a long time before she could get herself attended to. She bought a dozen of mixed penny cakes, and at last came out of the shop laden with a big bag. Then she thought what else would she buy: she wanted to buy something really nice. They would be sure to have plenty of apples and nuts. It was hard to know what to buy and all she could think of was cake. She decided to buy some plumcake but Downes's plumcake had not enough almond icing on top of it so she went over to a shop in Henry Street. Here she was a long time in suiting herself and the stylish young lady behind the counter, who was evidently a little annoyed by her, asked her was it wedding-cake she wanted to buy. That made Maria blush and smile at the young lady; but the young lady took it all very seriously and finally cut a thick slice of plumcake, parcelled it up and said:

"Two-and-four, please."

She thought she would have to stand in the Drumcondra tram because none of the young men seemed to notice her but an elderly gentleman made room for her. He was a stout gentleman and he wore a brown hard hat; he had a square red face and a greyish moustache. Maria thought he was a colonel-looking gentleman and she reflected how much more polite he was than the young men who simply stared straight before them. The gentleman began to chat with her about Hallow Eve and the rainy weather. He supposed the bag was full of good things for the little ones and said it was only right that the youngsters should enjoy themselves while they were young. Maria agreed with him and favoured him with demure nods and hems. He was very nice with her, and when she was getting out at the Canal Bridge she thanked him and bowed, and he bowed to her and raised his hat and smiled agreeably; and while she was going up along the terrace, bending her tiny head under the rain, she thought how easy it was to know a gentleman even when he has a drop taken.

Everybody said: *"O, here's Maria!"* when she came to Joe's house. Joe was there, having come home from business, and all the children had their Sunday dresses on. There were two big girls in from next door and games were going on. Maria gave the bag of cakes to the eldest boy, Alphy, to divide and Mrs. Donnelly said it was too good of her to bring such a big bag of cakes and made all the children say:

"Thanks, Maria."

But Maria said she had brought something special for papa and mamma, something they would be sure to like, and she began to look for her plumcake. She tried in Downes's bag and then in the pockets of her waterproof and then on the hallstand but nowhere could she find it. Then she asked all the children had any of them eaten it—by mistake, of course—but the children all said no and looked as if they did not like to eat cakes if they were to be accused of stealing. Everybody had a solution for the mystery and Mrs. Donnelly said it was plain that Maria had left it behind her in the tram. Maria, remembering how confused the gentleman with greyish moustache had made her, coloured with shame and vexation and disappointment. At the thought of the failure of her little surprise and of the two and four-pence she had thrown away for nothing she nearly cried outright.

But Joe said it didn't matter and made her sit down by the fire. He was very nice with her. He told her all that went on in his office, repeating for her a smart answer which he had made to the manager. Maria did not understand why Joe laughed so much over the answer he had made but she said that the manager must have been a very overbearing person to deal with. Joe said he wasn't so bad when you knew how to take him, that he was a decent sort so long as you didn't rub him the wrong way. Mrs. Donnelly played the piano for the children and they danced and sang. Then the two next-door girls handed round the nuts. Nobody could find the nutcrackers and Joe was nearly getting cross over it and asked how did they expect Maria to crack nuts without a nutcracker. But Maria said she didn't like nuts and that they weren't to bother about her. Then Joe asked would she take a bottle of stout and Mrs. Donnelly said there was port wine too in the house if she would prefer that. Maria said she would rather they didn't ask her to take anything: but Joe insisted.

So Maria let him have his way and they sat by the fire talking over old times and Maria thought she would put in a good word for Alphy. But Joe cried that God might strike him stone dead if ever he spoke a word to his brother again and Maria said she was sorry she had mentioned the matter. Mrs. Donnelly told her husband it was a great shame for him to speak that way of his own flesh and blood but Joe said that Alphy was no brother of his and there was nearly being a row on the head of it. But Joe said he would not lose his temper on account of the night it was and asked his wife to open some more stout. The two next-door girls had arranged some Hallow Eve games and soon everything was merry again. Maria was delighted to see the children so merry and Joe and his wife in such good spirits. The next-door girls put some saucers on the table and then led the children up to the table, blindfold. One got the prayer-book and the other three got the water; and when one of the next-door girls got the ring Mrs. Donnelly shook her finger at the blushing girl as much as to say: *O, I know all about it!* They insisted then on blindfolding Maria and leading her up to the table to see what she would get; and, while they were putting on the bandage, Maria laughed and laughed again till the tip of her nose nearly met the tip of her chin.

They led her up to the table amid laughing and joking and she put her hand out in the air as she was told to do. She moved her hand about here and there in the air and descended on one of the saucers. She felt a soft wet substance with her fingers and was surprised that nobody spoke or took off her bandage. There was a pause for a few seconds; and then a great deal of scuffling and whispering. Somebody said something about the garden, and at last Mrs. Donnelly said something very cross to one of the next-door girls and told her to throw it out at once: that was no play. Maria understood that it was wrong that time and so she had to do it over again: and this time she got the prayer-book.

After that Mrs. Donnelly played Miss McCloud's Reel for the children and Joe made Maria take a glass of wine. Soon they were all quite merry again and Mrs. Donnelly said Maria would enter a convent before the year was out because she had got the prayer-book. Maria had never seen Joe so nice to her as he was that night, so full of pleasant talk and reminiscences. She said they were all very good to her.

At last the children grew tired and sleepy and Joe asked Maria would she not sing some little song before she went, one of the old songs. Mrs. Donnelly said "*Do, please, Maria!*" and so Maria had to get up and stand beside the piano. Mrs. Donnelly bade the children be quiet and listen to Maria's song. Then she played the prelude and said "*Now, Maria!*" and Maria, blushing very much, began to sing in a tiny quavering voice. She sang *I Dreamt that I Dwelt,* and when she came to the second verse she sang again:

> "I dreamt that I dwelt in marble halls
> With vassals and serfs at my side
> And of all who assembled within those walls
> That I was the hope and the pride.
>
> "I had riches too great to count, could boast
> Of a high ancestral name,
> But I also dreamt, which pleased me most,
> That you loved me still the same."

But no one tried to show her her mistake;[1] and when she had ended her song Joe was very much moved. He said that there was no time like the long ago and no music for him like poor old Balfe, whatever other people might say; and his eyes filled up so much with tears that he could not find what he was looking for and in the end he had to ask his wife to tell him where the corkscrew was.

Discussion of "Clay"[2]

Earlier in this volume we printed a brief discussion of "Counterparts" by the great James Joyce. Now we have another of his excellent stories—even subtler, more challenging to analyze, and more carefully controlled. First, however, a few general comments about Joyce.

James Joyce (1882-1941) is one of the greatest and most controversial writers produced by Ireland. With incredible power and virtuosity in his use of language, and with equally impressive penetration in his psychological portrayal of human character, Joyce is recognized throughout the world as one of the most influential writers of our century. Especially was he important as a forerunner in the

[1]Repeating the first verse instead of singing the second verse.

[2]Several of the ideas explored in this analysis were suggested by Cleanth Brooks, John Purser, and Robert Penn Warren, *An Approach to Literature,* Third Edition (New York: Appleton-Century-Crofts, 1952), pp. 137-140.

development of the stream-of-consciousness movement in prose fiction.[3] Also notable is the rebellion throughout his writing against the bigotry and narrowness that he felt characterized his Irish Roman Catholic background. In 1912 he fled Ireland never to return, living for the rest of his life at various places in continental Europe. However, although he repudiated Ireland, he is still a celebrated Irish writer, and the city of Dublin forms the heart of most of his work, even that written long after he left Ireland.

Poems and plays are part of his total writing, but it is principally as a novelist and short-story writer that Joyce is famous. His novels—*Portrait of the Artist as a Young Man, Ulysses,* and *Finnegans Wake*—become increasingly experimental and massively complex. The short stories, published in the volume *Dubliners* (1914), are earlier (written when Joyce was in his early twenties) and less difficult, but still brilliantly deep. Among them are some of the best stories of the world—"Araby," "Ivy Day in the Committee Room," "A Little Cloud," and a dozen others, including "The Dead," his great symbolic study of a marriage that has failed because it exists on the social and physical levels only, with little fulfillment or understanding emotionally, intellectually, and spiritually.

Readers' first reaction to "Clay" is likely to be that "nothing happens," that although it is an interesting character study of Maria with many authentic details of setting drawn from early-twentieth-century Ireland, still nothing significant really happens and there is neither drama nor plot of any consequence. Only a close study of the story will make us realize that indeed significant things do happen, involving tension and conflict, and giving vital, even fatal direction to Maria's future.

Since the story is principally Maria's, we need to see her clearly—a homely, undersized old maid with sharp features. ("She had a very long nose and a very long chin,"

[3]See p. 174 of Volume 1 of *Out of the Best Books.*

so long that when she laughed "the tip of her nose nearly met the tip of her chin.") Moreover, her life obviously is as drab as her appearance: she works in a laundry kitchen, a job arranged for her by Joe and Alphy, who grudgingly feel responsible to see that she is taken care of. At the laundry, and in her occasional visits with Joe's family, she imagines that she is happy, that people are delighted with her company. But is she fooling anyone? Perhaps herself. Certainly not the reader. We see that she is little better off than the tub-women whom she looks down on as coarser than herself. We also see that Joe and his family tolerate her for an evening but hardly more: Joe feels an obligation to her, Joe's wife is politely formal, and the children, although enjoying games with Maria, feel free to play mean tricks on her. The result is that we are won in sympathy to Maria—the pathos of her dull, drab, lonely life and her pitiable yielding to every pressure upon her as other people manipulate her as if she were a piece of plastic clay.

To explore the rich subtleness in characterization and meaning of this story and relate it to the theme of obedience, we now approach the story through a series of questions and suggestions for discussion:

1. What is Maria's relationship to Joe and Alphy? Apparently she raised them when they were boys, taking care of them until the "break-up at home" caused the family to split and resulted in her getting a job at the laundry arranged by Joe and Alphy. Is she their older sister, or a servant who raised them, or what? Is it more likely that she is an older sister (or other close blood relative) rather than a servant or governess because a family of their social position would probably not have a servant or governess? Does the story become emotionally stronger if we see her as Joe's older sister rather than someone less personal?

2. Maria is portrayed throughout the story as a homely old maid with a drab life. Special emphasis is placed upon how small she is physically. Are her life, her

world, and her awareness of these as diminutive as her body?

3. Although Maria probably wouldn't admit it, either to herself or to anyone else, as readers we realize that deep in her heart she still dreams of the possibility of marrying and having a family. Indeed, much of the pathos of the story results from our awareness of this. What details unobtrusively woven into the plot let us know this? (Note, among other things, her pleasure in believing that "everyone was so fond" of her, that the matron once referred to her as "a veritable peace-maker," and that Joe used often to say "Mamma is Mamma but Maria is my proper mother." She yearns to be a mother and peace-maker. Note too her looking "with quaint affection" at her small figure which, "in spite of its years" she still thinks of as a "nice tidy little body." Also, note how she blushes when the sales girl asks her if she wants to buy a wedding cake, how embarrassed she is when others suggest that perhaps she will select the ring (indicating future marriage) in the blindfold Hallow Eve game, and how flustered she is when the elderly "colonel-looking gentleman" offers her his seat and chats briefly with her on the tram—so flustered that she forgets the plumcake she took so much pains to buy. Finally, note the romantic song she sings "in a tiny quavering voice" at the end of the story, particularly the "mistake" of repeating the first verse instead of singing the second verse; apparently she is so lost in reverie while singing that she doesn't realize she has made the mistake, even as she probably also doesn't realize how ironically inappropriate it is for her to sing a song so romantic.)

4. Obviously Maria likes Joe and his family very much. Point out evidences showing that Joe feels obligated to her but does not like her as much as she imagines, that Joe's wife is polite but distant, and that Joe's children as well as the neighbor children treat Maria as if she were a servant. (Note that Maria calls Joe by his first name but

calls Joe's wife Mrs. Donnelly even though Joe's wife is apparently much younger than Maria. What does this tell us about the relationship between the two women? Note also the nasty trick the children play on Maria in the blindfold game.)

5. Maria says that often Joe has told her he would like her to live with him and his family. Do you believe that he really wants this? If he said so, how did he probably say it?

6. In the blindfold game a number of articles are placed in saucers on the center of a table and the blindfolded person selects one article. Maria would like to select the ring, prophesying a marriage in her future. Instead she first selects a "soft wet substance" (clay or mud from the garden placed on the table as a joke by the children). Then on the second try she selects a prayer-book, prophesying that she will become a nun. Obviously all of this is just a game—but does it have ominous overtones of more than just a game? Does the clay of her first selection ironically foreshadow what really does lie ahead for her—a drab life, ending in death? And is it likely that Maria really will "enter a convent before the year is out" as Mrs. Donnelly says—"because she got the prayer-book"? Before answering "no" to this question, look back through the story. Note how fully other people manipulate Maria's life, how she has no will of her own but yields to every pressure upon her, especially the desires of Joe and his family. (Maria didn't want to drink port wine, but "Joe insisted, so Maria let him have his way." Maria wanted to say some good things about Alphy, with whom Joe had quarreled, but Joe grew angry, so "Maria said she was sorry she had mentioned the matter." Maria was hesitant to play the blindfold game, but "they insisted," so she *had to* play. When they tricked her into putting her hand on the messy clay, she "understood that it was wrong that time and so she *had to* do it over again." Finally, Maria apparently didn't

want to sing for the family but because they asked her she "had to.") For the time being Maria is provided for by her job at the laundry, but the time will come when somebody will need to take care of her. Sentimental Joe feels an obligation but hardly a desire to care for Maria, and Joe's wife perhaps not even much of an obligation. Wouldn't it be convenient if Maria were to enter a convent? Considering how she yields to pressure, is it not likely that they may indeed maneuver her into a convent? And perhaps even "before the year is out."

7. We have included this story in the section on obedience. Clearly we should be sensitive to and obedient to the righteous desires of those we love. Obedience, however, does not mean that we should have no will, no inner strength, yielding to every pressure from without, twisted and shaped like a piece of molding clay. Note the symbolism of the clay. In a general way it perhaps suggests drab living and death, but in this story it even more represents Maria's life in relation to those who manipulate her like clay. Obedience does not mean loss of individuality, integrity, dignity, and self-direction. In being obedient to those we love, we should also be careful that their desires for us are not evil or petty; for if we have to choose between obedience to God and obedience to man, our choice is clear.

8. We have referred to "Clay" as a story of pathos rather than tragedy. Tragedy is the spectacle of a heroic figure suffering heroically. In tragedy we both pity and admire. In pathos our feeling is mostly pity. Maria is not heroic enough for tragedy, but she genuinely earns our sympathy because she is a believable person trapped in the psychological paralysis of her own personality and hemmed in by narrowness and pressures she hardly even senses. Fortunately the story is written by a great artist with sufficient skill to present it objectively, saving it from sentimentality which probably would result if Maria were

self-pitying. How perceptive is Maria in seeing herself as she really is? Does she realize that she is as homely, lonely, and future-less as she really is? Do we see Maria better than she sees herself and understand her plight better than she understands it? Finally, why does her lack of awareness of the pathos of her situation increase rather than lessen the pathos and improve rather than weaken the story?

Discussion of "A Man for All Seasons"

For the past six years Robert Bolt's play *A Man for All Seasons* has been sweeping the drama world. Originally produced in London in 1960, the play had a great success there, and later during a three-year run in New York it won virtually every honor the theater world could bestow, including five Tony Awards and the New York Drama Critics "best play" award. Especially notable during both the London and New York seasons was the brilliant performance of Paul Scofield, eminent British actor, who played the starring role of Sir Thomas More, the great English statesman whom Henry the Eighth could crush in body but could not conquer in spirit.

Columbia Pictures then turned *A Man for All Seasons* into a motion picture, with Robert Bolt writing the screen adaptation of his own play, and with Paul Scofield again starring as Thomas More. And once more the honors came, including four Academy Award "Oscars." The movie itself won top honors as "best movie of the year" for 1966, Robert Bolt's screen adaptation was named "best screenplay of the year," Paul Scofield was named "best actor of the year," and Fred Zinnemann was named "best director of the year." The movie is now being shown throughout the world and is capturing the admiring applause of audiences everywhere.

Perhaps most readers do not know Robert Bolt by name, but they certainly know some of the work of this greatly talented British playwright, who is still a young man of only forty-two years. Among other things, he is the one who wrote the screenplays for both *Lawrence of Arabia* and Boris Pasternak's great novel *Doctor Zhivago* —and all the world knows the power of those two movies. In re-doing *A Man for All Seasons* for the movie version, Mr. Bolt made some substantial changes in the original stage play, but in either version the work is excellent.

Neither space nor copyright privileges permit our printing *A Man for All Seasons* in this volume. However, many readers will be familiar with it through movie and stage productions. Therefore, and because the play so profoundly and powerfully emphasizes obedience to principle, we have decided to include a discussion of it here.

The work centers around the life of Sir Thomas More (1478-1535), great English statesman, scholar, humanist, and writer of the Renaissance. His most famous work was *Utopia* (1516), but he also wrote many other major works. In public life he was one of the most esteemed statesmen of his time, both as a member of Parliament, and ultimately as Lord Chancellor of England. Although More had been a friend of King Henry VIII, he refused to take an oath to the Act of Supremacy acknowledging the King to be the supreme authority of the English Church, a maneuver King Henry felt necessary in order to circumvent the Pope's refusal to permit the King to divorce Queen Catherine and marry Anne Boleyn. More was a devout churchman and felt that he could not sign the Act of Supremacy, for which he was beheaded as a traitor in 1535.

If ever a play dramatized the ideal of being obedient to principle and to one's conscience, *A Man for All Seasons* surely does. Thomas More is surrounded on all sides by a world of corruption, conspiracy, compromise, rationalization, bribery, threats, intrigue, and conflicting allegiances. As one of the characters says, "Every man has his price": money, titles, pleasure, women, the threat of suffering—something for which he will yield. But More has no price! Although a mild and mellow man, with a sensitive intelligence, a delightful sense of humor, and a great desire to live, he will not violate principle at any cost. He will use every maneuver "within honor" to save himself and his family, but he will not betray his conscience no matter what the consequences. As he says to Cardinal Wolsey, "When statesmen forsake their own private conscience for the sake of their public duties—they lead their country by a short route to chaos."

When Henry VIII tries to persuade, bribe, and threaten Thomas More into yielding to the King's wishes, More holds out his arm and says, "There is my right arm. Take your dagger and saw it through my shoulder, and I will laugh and be thankful, if by that means I can come with a clear conscience." The key to all his actions is obedience to a "clear conscience." Not what is practical but what is moral governs his life, and every action in his life. When, for example, the Duke of Norfolk tries to persuade More to do what his conscience tells him is wrong by urging, "Can't you do what I did, and come with us for fellowship?" More answers, "And when we stand before God, and you are sent to Paradise for doing according to your conscience, and I am damned for not doing according to mine, will you come with me for fellowship?" Even when the pressures are massive against him, he has a sense of humor—but he will not betray his obedience to principle and conscience. Others may live by the rule "Better a live rat than a dead lion," but not More. Although he has enjoyed the cultured life of a scholar-gentleman, not even imprisonment and the threat of torture will make him compromise his principles. Friends, loved ones, everybody presses him to compromise, but he will not yield, not even to preserve an old friendship nor save his family from suffering.

Thomas More is a quiet man, but in his silence there is great strength, inviolable and wonderful to observe as the drama unfolds. Near the end of the play he is dismissed as Lord Chancellor, stripped of all his titles and possessions, and finally thrown for months into a water-soaked dungeon. There his faithful wife Alice and beloved daughter Margaret are permitted just once to visit him. They plead with him to save himself and them by swearing to the Act of Supremacy. In their efforts to persuade him they remind him that he has always told them, "God more regards the thoughts of the heart than the words of the mouth." Margaret pleads, "Then say the words of the oath, and in your heart think otherwise." But More answers, "What is an oath, then, but words that we say to God?" A little later he adds, "When a man takes an oath, he's holding his own life in his own hands. Like water. [He holds his hands in the shape of a cup to illustrate.] And if he opens his fingers then—he needn't hope to find himself again."

In their efforts to persuade him to say the few words necessary to gain his freedom and save himself and his family from suffering, More's wife and daughter (especially his wife) grow outwardly impatient with him, implying that he is stubborn, selfish, and even inconsiderate of their well-being, but More says, "I am faint when I think of the worst that they may do to me. But worse than that would be to go"—by which he means that worse than whatever punishment they may give him would be to gain freedom by betraying his conscience.

At the very end of the play More is found guilty of high treason and beheaded. At any moment even to the very last he could have saved himself by merely saying a few words. Indeed, almost everyone in the play wants him to say the words that will save his life, for all know that with him will die more honesty than any of them can look inward and see. He cannot, however, swear an oath against his conscience. He knows that he dies having been true to his convictions. Thus he can say to the executioner, as he places his neck upon the chopping block and the terrible axe is raised aloft, "Friend, be not afraid of your office. You send me to God."

Anyone experiencing this play, either by reading it (published by Random House, Vintage Books, and Samuel French), by seeing it in a stage production, or by attending the excellent movie, will have an unforgettable experience. It is not only a great play but a play with a great message.

Thoughts and Questions for Discussion:

1. The central point we wish to make through discussion of this play is that in planning our lives we need to be *wisely* obedient, not just blindly, foolishly, or selfishly obedient. If we are obedient to people, we need to choose people who deserve to be followed because of their righteous living and honorable leadership. If we are obedient to principles, we need to choose principles that merit obedience because they are in harmony with Christian ideals. Simply to be obedient is not enough—in fact is not even wise—if we are obedient to the wrong things, either the wrong people or the wrong principles. This play—and the world—are filled with people who are obedient to the wrong masters and the wrong standards. That is why the moral courage of Sir Thomas More stands out so nobly throughout the play.

2. At one point in the play Thomas More says, "I have no window to look into another man's conscience." What does this suggest about the danger of setting ourselves up as judges of each other's conduct and motives—at least unless we are confident that we are guided by inspiration in our judgments?

3. In the play Richard Rich several times accepts bribes, betraying different people, each time at a higher price. What does this suggest about the nature and evil of yielding to bribery and starting down the roadway of deceit? What kind of bribes (hiding under various disguises) confront us in our twentieth-century world?

4. In order to be obedient to his conscience Thomas More refuses to be obedient to King Henry and the pressures many others, including his own family, exert upon him. In our own lives must we sometimes choose between allegiances? Are we sometimes faced with the problem of being disobedient to the pressures of social groups or customs or even those we love in order to be obedient to the principles we know to be right? Should we ever compromise

principles in order to save those we love from suffering? More refuses to do this. Do you feel he is right or wrong in the stand he takes?

5. Part of the pressure both for good and bad on More in this play is that he is surrounded by traditions, which themselves may be either good or bad. Point out some traditions in your own cultural heritage that should be followed because they are good and others that should be resisted because they are bad.

6. Thomas More disciplines his life totally through obedience to the whisperings of his conscience. Is this a good standard to live by? Can we always trust our "conscience"? How do we need to live in order to rely safely upon "conscience" as a guide?

A Loving Heart

by Bruce B. Clark

A LOVING HEART

"A loving heart is the beginning of all knowledge."
—Thomas Carlyle

Introductory Comments

Surely love is the most universal subject of literature, as well as one of the great principles of the gospel. Thousands of novels, stories, poems, dramas, essays, sermons, and scriptures have been published emphasizing the values of love and exploring its many variations—romantic love, family love, God's love, our love of God, love of truth, self love, friendship, etc., including such counterfeits of genuine love as pride, pity, lust, and greed. Indeed, so much has been written on love that it is difficult not to be trite, especially in discussion. Therefore, rather than have a lengthy general introduction to this section, the wisest thing is to get out of the way and let the literature speak for itself.

Before this, however, one observation needs to be made that is not covered in the discussion of selections that follow. Even as hate damages the one who hates more than it damages the one hated, so love benefits the one who loves at least as much as it benefits the one loved. Hate corrodes the one who hates whether the one who is hated returns the hate or not, even as love refines the one who loves whether the one who is loved returns the love or not. The value of love is at least as much in the wonder of loving as in the wonder of being loved. This is the magic, the mystery, and the miracle of love.

The section that now follows is divided into four subsections: First, Burns's "The Cotter's Saturday Night" as a beautiful description in poetry of a family united by deep love and firm parental guidance. Second, "The Parable of the Prodigal Son" as an example of parental love that is genuine and unconditional, after the manner of God's love for His children. Third, Chekhov's "The Darling" as an example of a woman's love that may at first appear admirably unselfish but on closer analysis is seen to be unwholesomely possessive. Fourth, a group of love lyrics—for delight, for beauty, and for a stimulating variety of thoughts.[1]

[1]In addition to the selections on love included in this section, quite a few selections have been printed in previous volumes of *Out of the Best Books* which readers may wish to review. In Volume 1 see especially "An Epistle of Karshish" by Robert Browning (pp. 80-90), "Still Falls the Rain" by Edith Sitwell (pp.105-107), "Birthday Party" by Katharine Brush (pp. 176-178), "Abou Ben Adhem" by Leigh Hunt (p. 233), "A Christmas Carol" by Charles Dickens (pp. 246-274), "The Rime of the Ancient Mariner" by S. T. Coleridge (pp. 304-328), "The Happy Prince" by Oscar Wilde (pp. 352-360), "Michael" by William Wordsworth (pp. 405-419), and "Prospice" by Robert Browning (pp. 459-460). In Volume 2 see especially "My Little Boy" by Carl Ewald (pp. 8-23), "Sixteen" by Jessamyn West (pp. 24-32), "Ruth" (pp. 33-40), "Sonnets from the Portuguese" by E. B. Browning (pp. 46-61), "The Eve of St. Agnes" by John Keats (pp. 77-90), "Mother" by Kathleen Norris (pp. 133-151), "My Last Duchess" by Robert Browning (pp. 190-195), and "Where Love Is, There God Is Also" by Leo Tolstoy (pp. 270-282).

Introduction to "The Cotter's Saturday Night"

In Volume 1 of *Out of the Best Books* we saw Robert Burns (1759-1796) as a stinging satirist of self-righteousness and a strong defender of genuine manliness.[1] Now we see him in "The Cotter's Saturday Night" describing a hard-working Scottish cottager and his family during an evening at home.

All things considered, Burns is probably the greatest poet Scotland ever produced, and one of the world's great song-writers. Although his personal life was rather loose and undisciplined, in his poetry Burns was an idealist with strong faith in God and in the fundamental goodness of man. The best of his many little poems are generally either beautiful lyics of love and friendship (such as "Mary Morison," "John Anderson, My Jo," "My Luve Is Like a Red, Red Rose," "Auld Lang Syne," "Sweet Afton," "To Highland Mary," etc.) or delightful satires attractively mixing humor with sharp criticism (such as "The Holy Fair," "To a Louse," "Holy Willie's Prayer," "Address to the Deil," "Address to the Unco Guid," etc.). He also wrote several excellent narrative poems, of which "The Cotter's Saturday Night" is the most famous.

Although this poem is generally successful as literature in both style and substance, it has some problems and weaknesses that are barriers to most modern readers. One problem is that much of it—indeed, the best of it—is in Scottish dialect, which interferes with immediate understanding in many spots and makes some footnoting necessary. For another thing, when it is not in dialect it shifts into genteel, neo-classic language that most readers find somewhat stiff, flat, and artificial (for example, stanza 1) or sentimental and preachy (for example, stanzas 9 and 10). The result is an uneven poem, with the descriptive and

---

[1]See pages 223-228 of Volume 1.

narrative passages in Scottish dialect which comprise the bulk of the poem generally better than the occasional moralizing interludes. Moreover, throughout the poem one feels at times that Burns is too consciously imitating some earlier poems, including Thomas Gray's "Elegy Written in a Country Churchyard." Indeed, this is often pointed to by critics as the most imitative of Burns's poems.

But the strengths far outweigh the weaknesses and problems. Beginning with stanza 2, the rich Scottish dialect takes over as Burns describes the humble cotter (cottager) and his wife and children during an evening in their home. The poetry is musical and spontaneously attractive, the descriptions are vivid in their realistic detail (note the cow chewing her cud), and the whole scene is authentic and lovely. As the cold November wind blows outside, all is warm and filled with love within the cottage where family and friends gather round the small hearth-fire to talk, play games, sing songs, read scripture, and pray during several hours of a Saturday evening prior to a day of rest on the Sabbath. Burns obviously had never heard of an L. D. S. Family Home Evening; even so, he does a good job of setting a pattern for one.

As we move through the poem, several valuable reminders of what an ideal family relationship should be impress themselves upon us: (1) the rich joy that all family members have in each other, (2) the genuine love that so abundantly fills the house and binds the family together (remember the song "There Is Beauty All Around When There's Love at Home"), (3) the strong family unity with the mother and the father at the head, (4) the concern of each family member for the welfare of all the others, including the neighbors, (5) the working of the children to help contribute to the needs of the family with each family member, including both parents and children, having a sense of duty and obedience, (6) a sincere joy of living, but an abiding seriousness too, (7) the deep religiousness of the whole family, led by the father, who recognizes his responsibility to study the scriptures with his children and to build character in them, (8) the interest and concern when it is discovered that Jenny has a boyfriend, and the desire to unite him with the family rather than have Jenny and her suitor separate from the family for their entertainment, (9) the conclusion of the evening with Bible reading, the singing of hymns, and finally the kneeling of the family in prayer as they simply but movingly speak to God in "the language of the soul" (stanza 17). And even after the gathering has ended, the father and mother continue close to God and to each other as they kneel in private prayer (stanza 18), thanking God for all their blessings and asking Him "in the way His wisdom sees the best" to provide for themselves and for their little ones. Because the whole scene is so lovely, we can even forgive Burns a slightly over-exuberant burst of patriotism in the closing three stanzas as he speaks with pride of Scotland and her special virtues. Indeed he has created for all the world a model family bound together by love and religion—all things simple and genuine, far removed from outward show and ceremony, which Burns scorned so much. Altogether the poem is a beautiful portrayal of the ideal that parents should be affectionate and tenderly loving in all their relationships with each other and with their children, even in times when firm discipline is necessary.

A few words on form may help those who want to study the poem as a work of art. Burns wrote it in Spenserian stanzas, which are nine-line stanzas rhyming ababbcbcc. The first eight lines are iambic pentameter, and the ninth line is iambic hexameter—as is characteristic of the Spenserian stanza. Traditionally this is a form of poetry inappropriate for speedy narration but ideally suited for rich description and quiet story—and Burns handles the style with great skill. The result is—in spite of some weak spots—a warm and beautiful poem of family love, a little old-fashioned perhaps, but filled with all the old-fashioned values and virtues that should not be lost in our rushing twentieth-century world.

The Cotter's Saturday Night

by Robert Burns

1

My lov'd, my honour'd, much respected friend![1]
No mercenary bard his homage pays:
With honest pride I scorn each selfish end,
My dearest meed a friend's esteem and praise:
To you I sing, in simple Scottish lays,
The lowly train in life's sequester'd scene;
The native feeling strong, the guileless ways;
What Aiken in a cottage would have been—
Ah! tho' his worth unknown, far happier there, I ween!

2

November chill blaws loud wi' angry sough;[2]
The short'ning winter-day is near a close;
The miry[3] beasts retreating frae the pleugh;
The black'ning trains o' craws[4] to their repose:
The toil-worn Cotter frae his labour goes,
This night his weekly moil[5] is at an end,
Collects his spades, his mattocks, and his hoes,
Hoping the morn in ease and rest to spend,
And weary, o'er the moor, his course does hameward bend.

3

At length his lonely cot[6] appears in view,
Beneath the shelter of an agèd tree;
Th' expectant wee things, toddlin', stacher[7] through
To meet their Dad, wi' flichterin'[8] noise an' glee.
His wee bit ingle,[9] blinkin bonnilie,
His clean hearth-stane, his thrifty wifie's smile,
The lisping infant prattling on his knee,

---

[1]Burns addressed the poem to Robert Aiken, a lawyer from Ayr, who was a friend and admirer.
[2]sound
[3]mud-covered
[4]crows
[5]heavy work
[6]cottage
[7]stagger
[8]fluttering
[9]fire

Does a' his weary kiaugh[10] and care beguile,
An' makes him quite forget his labour an' his toil.

4

Belyve,[11] the elder bairns[12] come drapping in,
At service out, amang the farmers roun';
Some ca'[13] the pleugh, some herd, some tentie[14] rin
A cannie[15] errand to a neibor town:
Their eldest hope, their Jenny, woman-grown,
In youthfu' bloom, love sparkling in her e'e,
Comes hame, perhaps to shew a braw[16] new gown,
Or deposite her sair-won penny-fee,[17]
To help her parents dear, if they in hardship be.

5

With joy unfeign'd brothers and sisters meet,
An' each for other's weelfare kindly spiers:[18]
The social hours, swift-wing'd, unnotic'd fleet;
Each tells the uncos[19] that he sees or hears;
The parents, partial, eye their hopeful years;
Anticipation forward points the view.
The mother, wi' her needle an' her sheers,
Gars auld claes look amaist[20] as well's the new;
The father mixes a' wi' admonition due.

6

Their master's an' their mistress's command,
The younkers[21] a' are warnèd to obey;
An' mind their labours wi' an eydent[22] hand,
An' ne'er, tho' out o' sight, to jauk[23] or play:
'And O! be sure to fear the Lord alway,

---

[10]worry
[11]soon
[12]children
[13]drive
[14]heedful
[15]careful
[16]fine
[17]hard-won wages
[18]asks
[19]news
[20]makes old clothes look almost
[21]youngsters
[22]diligent
[23]trifle

An' mind your duty, duly, morn an' night!
Lest in temptation's path ye gang astray,
Implore His counsel and assisting might:
They never sought in vain that sought the Lord aright!'

7

But hark! a rap comes gently to the door;
Jenny, wha kens[24] the meaning o' the same,
Tells how a neibor lad cam o'er the moor,
To do some errands, and convoy her hame.
The wily mother sees the conscious flame
Sparkle in Jenny's e'e, and flush her cheek;
Wi' heart-struck anxious care, inquires his name,
While Jenny hafflins[25] is afraid to speak;
Weel pleas'd the mother hears it's nae wild worthless rake.

8

Wi' kindly welcome, Jenny brings him ben:[26]
A strappin' youth; he takes the mother's eye;
Blythe Jenny sees the visit's no ill ta'en;
The father cracks[27] of horses, pleughs, and kye[28]
The youngster's artless heart o'erflows wi' joy,
But blate and laithfu',[29] scarce can weel behave;
The mother, wi' a woman's wiles, can spy
What makes the youth sae bashfu' an' sae grave;
Weel-pleased to think her bairn's respected like the lave.[30]

9

O happy love! where love like this is found;
O heart-felt raptures! bliss beyond compare!
I've pacèd much this weary mortal round
And sage experience bids me this declare—
'If Heaven a draught of heavenly pleasure spare,

---

[24]who knows
[25]half
[26]into the parlor
[27]talks
[28]cows
[29]shy and bashful
[30]others

One cordial in this melancholy vale,
'Tis when a youthful, loving, modest pair
In other's arms breathe out the tender tale,
Beneath the milk-white thorn that scents the evening gale.'

10

Is there, in human form, that bears a heart—
A wretch, a villain, lost to love and truth—
That can, with studied, sly ensnaring art,
Betray sweet Jenny's unsuspecting youth?
Curse on his perjur'd arts, dissembling smooth!
Are honour, virtue, conscience, all exil'd?
Is there no pity, no relenting ruth,
Points to the parents fondling o'er their child?
Then paints the ruin'd maid, and their distraction wild?

11

But now the supper crowns their simple board,
The halesome parritch,[31] chief of Scotia's food:
The sowpe[32] their only hawkie [33] does afford,
That 'yont the hallan[34] snugly chows her cood;
The dame brings forth in complimental mood,
To grace the lad, her weel-hain'd kebbuck, fell;[35]
And aft he's prest, and aft he ca's it good;
The frugal wifie, garrulous, will tell
How 'twas a towmond[36] auld sin' lint was i' the bell.[37]

12

The cheerfu' supper done, wi' serious face
They round the ingle form a circle wide;

---

[31]oatmeal porridge
[32]milk
[33]cow
[34]beyond the partition
[35]well-saved, strong cheese
[36]twelvemonth
[37]since flax was in bloom

The sire turns o'er, wi' patriarchal grace,
The big ha'-Bible[38] ance his father's pride:
His bonnet rev'rently is laid aside,
His lyart haffets[39] wearing thin an' bare;
Those strains that once did sweet in Zion glide—
He wales[40] a portion with judicious care,
And 'Let us worship God!' he says with solemn air.

13

They chant their artless notes in simple guise;
They tune their hearts, by far the noblest aim:
Perhaps Dundee's[41] wild warbling measures rise,
Or plaintive Martyrs,[41] worthy of the name;
Or noble Elgin[41] beets[42] the heav'nward flame,
The sweetest far of Scotia's holy lays:
Compar'd with these, Italian trills are tame;
The tickl'd ears no heartfelt raptures raise;
Nae unison hae they with our Creator's praise.

14

The priest-like father reads the sacred page,
How Abram was the friend of God on high;
Or Moses bade eternal warfare wage
With Amalek's ungracious progeny;
Or how the royal bard[43] did groaning lie
Beneath the stroke of Heaven's avenging ire;
Or Job's pathetic plaint, and wailing cry;
Or rapt Isaiah's wild seraphic fire;
Or other holy seers that tune the sacred lyre.

15

Perhaps the Christian volume is the theme,
How guiltless blood for guilty man was shed;

---

[38]hall-Bible
[39]gray locks
[40]chooses
[41]sacred melodies
[42]kindles
[43]David

How He[44] who bore in Heaven the second name
Had not on earth whereon to lay His head;
How His first followers and servants sped;
The precepts sage they wrote to many a land:
How he,[45] was lone in Patmos banishèd,
Saw in the sun a mighty angel stand,
And heard great Bab'lon's doom pronounc'd by Heaven's command.

16

Then kneeling down to Heaven's Eternal King
The saint, the father, and the husband prays:
Hope 'springs exulting on triumphant wing'[46]
That thus they all shall meet in future days:
There ever bask in uncreated rays,
No more to sigh, or shed the bitter tear,
Together hymning their Creator's praise,
In such society, yet still more dear;
While circling Time moves round in an eternal sphere.

17

Compar'd with this, how poor Religion's pride,
In all the pomp of method and of art,
When men display to congregations wide
Devotion's ev'ry grace, except the heart!
The Power, incens'd, the pageant will desert,
The pompous strain, the sacerdotal stole;[47]
But haply, in some cottage far apart,
May hear, well pleas'd, the language of the soul;
And in His Book of Life the inmates poor enrol.

18

Then homeward all take off their sev'ral way;
The youngling cottagers retire to rest:
The parent-pair their secret homage pay,
And proffer up to Heav'n the warm request,
That He who stills the raven's clamorous nest,[48]

---

[44]Christ
[45]John
[46]Alexander Pope, *Windsor Forest,* l. 112.
[47]priestly vestment
[48]See Psalms, 147:9

And decks the lily fair in flow'ry pride,[49]
Would, in the way His wisdom sees the best,
For them and for their little ones provide;
But chiefly in the hearts with Grace Divine preside.

19

From scenes like these old Scotia's grandeur springs,
That makes her lov'd at home, rever'd abroad:
Princes and lords are but the breath of kings,
'An honest man's the noblest work of God';[50]
And certes, in fair Virtue's heavenly road,
The cottage leaves the palace far behind;
What is a lordling's pomp? a cumbrous load,
Disguising oft the wretch of human kind,
Studied in arts of Hell, in wickedness refin'd!

20

O Scotia! my dear, my native soil!
For whom my warmest wish to Heaven is sent!
Long may thy hardy sons of rustic toil
Be blest with health, and peace, and sweet content!
And O! may Heaven their simple lives prevent
From Luxury's contagion, weak and vile;
Then, howe'er crowns and coronets be rent,
A virtuous populace may rise the while,
And stand a wall of fire around their much-lov'd isle.

21

O Thou! who pour'd the patriotic tide
That stream'd thro' Wallace's[51] undaunted heart,
Who dared to nobly stem tyrannic pride,
Or nobly die—the second glorious part,
(The patriot's God, peculiarly Thou art,
His friend, inspirer, guardian, and reward!)
O never, never Scotia's realm desert;
But still the patriot, and the patriot-bard,
In bright succession raise, her ornament and guard!

---

[49]See Matthew, 6:28-29
[50]Alexander Pope, *Essay on Man,* IV, 248.
[51]Thirteenth-century Scottish patriot.

Introduction to the Parable of the Prodigal Son

The greatest, wisest, most skillful teacher the world has ever known was Jesus Christ, and it is significant that He taught many of His most memorable lessons through short stories, or parables as He called them. Surely He knew the power of literature to dramatize truth, implant it vividly in the mind and heart, and make it a living force in the lives of his listeners. Had He not believed in the power of literature He would not have used it as an instrument through which to dramatize so many of His messages.

Because the Parable of the Prodigal Son explores some serious family problems and sensitive family relationships relating to love, we have included it for study here. The story is generally simple and self-explanatory, but several points need analysis.

First, note that the younger or "prodigal" son has both good and bad qualities. Obviously he has sinned seriously and lengthily, wasting his money on riotous living, including (if we can believe the elder brother) squandering it on harlots. Apparently also his repentance is not as admirable as it could be. For one thing, it comes only in desperation after he has lost all his money and is starving. For another thing, even when he does return to his home, the repentant return may be motivated at least in part by selfish thoughts of what he can get out of his father. Certainly he is not altogether admirable. But he does return. And he is at least partly sincere in his repentance. He does confess his sins and acknowledge his unworthiness, and he does humble himself before his father and before God. He has at least started down the long road of redemption.

The elder brother also has both good and bad qualities. On the positive side, for years he has obediently lived the commandments of the family, and for years he has worked hard and faithfully on the family farm. But his attitudes are not as they should be. He shows anger and jealousy, and he is unforgiving towards his brother. Moreover, in his relations with his father he seems to feel that love is a thing to be bought.

More important than what happens to either of the sons so far as the message of this story is concerned is the attitude of the father. He beautifully displays what Jesus taught in another brief parable immediately preceding this one, The Parable of the Lost Sheep.

> What man of you, having an hundred sheep, if he lose one of them doth not leave the ninety and nine in the wilderness, and go after that which is lost, until he find it? And when he hath found it, he layeth it on his shoulders, rejoicing. And when he cometh home, he calleth together his friends and neighbours, saying unto them, Rejoice with me; for I have found my sheep which was lost.
>
> I say unto you, that likewise joy shall be in heaven over one sinner that repenteth, more than over ninety and nine just persons, which need no repentance. —St. Luke 15:4-7.

Both of these parables illustrate the nature of true love. Love, genuine love, unconditional love, divine love, is a gift that is not dependent on the worthiness of those who are loved. If we loved—or if God loved—only those who earn that love by righteousness and obedience, then the love would not be genuine and unconditional. God loves everyone. Similarly, a father or mother does not stop loving a child—at least should not—because the child betrays a trust or turns out to be different from what the parents desire. The child who strays or otherwise sins is loved no less than the one who remains faithful, and the faithful one should rejoice over the repentance of the one who has sinned, not resent him as does the older brother in this parable. That is, as God has set the pattern in love for His children, so should be the relationships one to another of all of us who are His children.

(Note: For these two parables the King James translation of the Bible is used—both because this is the translation most widely used by L.D.S. readers and because it has the most beautiful literary style of all English translations.)

Parable of the Prodigal Son

And he said, "A certain man had two sons: And the younger of them said to his father, 'Father, give me the portion of goods that falleth to me.' And he divided unto them his living.

"And not many days after the younger son gathered all together, and took his journey into a far country, and there wasted his substance with riotous living. And when he had spent all, there arose a mighty famine in that land; and he began to be in want. And he went and joined himself to a citizen of that country; and he sent him into his fields to feed swine. And he would fain have filled his belly with the husks that the swine did eat; and no man gave unto him.

"And when he came to himself, he said, 'How many hired servants of my father's have bread enough and to spare, and I perish with hunger! I will arise and go to my father, and will say unto him, "Father, I have sinned against heaven and before thee, and am no more worthy to be called thy son: make me as one of thy hired servants." '

"And he arose, and came to his father. But when he was yet a great way off, his father saw him, and had compassion, and ran, and fell on his neck, and kissed him. And the son said unto him, 'Father, I have sinned against heaven, and in thy sight, and am no more worthy to be called thy son.' But the father said to his servants, 'Bring forth the best robe, and put it on him; and put a ring on his hand, and shoes on his feet: and bring hither the fatted calf, and kill it; and let us eat, and be merry: for this my son was dead, and is alive again; he was lost, and is found.' And they began to be merry.

"Now his elder son was in the field: and as he came and drew nigh to the house, he heard music and dancing. And he called one of the servants and asked what these things meant. And he said unto him, 'Thy brother is come; and thy father hath killed the fatted calf, because he hath received him safe and sound.' And he was angry, and would not go in: therefore came his father out, and intreated him. And he answering said to his father, 'Lo, these many years do I serve thee, neither transgressed I at any time thy commandment: and yet thou never gavest me a kid, that I might make merry with my friends: but as soon as this thy son was come, which hath devoured thy living with harlots, thou hast killed for him the fatted calf.'

"And he said unto him, 'Son, thou art ever with me, and all that I have is thine. It was meet that we should make merry, and be glad: for this thy brother was dead, and is alive again; and was lost, and is found.' "

—St. Luke 15:11-32

Introduction to "The Darling"

William Blake (1757-1827) once wrote a little poem called "The Clod and the Pebble" in which he described two opposite kinds of love:

> "Love seeketh not itself to please,
> Nor for itself hath any care,
> But for another gives its ease,
> And builds a Heaven in Hell's despair."
>
> So sung a little Clod of Clay
> Trodden with the cattle's feet,
> But a Pebble of the brook
> Warbled out these metres meet:
>
> "Love seeketh only self to please,
> To bind another to its delight,
> Joys in another's loss of ease,
> And builds a Hell in Heaven's despite."

The clod, of course, represents unselfish love, and the pebble represents selfish love. Within the poem Blake lets each speak for itself, without identifying the narrowness of the selfish love as contrasted with the breadth of the unselfish love. But later, in another poem ("Visions of the Daughters of Albion"), Blake emphasizes the evil of selfish love:

> Can that be love, that drinks another as a sponge drinks water,
> That clouds with jealousy his nights, with weepings all the day . . .?
> Such is self-love that envies all, a creeping skeleton,
> With lamp-like eyes watching around the frozen marriage bed!

These little poems are quoted to remind us that love may be of many kinds, and not all kinds are beautiful and admirable. Not only may we have selfish and unselfish love, but there are such counterfeit emotions as lust, greed, jealousy, passion, possessiveness, etc., which are perversions of true love.

Placing the needs and happiness of those we love ahead of our own desires and comforts is essential to ideal family relationships and is an expression of ideal family love—the complete unity of husband and wife in marriage.

> From the beginning of the creation God made them male and female. For this cause shall a man leave his father and mother, and cleave to his wife; and they twain shall be one flesh: so then they are no more twain, but one flesh." —St. Mark 10:6-8.

Husbands and wives must follow this scripture to be obedient to the most fundamental law of love and marriage. The resulting relationship, however, should be one of equal respect, not of subservience one to the other.

And so we turn to "The Darling" by Anton Chekhov (1860-1904). This is one of the best known stories by one of Russia's greatest authors. In style it is what we call a "slice-of-life" story, without definite beginning or ending, as if we took a motion picture of a person's life and then with scissors cut a section out of the middle for viewing. What we see of Olenka, the central character, is typical of what has gone on before the story begins and will continue after the story ends. That is to say, primarily the story is a character study.

Olenka is called "the darling" by everyone because, we are told, "She was always fond of someone, and could not exist without loving." Within limits this need to love and be loved is natural, even admirable. Certainly selfish aloneness is not a proper way of life. But she carries her need for others too far. She has no life, no personality, no mind of her own. Unless she can live in other people's lives, she has no existence of her own.

And so a succession of men fill her life. In the background of the story there are her father, her French master, and others. In the story itself she first marries Kukin, the theater manager; and while he is alive she thinks and talks only the language of the theater. Then he dies, and her life is completely empty until a few months later when she "falls in love" with a timber merchant. Now for a time he totally absorbs her life. "The theater, who wants to waste time on the theater?" she asks. "We have no time for nonsense." She thinks, and even dreams, only in board feet. She has no ideas of her own, nor even opinions. However, the timber merchant also dies after a while, and again her life is desolate. At least this is so until Smirnin, an army veterinary surgeon, comes into her life. Then once again she yields her individuality and becomes a faceless part of his life. "It was evident that she could not live a year without some attachment." When the veterinary surgeon is transferred to a distant post and pulls out of her life, Olenka once again is empty and desolate. "Worst of all, she had no opinions of any sort. . . . She wanted a love that would absorb her whole being, her whole soul and reason—that would give her ideas and an object in life, and would warm her blood." So desperate is she to attach herself to someone that she even echoes the opinions of Mavra, the cook. Then Sasha, the veterinary surgeon's little boy, comes to live with her, and once again she comes alive as a person. However, now her opinions are all about the cruelty of school teachers and the harshness of schools. Thus the story ends, with Olenka smothering Sasha with her love, and Sasha trying to escape her over-possessiveness, even in his sleep.

Is Olenka's love beautiful, healthy? Certainly there is something beautiful about sacrifice in behalf of others, about unselfishly doing things for others and even thinking in unity with those we love. But is Olenka's love too self-sacrificing, too possessive, too smothering? Does it, in fact, become almost leech-like as she attaches herself to those she loves, clinging to them not so much for their sake as for herself?

Ideal love involves unselfishness and unity, but as children of God we also need to maintain a dignity of individual personality. Marriage is a union of souls, but not a loss of personal identity, and not a sacrifice of oneself to the extent that if death comes to the marriage partner one's total personality and purpose die also. Can love become so possessive, so dependent, so smothering that it is unhealthy rather than healthy? Does obedience to the authority of one's husband mean total subservience to his personality?

Thoughts and Questions for Further Discussion after Reading "The Darling:"

1. Distinguish between (a) unselfishness that is good in love and marriage and (b) loss of self that is bad.

2. To what extent is Olenka's love unselfish, healthy, wholesome, and admirable? To what extent is it selfish, unhealthy, unwholesome, and pitiable? Discuss fully, pointing out evidences of both kinds of love in her life.

3. When Christ said, "He that loses his life shall find it," did He mean that a person should lose his individual personality? If not, what did He mean?

page 219

The Darling

by Anton Chekhov

Olenka, the daughter of the retired collegiate assessor, Plemyanniakov, was sitting in her back porch, lost in thought. It was hot, the flies were persistent and teasing, and it was pleasant to reflect that it would soon be evening. Dark rainclouds were gathering from the east, and bringing from time to time a breath of moisture in the air.

Kukin, who was the manager of an open-air theater called the Tivoli, and who lived in the lodge, was standing in the middle of the garden looking at the sky.

"Again!" he observed despairingly. "It's going to rain again! Rain every day, as though to spite me. I might as well hang myself! It's ruin! Fearful losses every day."

He flung up his hands, and went on, addressing Olenka:

"There! That's the life we lead, Olga Semyonovna.[1] It's enough to make one cry. One works and does one's utmost; one wears oneself out, getting no sleep at night, and racks one's brain what to do for the best. And then what happens? To begin with, one's public is ignorant, boorish. I give them the very best operetta, a dainty masque, first rate music-hall artists. But do you suppose that's what they want! They don't understand anything of that sort. They want a clown; what they ask for is vulgarity. And then look at the weather! Almost every evening it rains. It started on the tenth of May, and it's kept it up all May and June. It's simply awful! The public doesn't come, but I've to pay the rent just the same, and pay the artists."

The next evening the clouds would gather again, and Kukin would say with an hysterical laugh:

"Well, rain away, then! Flood the garden, drown me! Damn my luck in this world and the next! Let the artists have me up! Send me to prison!—to Siberia!—the scaffold! ha, ha, ha!"

And next day the same thing.

Olenka listened to Kukin with silent gravity, and sometimes tears came into her eyes. In the end his misfortunes touched her; she grew to love him. He was a small thin man, with a yellow face, and curls combed forward on his forehead. He spoke in a thin tenor; as he talked his mouth worked on one side, and there was always an expression of despair on his face; yet he aroused a deep and genuine affection in her. She was always fond of some one, and could not exist without loving. In earlier days she had loved her papa, who now sat

---

[1]Russian names are confusing. Each person has a formal name, such as Olga Semyonovna, and a familiar name or nickname, such as Olenka.

in a darkened room, breathing with difficulty; she had loved her aunt who used to come every other year from Bryansk; and before that, when she was at school, she had loved her French master. She was a gentle, soft-hearted, compassionate girl, with mild, tender eyes and very good health. At the sight of her full rosy cheeks, her soft white neck with a little dark mole on it, and the kind, naive smile, which came into her face when she listened to anything pleasant, men thought, "Yes, not half bad," and smiled too, while lady visitors could not refrain from seizing her hand in the middle of a conversation, exclaiming in a gush of delight, "You darling!"

The house in which she had lived from her birth upwards, and which was left her in her father's will, was at the extreme end of the town, not far from the Tivoli. In the evenings and at night she could hear the band playing, and the crackling and banging of fireworks, and it seemed to her that it was Kukin struggling with his destiny, storming the entrenchments of his chief foe, the indifferent public; there was a sweet thrill at her heart, she had no desire to sleep, and when he returned home at daybreak, she tapped softly at her bedroom window, and showing him only her face and one shoulder through the curtain, she gave him a friendly smile. . . .

He proposed to her, and they were married. And when he had a closer view of her neck and her plump, fine shoulders, he threw up his hands, and said: "You darling!"

He was happy, but as it rained on the day and night of his wedding, his face still retained an expression of despair.

They got on very well together. She used to sit in his office, to look after things in the Tivoli, to put down the accounts and pay the wages. And her rosy cheeks, her sweet, naive, radiant smile, were to be seen now at the office window, now in the refreshment bar or behind the scenes of the theater. And already she used to say to her acquaintances that the theater was the chief and most important thing in life, and that it was only through the drama that one could derive true enjoyment and become cultivated and humane.

"But do you suppose the public understands that?" she used to say. "What they want is a clown. Yesterday we gave *Faust Inside Out*, and almost all the boxes were empty; but if Vanitchka and I had been producing some vulgar thing, I assure you the theater would have been packed. Tomorrow Vanitchka and I are doing *Orpheus in Hell*. Do come."

And what Kukin said about the theater and the actors she repeated. Like him she despised the public for their ignorance and their indifference to art; she took part in the rehearsals, she corrected the actors, she kept an eye on the behavior of the musicians, and when there was an unfavorable notice in the local paper, she shed tears, and then went to the editor's office to set things right.

The actors were fond of her and used to call her "Vanitchka and I" and "the darling"; she was sorry for them and used to lend them small sums of money, and if they deceived her, she used to shed a few tears in private, but did not complain to her husband.

They got on well in the winter too. They took the theater in the town for the whole winter, and let it for short terms to a Little Russian company, or to a conjurer, or to a local dramatic society. Olenka grew stouter, and was always beaming with satisfaction, while Kukin grew thinner and yellower, and continually complained of their terrible losses, although he had not done badly all the winter. He used to cough at night, and she used to give him hot raspberry tea or lime-flower water, to rub him with eau de Cologne and to wrap him in her warm shawls.

"You're such a sweet pet!" she used to say with perfect sincerity, stroking his hair. "You're such a pretty dear!"

Towards Lent he went to Moscow to collect a new troupe, and without him she could not sleep, but sat all night at her window, looking at the stars, and she compared herself to the hens, who are awake all night and uneasy when the cock is not in the henhouse. Kukin was detained in Moscow, and wrote that he would be back at Easter, adding some instructions about the Tivoli. But on the Sunday before Easter, late in the evening, came a sudden ominous knock at the gate; some one was hammering on the gate as though on a barrel —boom, boom boom! The drowsy cook went flopping with her bare feet through the puddles, as she ran to open the gate.

"Please open," said some one outside in a thick bass. "There is a telegram for you."

Olenka had received telegrams from her husband before, but this time for some reason she felt numb with terror. With shaking hands she opened the telegram and read as follows:

"Ivan Petrovitch died suddenly today. Awaiting immate instructions fufuneral Tuesday."

That was how it was written in the telegram—"fufuneral," and the utterly incomprehensible word "immate." It was signed by the stage manager of the operatic company.

"My darling!" sobbed Olenka. "Vanitchka, my precious, my darling! Why did I ever meet you! Why did I know you and love you! Your poor heartbroken Olenka is all alone without you!"

Kukin's funeral took place on Tuesday in Moscow, Olenka returned home on Wednesday, and as soon as she got indoors she threw herself on her bed and sobbed so loudly that it could be heard next door, and in the street.

"Poor darling!" the neighbors said, as they crossed themselves. "Olga Semyonovna, poor darling! How she does take on!"

Three months later Olenka was coming home from mass, melancholy and in deep mourning. It happened that one of her neighbors, Vassily Andreitch Pustovalov, returning home from church, walked back beside her. He was the manager at Babakayev's, the timber merchant's. He wore a straw hat, a white waistcoat, and a gold watch-chain, and looked more like a country gentleman than a man in trade.

"Everything happens as it is ordained, Olga Semyonovna," he said gravely, with a sympathetic note in his voice; "and if any of our dear ones die, it must be because it is the will of God, so we ought to have fortitude and bear it submissively."

After seeing Olenka to her gate, he said good-by and went on. All day afterwards she heard his sedately dignified voice, and whenever she shut her eyes she saw his dark beard. She liked him very much. And apparently she had made an impression on him too, for not long afterwards an elderly lady, with whom she was only slightly acquainted, came to drink coffee with her, and as soon as she was seated at table began to talk about Pustovalov, saying that he was an excellent man whom one could thoroughly depend upon, and that any girl would be glad to marry him. Three days later Pustovalov came himself. He did not stay long, only about ten minutes, and he did not say much, but when he left, Olenka loved him—loved him so much that she lay awake all night in a perfect fever, and in the morning she sent for the elderly lady. The match was quickly arranged, and then came the wedding.

Pustovalov and Olenka got on very well together when they were married.

Usually he sat in the office till dinnertime, then he went out on business, while Olenka took his place, and sat in the office till evening, making up accounts and booking orders.

"Timber gets dearer every year; the price rises twenty per cent," she would say to her customers and friends. "Only fancy we used to sell local timber, and now Vassitchka always has to go for wood to the Mogilov district. And the freight!" she would add, covering her cheeks with her hands in horror. "The freight!"

It seemed to her that she had been in the timber trade for ages and ages, and that the most important and necessary thing in life was timber; and there was something intimate and touching to her in the very sound of words such as "baulk," "post," "beam," "pole," "scantling," "batten," "lath," "plank," etc.

At night when she was asleep she dreamed of perfect mountains of planks and boards, and long strings of wagons, carting timber somewhere far away. She dreamed that a whole regiment of six-inch beams forty feet high, standing on end, was marching upon the timber-yard; that logs, beams, and boards knocked together with the resounding crash of dry wood, kept falling and getting up again, piling themselves on each other. Olenka cried out in her sleep, and Pustovalov said to her tenderly: "Olenka, what's the matter, darling? Cross yourself!"

Her husband's ideas were hers. If he thought the room was too hot, or that business was slack, she thought the same. Her husband did not care for entertainments, and on holidays he stayed at home. She did likewise.

"You are always at home or in the office," her friends said to her. "You should go to the theater, darling, or to the circus."

"Vassitchka and I have no time to go to theaters," she would answer sedately. "We have no time for nonsense. What's the use of those theaters?"

On Saturdays Pustovalov and she used to go to the evening service; on holidays to early mass, and they walked side by side with softened faces as they came home from church. There was a pleasant fragrance about them both, and her silk dress rustled agreeably. At home they drank tea, with fancy bread and jams of various kinds, and afterwards they ate pie. Every day at twelve o'clock there was a savory smell of beet-root soup and of mutton or duck in their yard, and on fast-days of fish, and no one could pass the gate without feeling hungry. In the office the samovar was always boiling, and customers were regaled with tea and cracknels. Once a week the couple went to the baths and returned side by side, both red in the face.

"Yes, we have nothing to complain of, thank God," Olenka used to say to her acquaintances. "I wish every one were as well off as Vassitchka and I."

When Pustovalov went away to buy wood in the Mogilev district, she missed him dreadfully, lay awake and cried. A young veterinary surgeon in the army, called Smirnin, to whom they had let their lodge, used sometimes to come in in the evening. He used to talk to her and play cards with her, and this entertained her in her husband's absence. She was particularly interested in what he told her of his home life. He was married and had a little boy, but was separated from his wife because she had been unfaithful to him, and now he hated her and used to send her forty roubles a month for the maintenance of their son. And hearing of all this, Olenka sighed and shook her head. She was sorry for him.

"Well, God keep you," she used to say to him at parting, as she lighted him down the stairs with a candle. "Thank you for coming to cheer me up, and may the Mother of God give you health."

And she always expressed herself with the same sedateness and dignity, the same reasonableness, in imitation of her husband. As the veterinary surgeon was disappearing behind the door below, she would say:

"You know, Vladimir Platonitch, you'd better make it up with your wife. You should forgive her for the sake of your son. You may be sure the little fellow understands."

And when Pustovalov came back, she told him in a low voice about the veterinary surgeon and his unhappy home life, and both sighed and shook their heads and talked about the boy, who, no doubt, missed his father, and by some strange connection of ideas, they went up to the holy ikons, bowed to the ground before them and prayed that God would give them children.

And so the Pustovalovs lived for six years quietly and peaceably in love and complete harmony.

But behold! one winter day after drinking hot tea in the office, Vassily Andreitch went out into the yard without his cap on to see about sending off some timber, caught cold and was taken ill. He had the best doctors, but he grew worse and died after four months' illness. And Olenka was a widow once more.

"I've nobody, now you've left me, my Darling," she sobbed, after her husband's funeral. "How can I live without you, in wretchedness and misery! Pity me, good people, all alone in the world!"

She went about dressed in black with long "weepers," and gave up wearing hat and gloves for good. She hardly ever went out, except to church, or to her husband's grave, and led the life of a nun. It was not till six months later that she took off the weepers and opened the shutters of the windows. She was sometimes seen in the mornings, going with her cook to market for provisions, but what went on in her house and how she lived now could only be surmised. People guessed, from seeing her drinking tea in her garden with the veterinary surgeon, who read the newspaper aloud to her, and from the fact that, meeting a lady she knew at the post office, she said to her:

"There is no proper veterinary inspection in our town, and that's the cause of all sorts of epidemics. One is always hearing of people's getting infection from the milk supply, or catching diseases from horses and cows. The health of domestic animals ought to be as well cared for as the health of human beings."

She repeated the veterinary surgeon's words, and was of the

same opinion as he about everything. It was evident that she could not live a year without some attachment, and had found new happiness in the lodge. In any one else this would have been censured, but no one could think ill of Olenka; everything she did was so natural. Neither she nor the veterinary surgeon said anything to other people of the change in their relations, and tried, indeed, to conceal it, but without success, for Olenka could not keep a secret. When he had visitors, men serving in his regiment, and she poured out tea or served the supper, she would begin talking of the cattle plague, of the foot and mouth disease, and of the municipal slaughter-houses. He was dreadfully embarrassed, and when the guests had gone, he would seize her by the hand and hiss angrily:

"I've asked you before not to talk about what you don't understand. When we veterinary surgeons are talking among ourselves, please don't put your word in. It's really annoying."

And she would look at him with astonishment and dismay, and ask him in alarm: "But, Voloditchka, what *am* I to talk about?"

And with tears in her eyes she would embrace him, begging him not to be angry, and they were both happy.

But this happiness did not last long. The veterinary surgeon departed, departed forever with his regiment, when it was transferred to a distant place—to Siberia, it may be. And Olenka was left alone.

Now she was absolutely alone. Her father had long been dead, and his armchair lay in the attic, covered with dust and lame of one leg. She got thinner and plainer, and when people met her in the street they did not look at her as they used to, and did not smile to her; evidently her best years were over and left behind, and now a new sort of life had begun for her, which did not bear thinking about. In the evening Olenka sat in the porch, and heard the band playing and the fireworks popping in the Tivoli, but now the sound stirred no response. She looked into her yard without interest, thought of nothing, wished for nothing, and afterwards, when night came on she went to bed and dreamed of her empty yard. She ate and drank as it were unwillingly.

And what was worst of all, she had no opinions of any sort. She saw the objects about her and understood what she saw, but could not form any opinion about them, and did not know what to talk about. And how awful it is not to have any opinions! One sees a bottle, for instance, or the rain, or a peasant driving in his cart, but what the bottle is for, or the rain, or the peasant, and what is the meaning of it, one can't say, and could not even for a thousand roubles. When she had Kukin, or Pustovalov, or the veterinary surgeon, Olenka could explain everything, and give her opinion about anything you like, but now there was the same emptiness in her brain and in her heart as there was in her yard outside. And it was as harsh and as bitter as wormwood in the mouth.

Little by little the town grew in all directions. The road became a street, and where the Tivoli and the timber-yard had been there were new turnings and houses. How rapidly time passes! Olenka's house grew dingy, the roof got rusty, the shed sank on one side, and the whole yard was overgrown with docks and stinging-nettles. Olenka herself had grown plain and elderly; in summer she sat in the porch, and her soul, as before, was empty and dreary and full of bitterness. In winter she sat at her window and looked at the snow. When she caught the scent of spring, or heard the chime of the church bells, a sudden rush of memories from the past came over her, there was a tender ache in her heart, and her eyes brimmed over with tears; but this was only for a minute, and then came emptiness again and the sense of the futility of life. The black kitten, Briska, rubbed against her and purred softly, but Olenka was not touched by these feline caresses. That was not what she needed. She wanted a love that would absorb her whole being, her whole soul and reason—that would give her ideas and an object in life, and would warm her old blood. And she would shake the kitten off her skirt and say with vexation:

"Get along: I don't want you!"

And so it was, day after day and year after year, and no joy, and no opinions. Whatever Mavra, the cook, said she accepted.

One hot July day, towards evening, just as the cattle were being driven away, and the whole yard was full of dust, some one suddenly knocked at the gate. Olenka went to open it herself and was dumbfounded when she looked out: she saw Smirnin, the veterinary surgeon, gray-headed, and dressed as a civilian. She suddenly remembered everything. She could not help crying and letting her head fall on his breast without uttering a word, and in the violence of her feeling she did not notice how they both walked into the house and sat down to tea.

"My dear Vladimir Platonitch! what fate has brought you?" she muttered, trembling with joy.

"I want to settle here for good, Olga Semyonovna," he told her. "I have resigned my post, and have come to settle down and try my luck on my own account. Besides, it's time for my boy to go to school. He's a big boy. I am reconciled with my wife, you know."

"Where is she?" asked Olenka.

"She's at the hotel with the boy, and I'm looking for lodgings."

"Good gracious, my dear soul! Lodgings? Why not have my

house? Why shouldn't that suit you? Why, my goodness, I wouldn't take any rent!" cried Olenka in a flutter, beginning to cry again. "You live here, and the lodge will do nicely for me. Oh, dear! how glad I am!"

Next day the roof was painted and the walls were whitewashed, and Olenka, with her arms akimbo, walked about the yard giving directions. Her face was beaming with her old smile, and she was brisk and alert as though she had waked from a long sleep. The veterinary's wife arrived—a thin, plain lady, with short hair and a peevish expression. With her was her little Sasha, a boy of ten, small for his age, blue-eyed, chubby, with dimples in his cheeks. And scarcely had the boy walked into the yard when he ran after the cat, and at once there was the sound of his gay, joyous laugh.

"Is that your puss, Auntie?" he asked Olenka. "When she has little ones, do give us a kitten. Mamma is awful afraid of mice."

Olenka talked to him, and gave him tea. Her heart warmed and there was a sweet ache in her bosom, as though the boy had been her own child. And when he sat at the table in the evening, going over his lessons, she looked at him with deep tenderness and pity as she murmured to herself:

"You pretty pet! . . . my precious! . . . Such a fair little thing, and so clever."

"'An island is a piece of land which is entirely surrounded by water,'" he read aloud.

"An island is a piece of land," she repeated, and this was the first opinion to which she gave utterance with positive conviction after so many years of silence and dearth of ideas.

Now she had opinions of her own, and at supper she talked to Sasha's parents, saying how difficult the lessons were at the high school, but that yet the high school was better than a commercial one, since with a high school education all careers were open to one, such as being a doctor or an engineer.

Sasha began going to the high school. His mother departed to Harkov to her sister's and did not return; his father used to go off every day to inspect cattle, and would often be away from home for three days together, and it seemed to Olenka as though Sasha was entirely abandoned, that he was not wanted at home, that he was being starved, and she carried him off to her lodge and gave him a little room there.

And for six months Sasha had lived in the lodge with her. Every morning Olenka came into his bedroom and found him fast asleep, sleeping noiselessly with his hand under his cheek. She was sorry to wake him.

"Sashenka," she would say mournfully, "get up, Darling. It's time for school."

He would get up, dress and say his prayers, and then sit down to breakfast, drink three glasses of tea, and eat two large cracknels and half a buttered roll. All this time he was hardly awake and a little ill-humored in consequence.

"You don't quite know your fable, Sashenka," Olenka would say, looking at him as though he were about to set off on a long journey. "What a lot of trouble I have with you! You must work and do your best, Darling, and obey your teachers."

"Oh do leave me alone!" Sasha would say.

Then he would go down the street to school, a little figure, wearing a big cap and carrying a satchel on his shoulder. Olenka would follow him noiselessly.

"Sashenka!" she would call after him, and she would pop into his hand a date or a caramel. When he reached the street where the school was, he would feel ashamed of being followed by a tall, stout woman; he would turn round and say:

"You'd better go home, Auntie. I can go the rest of the way alone."

She would stand still and look after him fixedly till he had disappeared at the school gate.

Ah, how she loved him! Of her former attachments not one had been so deep; never had her soul surrendered to any feeling so spontaneously, so disinterestedly, and so joyously as now that her maternal instincts were aroused. For this little boy with the dimple in his cheek and the big school cap she would have given her whole life, she would have given it with joy and tears of tenderness. Why? Who can tell why?

When she had seen the last of Sasha, she returned home, contented and serene, brimming over with love; her face, which had grown younger during the last six months, smiled and beamed; people meeting her looked at her with pleasure.

"Good morning, Olga Semyonovna, Darling. How are you, Darling?"

"The lessons at the high school are very difficult now," she would relate at the market. "It's too much; in the first class yesterday they gave him a fable to learn by heart, and a Latin translation and a problem. You know it's too much for a little chap."

And she would begin talking about the teachers, the lessons, and the school books, saying just what Sasha said.

At three o'clock they had dinner together; in the evening they learned their lessons together and cried. When she put him to bed she would stay a long time making the cross over him and murmuring a prayer; then she would go to bed and dream of that far-away, misty future when Sasha would finish his studies and become a doctor or an engineer, would have a big house of his own with horses and a carriage, would get married and have children. . . . She would fall asleep still thinking of the same thing, and tears would run down her cheeks from her closed eyes, while the black cat lay purring beside her: "Mrr, mrr, mrr."

Suddenly there would come a loud knock at the gate.

Olenka would wake up breathless with alarm, her heart throbbing. Half a minute later would come another knock.

"It must be a telegram from Harkov," she would think, beginning to tremble from head to foot. "Sasha's mother is sending for him from Harkov. . . . Oh, mercy on us!"

She was in despair. Her head, her hands, and her feet would turn chill, and she would feel that she was the most unhappy woman in the world. But another minute would pass, voices would be heard: it would turn out to be the veterinary surgeon coming home from the club.

"Well, thank God!" she would think.

And gradually the load in her heart would pass off, and she would feel at ease. She would go back to bed thinking of Sasha, who lay sound asleep in the next room, sometimes crying out in his sleep:

"I'll give it you! Get away! Shut up!"

Introduction to a Garland of Love Lyrics

From the thousands of lyric poems reflecting all facets of love's variety, we now select a few examples illustrating the delight, the beauty, the idealism, and the stimulating thought-richness of the world's heritage of love poetry. Some of these have been set to music, and others are beloved the world over as folk poems. Still others may not be so familiar but are attractive through the crisp freshness of their thought.

The intent in this brief sampling is to show variety, for love is indeed "a many-splendored thing." The earliest of the poems are several hundred years old, written in the English Renaissance, when love poetry was at its most delightsome; later poems are from the Age of Romanticism; and still later ones are from our twentieth-century world. The arrangement is simply chronological, the oldest poems first, the most recent last.

Generally the poems speak for themselves and need no explanation. Indeed, explanation would ruin them. However, perhaps a few brief comments will be useful. The first three lyrics—by Sidney, Marlowe, and Shakespeare—simply express, in exquisite music, the ecstasy of romantic love. Then Shakespeare's Sonnet 116 deepens in thought to emphasize the constancy and stability of genuine love that surmounts both time, change, and adversity. Drayton's Sonnet 61, also very serious, explores a love that is supposedly dead but obviously still lives—and has power to redeem. Next Campion's charming little poem is intended as advice to women on what to expect from their husbands in marriage. And Herbert's "Love" lifts us from earthly love to the divine love of Christ.

Anne Bradstreet, one of America's earliest poets, attractively expresses deep love for her husband in her little poem; followed by Lovelace's similar poem stressing that true lovers, even though far apart, are still together, for genuine love survives time and separation to live on in life after death.[1] Next appear three poems by Robert Burns, one of the world's greatest love-song poets. The first again expresses the ecstasy of romantic love; the second ("Highland Mary") beautifully shows love that continues for a loved one who has died; and the third ("John Anderson, My Jo") with equal beauty shows love between husband and wife that endures into old age, sweethearts always, much like President and Sister McKay.

Wordsworth's "She Was a Phantom of Delight" was written to his wife describing her as a "perfect woman." Coleridge's sonnet also is written to his wife, telling how—in spite of problems between them—the birth of their baby drew them close together in love. Landor's little poem that follows is very different—a humorous poem, intended mostly for fun, but also painfully true. And in Moore's beautiful song we again find love that endures forever, growing deeper when youth and beauty fade. Following this, the brief excerpt from Byron and Shelley's first poem are self-explanatory, but the passage from Shelley's *Epipsychidion* is more complex, suggesting the spiritual nature of love, which does not decrease when divided.

Mrs. Browning's Sonnet 14 is repeated here from Volume 2 because it is such a lovely expression of a woman's (or man's) desire to be loved for herself alone, and the excerpt from Tennyson's *In Memoriam* is at least equally famous in the thought it encompasses. Exquisite loveliness characterizes the little stanza by Christina Rossetti, followed by two more little poems by Bourdillon and Markham illustrating that profound truths can be very simply expressed, and by Housman's lyric which is endlessly charming in its lighter tone. Next is a fragile love lyric by that greatest of Irish lyric poets, William Butler Yeats, and this is followed by a story poem by Edgar Lee

[1]For an even stronger expression of this idea, see Browning's "Prospice" on pp. 459-460 of Volume 1 of *Out of the Best Books.*

Masters telling of a woman who has lived much and loved much through almost a century.

The two little poems by W. H. Davies and Sara Teasdale are again self-explanatory in their attractive, stimulating simplicity. Frances Cornford's delicate triolet is also simple, but startlingly different in idea as it suggests the ache of a lonely life without love. And the closing two poems by Edna St. Vincent Millay are both rich in illustrating the power of love, the first symbolically, the second dramatically.

No words, however, can begin to express the thoughts, emotions, and beauty of poetry as well as the poetry itself; so without further delay we print the poems, letting them speak for themselves.

A GARLAND OF LOVE LYRICS

"My True-Love Hath My Heart"

by Sir Philip Sidney (1554-1586)

My true-love hath my heart, and I have his,
By just exchange one for another given:
I hold his dear, and mine he cannot miss,
There never was a better bargain driven:
  My true-love hath my heart, and I have his.

His heart in me keeps him and me in one,
My heart in him his thoughts and senses guides:
He loves my heart, for once it was his own,
I cherish his because in me it bides:
  My true-love hath my heart, and I have his.

"The Passionate Shepherd to His Love"

by Christopher Marlowe (1564-1593)

Come live with me and be my love,
And we will all the pleasures prove
That valleys, groves, hills, and fields,
Woods, or steepy mountain yields.

And we will sit upon the rocks,
Seeing the shepherds feed their flocks,
By shallow rivers to whose falls
Melodious birds sing madrigals.

And I will make thee beds of roses
And a thousand fragrant posies,
A cap of flowers, and a kirtle
Embroidered all with leaves of myrtle;

A gown made of the finest wool
Which from our pretty lambs we pull;
Fair linèd slippers for the cold,
With buckles of the purest gold;

A belt of straw and ivy buds,
With coral clasps and amber studs;
And if these pleasures may thee move,
Come live with me, and be my love.

The shepherds' swains shall dance and sing
For thy delight each May morning:
If these delights thy mind may move,
Then live with me and be my love.

"O Mistress Mine" from "Twelfth Night"

by William Shakespeare (1564-1616)

O mistress mine, where are you roaming?
O, stay and hear; your true love's coming,
  That can sing both high and low.
Trip no further, pretty sweeting;
Journeys end in lovers meeting,
  Every wise man's son doth know.

What is love? 'Tis not hereafter;
Present mirth hath present laughter;
  What's to come is still unsure.
In delay there lies no plenty;
Then come kiss me, sweet and twenty!
  Youth's a stuff will not endure.

Sonnet 116

by William Shakespeare (1564-1616)

Let me not to the marriage of true minds
Admit impediments. Love is not love
Which alters when it alteration finds,
Or bends with the remover to remove:
O, no! it is an ever-fixèd mark,
That looks on tempests and is never shaken;
It is the star to every wandering bark,
Whose worth's unknown, although his height be taken.
Love's not Time's fool, though rosy lips and cheeks
Within his bending sickle's compass come;
Love alters not with his brief hours and weeks,
But bears it out even to the edge of doom.
  If this be error, and upon me proved,
  I never writ, nor no man ever loved.

Question for discussion: What are the strengths of love as suggested in this sonnet by Shakespeare?

Sonnet 61 from "Idea's Mirrour"

by Michael Drayton (1563-1631)

Since there's no help, come let us kiss and part;
Nay, I have done, you get no more of me,
And I am glad, yea glad with all my heart
That thus so cleanly I myself can free;
Shake hands for ever, cancel all our vows,
And when we meet at any time again,
Be it not seen in either of our brows
That we one jot of former love retain.
Now at the last gasp of love's latest breath,
When, his pulse failing, passion speechless lies,
When faith is kneeling by his bed of death,
And innocence is closing up his eyes,
  Now if thou wouldst, when all have given him over,
  From death to life thou mightst him yet recover.

Question for discussion: How do its last two lines change the meaning of Drayton's poem, reveal the speaker's true attitude, and suggest the redemptive power of love?

"Never Love Unless You Can"

by Thomas Campion (1567-1620)

Never love unless you can
Bear with all the faults of man;
Men sometimes will jealous be,
Though but little cause they see,
  And hang the head, as discontent,
  And speak what straight they will repent.

Men that but one saint adore
Make a show of love to more;
Beauty must be scorned in none,
Though but truly served in one;
  For what is courtship but disguise?
  True hearts may have dissembling eyes.

Men when their affairs require
Must a while themselves retire,
Sometimes hunt, and sometimes hawk,
And not ever sit and talk.
  If these and such-like you can bear,
  Then like, and love, and never fear.

Question for discussion: Is the advice to wives in Campion's poem wise or merely charming?

"Love"

by George Herbert (1593-1633)

Love bade me welcome; yet my soul drew back,
  Guilty of dust and sin.
But quick-eyed Love, observing me grow slack
  From my first entrance in,
Drew nearer to me, sweetly questioning
  If I lacked anything.

"A guest," I answered, "worthy to be here."
  Love said, "You shall be he."
"I, the unkind, ungrateful? Ah my dear,
  I cannot look on Thee."
Love took my hand, and smiling, did reply,
  "Who made the eyes but I?"

"Truth, Lord, but I have marred them; let my shame
  Go where it doth deserve."
"And know you not," says Love, "who bore the blame?"
  "My dear, then I will serve."
"You must sit down," says Love, "and taste my meat."
  So I did sit and eat.

Question for discussion: What does Herbert's poem suggest about the divine love of Christ?

"To My Dear and Loving Husband"

by Anne Bradstreet (1612?-1672)

If ever two were one, then surely we.
If ever man were loved by wife, then thee;
If ever wife was happy in a man,
Compare with me ye women if you can.
I prize thy love more than whole mines of gold,
Or all the riches that the East doth hold.
My love is such that rivers cannot quench,
Nor ought but love from thee give recompense.
Thy love is such I can no way repay;
The heavens reward thee manifold, I pray.
Then while we live, in love let's so persever,
That when we live no more we may live ever.

"To Lucasta, Going Beyond the Seas"

by Richard Lovelace (1618-1657?)

If to be absent were to be
Away from thee,
Or that when I am gone
You or I were alone,
Then, my Lucasta, might I crave
Pity from blust'ring wind or swallowing wave.

But I'll not sigh one blast or gale
To swell my sail,
Or pay a tear to 'suage
The foaming blue god's[1] rage;
For whether he will let me pass
Or no, I'm still as happy as I was.

Though seas and land betwixt us both,
Our faith and troth,
Like separated souls,
All time and space controls:
Above the highest sphere we meet,
Unseen, unknown, and greet as angels greet.

---

[1]Neptune's

So then we do anticipate
Our after-fate,
And are alive i' th' skies,
If thus our lips and eyes
Can speak like spirits unconfined,
In heav'n, their earthy bodies left behind.

"My Luve Is Like a Red, Red Rose"

by Robert Burns (1759-1796)

O, my luve is like a red, red rose
That's newly sprung in June:
O, my luve is like the melodie
That's sweetly play'd in tune.

So fair art thou, my bonnie lass,
So deep in luve am I:
And I will luve thee still, my dear,
Till a' the seas gang dry.

Till a' the seas gang dry, my dear,
And the rocks melt wi' the sun:
And I will luve thee still, my dear,
While the sands o' life shall run.

And fare thee weel, my only luve,
And fare thee weel awhile!
And I will come again, my luve,
Tho' it were ten thousand mile.

"Highland Mary"[1]

by Robert Burns (1759-1796)

Ye banks, and braes,[2] and streams around
The castle o' Montgomery,
Green be your woods, and fair your flowers,
Your waters never drumlie![3]
There Simmer first unfauld her robes.
And there the langest tarry;
For there I took the last fareweel
O' my sweet Highland Mary.

---

[1]Mary Campbell, whom Burns deeply loved long after she died.
[2]Hillsides.
[3]Muddy.

How sweetly bloom'd the gay green birk,[4]
  How rich the hawthorn's blossom,
As underneath their fragrant shade
  I clasp'd her to my bosom!
The golden hours on angel wings
  Flew o'er me and my dearie;
For dear to me as light and life
  Was my sweet Highland Mary.

Wi' mony a vow, and lock'd embrace,
  Our parting was fu' tender;
And, pledging aft to meet again,
  We tore oursels asunder;
But oh! fell Death's untimely frost,
  That nipt my flower sae early!
Now green's the sod, and cauld's the clay,
  That wraps my Highland Mary!

O pale, pale now, those rosy lips,
  I aft have kiss'd sae fondly!
And closed for aye the sparkling glance,
  That dwelt on me sae kindly!
And mould'ring now in silent dust,
  That heart that lo'ed me dearly!
But still within my bosom's core
  Shall live my Highland Mary.

"John Anderson My Jo"

by Robert Burns (1759-1796)

John Anderson my jo,[1] John,
  When we were first acquent,
Your locks were like the raven,
  Your bonnie brow was brent;[2]
But now your brow is beld,[3] John,
  Your locks are like the snow;
But blessings on your frosty pow,[4]
  John Anderson, my jo.

---

[4]Birch.
[1]Sweetheart.
[2]Unwrinkled.
[3]Bald.
[4]Head.

John Anderson my jo, John,
  We clamb the hill thegither;
And mony a canty[5] day, John,
  We've had wi' ane anither:
Now we maun totter down, John,
  And hand in hand we'll go,
And sleep thegither at the foot,
  John Anderson, my jo.

"She Was a Phantom of Delight"

by William Wordsworth (1770-1850)

She was a phantom of delight
When first she gleamed upon my sight;
A lovely apparition, sent
To be a moment's ornament;
Her eyes as stars of twilight fair;
Like twilight's, too, her dusky hair;
But all things else about her drawn
From Maytime and the cheerful dawn;
A dancing shape, an image gay,
To haunt, to startle, and waylay.

I saw her upon nearer view,
A spirit, yet a woman too!
Her household motions light and free,
And steps of virgin liberty;
A countenance in which did meet
Sweet records, promises as sweet;
A creature not too bright or good
For human nature's daily food;
For transient sorrows, simple wiles,
Praise, blame, love, kisses, tears, and smiles.

And now I see with eye serene
The very pulse of the machine;
A being breathing thoughtful breath,
A traveller between life and death;
The reason firm, the temperate will,
Endurance, foresight, strength, and skill;

[5]Happy.

A perfect woman, nobly planned,
To warn, to comfort, and command;
And yet a spirit still, and bright
With something of angelic light.

Question for discussion: This poem by Wordsworth was written as a tribute to his wife, whom he describes as a "perfect woman." But the poem, although generally complimentary, has problems. Would most wives be pleased if their husband referred to them as a "creature not too bright or good for human nature's daily food" (stanza 2) or as a "machine" (stanza 3)?

"Sonnet"

To a Friend Who Asked How I Felt When the Nurse First Presented My Infant to Me

by Samuel Taylor Coleridge (1772-1834)

Charles! my slow heart was only sad, when first
I scann'd that face of feeble infancy:
For dimly on my thoughtful spirit burst
All I had been, and all my child might be!
But when I saw it on its mother's arm,
And hanging at her bosom (she the while
Bent o'er its features with a tearful smile)
Then I was thrill'd and melted, and most warm
Impress'd a father's kiss: and all beguil'd
Of dark remembrance and presageful fear,
I seem'd to see an angel-form appear—
'Twas even thine, belovèd woman mild!
So for the mother's sake the child was dear,
And dearer was the mother for the child.

"Alas, How Soon the Hours"

by Walter Savage Landor (1775-1864)

Alas, how soon the hours are over,
Counted us out to play the lover!
And how much narrower is the stage,

Allotted us to play the sage!
But when we play the fool, how wide
The theatre expands; beside,
How long the audience sits before us!
How many prompters! what a chorus!

"Believe Me, If All Those Endearing Young Charms"

by Thomas Moore (1779-1852)

Believe me, if all those endearing young charms,
  Which I gaze on so fondly today,
Were to change by tomorrow, and fleet in my arms,
  Like fairy gifts fading away,
Thou wouldst still be adored, as this moment thou art,
  Let thy loveliness fade as it will,
And around the dear ruin each wish of my heart
  Would entwine itself verdantly still.

It is not while beauty and youth are thine own,
  And thy cheeks unprofaned by a tear,
That the fervor and faith of a soul can be known,
  To which time will but make thee more dear;
No, the heart that has truly loved never forgets,
  But as truly loves on to the close,
As the sunflower turns on her god, when he sets,
  The same look which she turned when he rose.

From "Don Juan"

by Lord Byron (1788-1824)

Man's love is of man's life a thing apart,
  'Tis woman's whole existence; man may range
The court, camp, church, the vessel, and the mart;
  Sword, gown, gain, glory, offer in exchange
Pride, fame, ambition, to fill up his heart,
  And few there are whom these cannot estrange;
Men have all these resources, we but one,
To love again, and be again undone.

"Love's Philosophy"

by Percy Bysshe Shelley (1792-1822)

The Fountains mingle with the River
And the Rivers with the Ocean,
The winds of Heaven mix for ever
With a sweet emotion;
Nothing in the world is single;
All things by a law divine
In one spirit meet and mingle.
Why not I with thine?

See the mountains kiss high Heaven
And the waves clasp one another;
No sister-flower would be forgiven
If it disdained its brother,
And the sunlight clasps the earth
And the moonbeams kiss the sea:
What is all this sweet work worth
If thou kiss not me?

From "Epipsychidion"

by Percy Bysshe Shelley (1792-1822)

True Love in this differs from gold and clay,
That to divide is not to take away.
Love is like understanding, that grows bright,
Gazing on many truths; 'tis like thy light,
Imagination! which from earth and sky,
And from the depths of human fantasy,
As from a thousand prisms and mirrors, fills
The Universe with glorious beams, and kills
Error, the worm, with many a sun-like arrow
Of its reverberated lightning. Narrow
The heart that loves, the brain that contemplates,
The life that wears, the spirit that creates
One object, and one form, and builds thereby
A sepulchre for its eternity.

Question for discussion: Shelley here suggests the spiritual quality of love, which may be divided without being diminished. For example, a mother does not love her first child less because she has other children. She loves them all equally, and each as much as if she had only one. This is the magic of love: the more it is drawn upon, the more it grows. However, are there obvious limits that must be placed upon this application of love outside the family?

Sonnet 14 from "Sonnets from the Portuguese"
by Elizabeth Barrett Browning (1806-1861)

If thou must love me, let it be for naught
Except for love's sake only. Do not say
"I love her for her smile—her look—her way
Of speaking gently—for a trick of thought
That falls in well with mine, and certes brought
A sense of pleasant ease on such a day"—
For these things in themselves, Belovèd, may
Be changed, or change for thee—and love, so wrought,
May be unwrought so. Neither love me for
Thine own dear pity's wiping my cheeks dry—
A creature might forget to weep, who bore
Thy comfort long, and lose thy love thereby!
But love me for love's sake, that evermore
Thou mayst love on, through love's eternity.

Section 27 from "In Memoriam"
by Alfred, Lord Tennyson (1809-1892)

I envy not in any moods
The captive void of noble rage,
The linnet born within the cage,
That never knew the summer woods;

I envy not the beast that takes
His license in the field of time,
Unfettered by the sense of crime,
To whom a conscience never wakes;

Nor, what may count itself as blest,
The heart that never plighted troth
But stagnates in the weeds of sloth;
Nor any want-begotten rest.

I hold it true, whate'er befall;
I feel it, when I sorrow most—
'Tis better to have loved and lost
Than never to have loved at all.

From "A Birthday"

by Christina Rossetti (1830-1894)

My heart is like a singing bird
Whose nest is in a watered shoot;
My heart is like an apple-tree
Whose boughs are bent with thickset fruit;
My heart is like a rainbow shell
That paddles in a halcyon sea;
My heart is gladder than all these
Because my love is come to me.

"The Night Has a Thousand Eyes"

by Francis William Bourdillon (1852-1921)

The night has a thousand eyes,
And the day but one;
Yet the light of the bright world dies
With the dying sun.

The mind has a thousand eyes,
And the heart but one;
Yet the light of a whole life dies
When love is done.

"Outwitted"

by Edwin Markham (1852-1940)

He drew a circle that shut me out—
Heretic, rebel, a thing to flout.
But Love and I had the wit to win:
We drew a circle that took him in!

Poem 13 from "A Shropshire Lad"
by A. E. Housman (1859-1936)

When I was one-and-twenty
  I heard a wise man say,
"Give crowns and pounds and guineas,
  But not your heart, away;
Give pearls away and rubies,
  But keep your fancy free."
But I was one-and-twenty—
  No use to talk to me.

When I was one-and-twenty
  I heard him say again,
"The heart out of the bosom
  Was never given in vain;
'Tis paid with sighs a plenty
  And sold for endless rue."
And I am two-and-twenty,
  And oh, 'tis true, 'tis true.

"Aedh Wishes for the Cloths of Heaven"
by William Butler Yeats (1865-1939)

Had I the heavens' embroidered cloths,
Enwrought with golden and silver light,
The blue and the dim and the dark cloths
Of night and light and the half-light,
I would spread the cloths under your feet;
But I, being poor, have only my dreams;
I have spread my dreams under your feet;
Tread softly because you tread on my dreams.

"Lucinda Matlock"
by Edgar Lee Masters (1869-1950)

I went to the dances at Chandlerville,
And played snap-out at Winchester.
One time we changed partners,
Driving home in the moonlight of middle June,
And then I found Davis.

We were married and lived together for seventy years,
Enjoying, working, raising the twelve children,
Eight of whom we lost
Ere I had reached the age of sixty.
I spun, I wove, I kept the house, I nursed the sick,
I made the garden, and for holiday
Rambled over the fields where sang the larks,
And by Spoon River gathering many a shell,
And many a flower and medicinal weed—
Shouting to the wooded hills, singing to the green valleys.
At ninety-six I had lived enough, that is all,
And passed to a sweet repose.
What is this I hear of sorrow and weariness,
Anger, discontent and drooping hopes?
Degenerate sons and daughters,
Life is too strong for you—
It takes life to love Life.

Question for discussion: Has her hard life drained Lucinda of capacity to love tenderly, or is her attitude simply the natural attitude of an old woman contrasting her life with the "soft" lives of younger people?

"Love, Like a Drop of Dew"

by William Henry Davies (1871-1940)

When I pass down the street and see
  The people smiling so,
It's clear enough that my true love
  Was there awhile ago.

Her lips that, following her two eyes,
  Go smiling here and there,
Seem newly kissed—but 'tis my faith
  That none but I would dare.

Love, like a drop of dew that joins
  Two blades of grass together,
Has made her mine, as I am hers,
  For ever and for ever.

"Faults"

by Sara Teasdale (1884-1933)

They came to tell your faults to me,
They named them over one by one;
I laughed aloud when they were done,
I knew them all so well before;—
Oh, they were blind, too blind to see
Your faults had made me love you more.

"To a Fat Lady Seen from the Train"

by Frances Cornford (1886-)

O why do you walk through the fields in gloves,
Missing so much and so much?
O fat white woman whom nobody loves,
Why do you walk through the fields in gloves,
When the grass is soft as the breast of doves
And shivering sweet to the touch?
O why do you walk through the fields in gloves,
Missing so much and so much?

Thought for discussion: Point out how Cornford uses the gloves as a symbol of the woman's withdrawal and insensitivity.

From "Renascence"

by Edna St. Vincent Millay (1892-1950)

The world stands out on either side
No wider than the heart is wide;
Above the world is stretched the sky,—
No higher than the soul is high.
The heart can push the sea and land
Farther away on either hand;
The soul can split the sky in two,
And let the face of God shine through.
But East and West will pinch the heart
That cannot keep them pushed apart;
And he whose soul is flat—the sky
Will cave in on him by and by.

Thought for discussion: Explore the meaning-through-symbolism in this thought-rich excerpt from "Renascence."

"Love Is Not All"

by Edna St. Vincent Millay (1892-1950)

Love is not all; it is not meat nor drink
Nor slumber nor a roof against the rain,
Nor yet a floating spar to men that sink
And rise and sink and rise and sink again;
Love can not fill the thickened lung with breath,
Nor clean the blood, nor set the fractured bone;
Yet many a man is making friends with death
Even as I speak, for lack of love alone.
It well may be that in a difficult hour,
Pinned down by pain and moaning for release,
Or nagged by want past resolution's power,
I might be driven to sell your love for peace,
Or trade the memory of this night for food.
It well may be. I do not think I would.

The Substance of Faith

by Robert K. Thomas

"Life from Death"

by Floyd E. Breinholt, American

Commentary by

Floyd E. Breinholt, Associate Professor of Art, Brigham Young University

Art is concerned with the expression of personal aesthetic or spiritual experiences. It is an attempt to make concrete some rather intangible truth discovered by the artist. Because each artist is different, his interpretation will be unique. In the search, discovery, and organization of this truth into perceptible form, man discovers joy—a feeling of well-being, of inner peace—that for which all men search. Joy is a result of the creative process. Perhaps the greatest joy one can receive in this life is to be a co-partner with God in the creation of another human soul.

The experience of joy is accompanied by a feeling of gratitude. Gratitude fosters faith—faith in oneself, faith in others, and faith in God. Art often becomes a hymn of praise or a prayer of gratitude.

I receive much joy from my work in art and as a teacher, and am grateful to the sisters of the General Board of the Relief Society for asking me to present one of my paintings here and to write this brief note. Perhaps a description of how this painting came to be will be of interest.

On each of our painting vacations to the Teton National Park, in Wyoming, over the past years, my family and I would drive by a large tree stump just off the highway near Jenny Lake. We finally stopped to look closer. The beautiful grays and soft textures of the old wood were fascinating. As we walked around it, we discovered a young tree growing from the decayed roots of the old one, and I decided to make a sketch and some color notes. Drawing forced me to look closer (drawing does this). The grains in the wood twisted and formed patterns around places where the branches had been. Some areas were bleached by the sun, and others, mellowed by decay, had become brilliant ochres and browns. As the sketch progressed, I was impressed with the strength of the old tree and how, even in death, it was sheltering, protecting, and nourishing the young one. Almost unconsciously I gradually began to dramatize this idea. By placing the horizon low and allowing the lone tree to project high into a stormy sky, it created a feeling of power, dimension, and mood.

Later, while working on this painting in my studio, I once again experienced the same feeling of awe and gratitude I often have

when alone in the mountains, deserts, or ghost towns—a feeling difficult to describe. It isn't really loneliness, but one of identification with something greater than myself—calm and peaceful. I wanted to be able to express what Harrison R. Merrill says in the first stanza of his poem, which I have tacked to the wall of my studio:

> Oh, God, let this be heaven. . . .
> I do not ask for golden streets
> Or long for jasper walls,
> Nor do I sigh for pearly shores
> Where twilight never falls;
> Just leave me here beside these peaks,
> In this rough western land.
> I love this dear old world of thine. . . .
> Dear God, you understand.

THE SUBSTANCE OF FAITH

"Faith is the substance of things hoped for."
—Hebrews 11:1

Introductory Comments

Those who have lost faith in God or who have never believed in Him usually suggest that the object of faith is not so important as faith itself. Their position seems to be that as long as we believe in *something,* we will have a base on which to build. The opening poem in this section is a famous and persuasive statement of this stand. Matthew Arnold's "Dover Beach" recounts the doubts which beset the Victorian age in memorable imagery. At least a major part of his conclusion is simply to substitute a belief in the supportive power of human love for a waning faith in religious certainties.

An emphatic denial that faith can ever be anything but faith in God is given in the excerpt from Joseph Mazzini's "Faith and the Future" which follows "Dover Beach." In rhetoric which crackles with the force of a rifle barrage, this famous Italian patriot disposes of those who fail to recognize the essentially religious nature of all positive, human activity.

A modern attempt to let family love and reliance upon nature substitute for conventional Christian faith is next seen in Philip Booth's "First Lesson." This tender poem seems to be less a repudiation of tenets which have proven to be unsatisfactory than the creation of a sustaining faith by someone who is trying to establish beliefs for himself as well as his daughter. If the picture we see here of a father and daughter learning together is an attractive one, the possible shortcomings of faith that has less than a focus on God are examined in George Santayana's "Sonnet III."

The American orator, William Jennings Bryan, next describes the types of faith that seem to him to exert a controlling influence on human lives. These are faith in oneself, others, one's country and one's God. Stephen Vincent Benèt's story "Jacob and the Indians" demonstrates all of these in a tale that is so charming we may not consciously recognize how emphatic its message of faith is.

The difficulty of keeping faith at full force, as presented by George Eliot in "The Tide of Faith," is in some contrast to the serenity exemplified in Francis Quarles' "A Good Night." Our final selection is part of a statement which has become a classic justification for faith.

After viewing faith from the facets which this section attempts to illuminate, we should be able to understand a little more clearly the significance of this basic principle. All of the authors who share their views with us here are animated by hope: Arnold is hoping to find something secure in a chaotic world; Mazzini hopes to establish freedom for his people on a lasting basis; Philip Booth would direct his daughter's development; Bryan hopes to shape his country's destiny, Benét would lead us to appreciate human possibilities; Santayana hopes to find something beyond his intellect; Eliot and Quarles seek fulfillment and peace, while James hopes to add a dimension to man's philosophical quest. The constant base underlying the variety of these hopes is faith, for hope without faith cannot be more than vague yearning. As the New Testament so graphically puts it, faith gives *substance* to hope.

It is worth noting that many of the objects of faith in the selections which follow are in the world. Faith need not be ethereal, but it is finally always spiritual, and it must be dynamic. We give evidence to things not seen when we become actively engaged in trying to realize our hopes. In the words of Henry David Thoreau, "by faithfulness faith is earned."

Dover Beach

by Matthew Arnold

The sea is calm to-night.
The tide is full, the moon lies fair
Upon the straits;—on the French coast the light
Gleams and is gone; the cliffs of England stand,
Glimmering and vast, out in the tranquil bay.
Come to the window, sweet is the night-air!
Only, from the long line of spray
Where the sea meets the moon-blanch'd land
Listen! you hear the grating roar
Of pebbles which the waves draw back, and fling
At their return, up the high stand,
Begin, and cease, and then again begin,
With tremulous cadence slow, and bring
The eternal note of sadness in.

Sophocles long ago
Heard it on the Aegean, and it brought
Into his mind the turbid ebb and flow
Of human misery; we
Find also in the sound a thought
Hearing it by this distant northern sea.
The sea of faith
Was once, too, at the full, and round earth's shore
Lay like the folds of a bright girdle furl'd.
But now I only hear
Its melancholy, long, withdrawing roar,
Retreating to the breath
Of the night-wind down the vast edges drear
And naked shingles of the world.

Ah, love, let us be true
To one another! for the world, which seems
To lie before us like a land of dreams,
So various, so beautiful, so new
Hath really neither joy, nor love, nor light,
Nor certitude, nor peace, nor help for pain;
And we are here as on a darkling plain
Swept with confused alarms of struggle and flight.
Where ignorant armies clash by night.

Discussion of "Dover Beach"

In a letter to his mother in 1869 Matthew Arnold (1822-1888) explained why he thought his poetry had not won much public recognition:

> It might be fairly urged that I have less poetical sentiment than Tennyson and less intellectual vigor than Browning; yet because I have perhaps more of a fusion of the two than either of them, I am likely enough to have my turn as they have had theirs.

In succeeding years he has had his turn. Perhaps more than any other English poet of his time he represented what he called the "main movement of mind" in the third quarter of the nineteenth century.

His father was headmaster at Rugby, and young Matthew soon came under the influence of the two great traditions, Christian and classical, which were to provide most of the substance of his thought. A scholarship student at Balliol College, he taught briefly at Rugby before becoming an Inspector of Schools in 1851. This position he held for virtually the remainder of his life.

"Dover Beach" is probably Arnold's best known poem, and it is typical of many poems in the later nineteenth century in its bleak sketch of the universe which man inhabits. The argument of Arnold's poem is that the old faith in a life securely and eternally guided by a benevolent God has begun to disappear, leaving many people with the feeling that they have nothing to depend on but the affection of beloved individuals.

The effect of calm beauty in the opening picture of Dover Beach and the sea at night soon submerges in the melancholy impression of the first stanza's closing lines. "Dover Beach" is not against delight in the world's beauty or religious faith. But this poem shows the fear which the new scientific developments of the century fostered in many of its most sensitive minds. There is a note of elegiac regret in "Dover Beach," a poignant awareness of beauty and trust which have passed and will probably never return.

In one sense this poem may have been written before its time. Only a few of Arnold's contemporaries were moved by it in spite of its metrical finesse and beautifully modulated imagery. It is the twentieth century to which this poem speaks its cosmic sadness.

Faith and the Future

by Joseph Mazzini

Faith requires an *aim* capable of embracing life as a whole, of concentrating all its manifestations, of directing its various modes of activity, or of repressing them all in favor of one alone. It requires an earnest, unalterable conviction that that aim will be realized; a profound belief in a mission, and the obligation to fulfil it; and the consciousness of a supreme power watching over the path of the faithful towards its accomplishment. These elements are indispensable to faith; and where any one of these is wanting, we shall have sects, schools, political parties, but no faith; no constant hourly sacrifice for the sake of a great religious idea.

Now we have no definite religious idea, no profound belief in an obligation entailed by a mission, no consciousness of a supreme protecting power. Our actual apostolate is a mere analytical opposition; our weapons are *interests,* and our chief instrument of action is a theory of rights. We are, all of us, notwithstanding our sublime presentiments, the sons of rebellion. We advance, like renegades, without a God, without a law, without a banner to lead us towards the future. Our former aim has vanished from our view; the new, dimly seen for an instant, is effaced by that doctrine of rights which alone directs our labors. We make of the *individual* both the means and the aim. We talk of Humanity—a formula essentially religious—and banish religion from our work. We talk of synthesis and yet neglect the most powerful and active element of human existence. Bold enough to be undaunted by the dream of the material unity of Europe, we thoughtlessly destroy its moral unity by failing to recognize the primary condition of all association,—uniformity of sanction and belief. And it is amidst such contradictions that we pretend to renew a world.

Right is the faith of the individual. Duty is the common collective faith. Right can but organize resistance: it may destroy, it cannot found. Duty builds up, associates, and unites; it is derived from a general law, whereas Right is derived only from human will. There is nothing therefore to forbid a struggle against Right: any individual may rebel against any right in another which is injurious to him; and the sole judge left between the adversaries is Force; and such, in fact, has frequently been the answer which societies based upon right have given to their opponents.

Societies based upon Duty would not be compelled to have recourse to force; duty, once admitted as the rule, excludes the possibility of struggle; and by rendering the individual subject to the general aim, it cuts at the very root of those evils which Right is unable to prevent, and only affects to cure. Moreover progress is not a necessary result of the doctrine of Right, it merely admits it as a fact. The exercise of rights being of necessity limited by capacity, progress is abandoned to the arbitrary rule of an unregulated and aimless liberty.

The doctrine of Rights puts an end to sacrifice, and cancels martyrdom from the world: in every theory of individual rights, interests become the governing and motive power, and martyrdom an absurdity, for what interest can endure beyond the tomb? Yet, how often has martyrdom been the initiation of progress, the baptism of a world!

Faith, which is intellect, energy, and love, will put an end to the discords existing in a society which has neither church nor leaders; which invokes a new world, but forgets to ask its secret, its Word, from God.

With faith will revive poetry, rendered fruitful by the breath of God, and by a holy creed. Poetry, exiled now from a world of prey to anarchy; poetry, the flower of the angels, nourished by the blood of martyrs, and watered by the tears of mothers, blossoming often among ruins, but ever colored by the rays of dawn; poetry a language prophetic of Humanity, European in essence, and national in form, will make known to us the fatherland of all the nations hitherto; translate the religious and social synthesis through art, and render still lovelier by its light.

The soul of man had fled: the senses reigned alone. The multitude demanded bread and the sports of the circus. Philosophy had sunk first into scepticism, then into epicureanism, then into subtlety and words. Poetry was transformed into satire.

Yet there were moments when men were terror-struck at the solitude around them, and trembled at their isolation. They ran to embrace the cold and naked statues of their once-venerated gods; to implore of them a spark of moral life, a ray of faith, even an illusion! They departed, their prayers unheard, with despair in their hearts and blasphemy upon their lips. Such were the times; they resembled our own.

Yet this was not the death agony of the world. It was the conclusion of one evolution of the world which had reached its ultimate expression. A great epoch was exhausted, and passing away to give place to another, the first utterances of which had already been heard in the north, and which awaited but the *Initiator,* to be revealed.

He came. The soul the most full of love, the most sacredly

virtuous, the most deeply inspired by God and the future, that men have yet seen on earth: Jesus. He bent over the corpse of the dead world, and whispered a word of faith. Over the clay that had lost all of man but the movement and the form, he uttered words until then unknown, *Love, Sacrifice, a heavenly origin.* And the dead arose. A new life circulated through the clay, which philosophy had tried in vain to reanimate. From that corpse arose the Christian world, the world of liberty and equality. From that clay arose the true Man, the image of God, the precursor of Humanity.

Discussion of "Faith and the Future"

Joseph, or Giuseppe, Mazzini (1805-1872) was born at Genoa, Italy. A precocious young man, he became a student of literature at the University of Genoa but soon gave most of his energies to the liberation of his country. He organized the movement entitled "Young Italy" which was devoted to the overthrow of domestic and foreign tyranny. During his intensely active life he was often in prison and more often an exile, but his zeal to proclaim freedom for his people never faltered.

During his years as an expatriate in London he earned his living by writing. Some of his articles from this period have been reprinted, and they reveal him to be a writer of skill and sensitivity. If his actions were often impulsive, his written work rarely suggests either haste or poor judgment. He had a gift for phrasing and an arresting style. When coupled with carefully thought ideas—as in the selection above—the whole can only be described as a literary achievement.

There is a convincing, eye-witness quality about his description of those who have given themselves to championing human rights, but what is most impressive is Mazzini's clear-eyed recognition that faith must have a focus which will justify supreme effort. It is easier to understand his repeated and abject failures when we see that Mazzini's faith was never simply in things of the earth, no matter how ardently he served practical causes.

In the final paragraph of the section we have quoted, Mazzini describes the advent of Christ as follows: "He bent over the corpse of the dead world, and whispered a word of faith. Over the clay that had lost all of man but the movement and the form, he uttered words until then unknown, *Love, Sacrifice,* a *heavenly origin.* And the dead arose." This is not only powerful imagery; it is an almost irresistible appeal. We, too, feel aroused, ready to justify our rebirth.

If history matter-of-factly records Mazzini's failures, it should not fail to note that this patriot's trumpet never gave an uncertain sound.

First Lesson

by Philip Booth

Lie back, daughter, let your head
be tipped back in the cup of my hand.
Gently, and I will hold you. Spread
your arms wide, lie out on the stream
and look high at the gulls. A dead-
man's-float is face down. You will dive
and swim soon enough where this tidewater
ebbs to the sea. Daughter, believe
me, when you tire on the long thrash
to your island, lie up, and survive.
As you float now, where I held you
and let go, remember when fear
cramps your heart what I told you:
lie gently and wide to the light-year
stars, lie back, and the sea will hold you.

Discussion of "First Lesson"

Philip Booth (1925-) has taught at Wellesley and at Syracuse University, where he is presently an Associate Professor of English. Among his honors and awards are the Lamont Poetry Prize of the American Academy of Poets in 1955 for his *Letter from a Distant Land* and a Guggenheim Fellowship in 1958.

"First Lesson" is obviously autobiographical. Introducing his young daughter to the water gives Prof. Booth a chance to turn a simple experience into a poetic assertion. The literal first swimming lesson becomes a basic lesson for all mankind: lie back in the bounty of nature and feel its support.

The faith that he asks his daughter to demonstrate is surely not misplaced. If there is any uneasiness in our reaction to this scene, it stems only from the implication that man's fundamental relationship to the world is adaptation. Few would suggest that man should not find his place. But adapting to the world is not overcoming it. A richer experience is possible if man both *makes* and *finds* his best relationship with the natural world.

If it be suggested that the real point of this poem is the necessity to develop faith, and that faith in nature is an obvious place to begin, our uneasiness doesn't entirely leave. Too great a trust in things of the world—whether natural or synthetic—can lead only to disillusionment. God alone warrants our total belief. Unreserved reliance upon Him must be our first, and last, lesson.

Sonnet III

by George Santayana

O world, thou choosest not the better part!
It is not wisdom to be only wise,
And on the inward vision close the eyes,
But it is wisdom to believe the heart.
Columbus found a world and had no chart,
Save one that faith deciphered in the skies;
To trust the soul's invincible surmise
Was all his science and his only art.
Our knowledge is a torch of smoky pine
That lights the pathway but one step ahead
Across a void of mystery and dread.
Bid, then, the tender light of faith to shine
By which alone the mortal heart is led
Unto the thinking of the thought divine.

Discussion of "Sonnet III"

George Santayana (1863-1952) was born in Madrid, Spain. Graduating from Harvard in 1886, he taught in the department of philosophy there from 1889 until 1912. After resigning from Harvard he returned to Europe and finally settled in Italy.

Although his *Life of Reason* stressed the primacy of reason in understanding life, much of his later work emphasized the role of faith as dominant in the life of man. Santayana insisted that the method of scientific analysis was the best resource available in the study of human affairs, but his own work has a tendency to refute this. His poetry, particularly, is deeply emotional.

In "Sonnet III," for instance, we see the emphasis of Santayana's life begin to shift. He has described his poetry as his "philosophy in the making," and this lovely poem clearly identifies a man who is questioning the values he has been holding. Since this sonnet is from a group composed before the turn of the century, we know that doubts about the intellectual focus of his life were planted early, to come to fruition over a quarter of a century later. How skillfully he extends the rather trite image of knowledge as a torch when he describes it as "a torch of smoky pine." If it gives light, it obscures almost as much as it reveals. At best it illuminates but a single step. Only the "tender light of faith" can set the heart to "thinking;" and, in so doing, reach beyond "science and art."

Faith

by William Jennings Bryan

Faith exerts a controlling influence over our lives. If it is argued that works are more important than faith, I reply that faith comes first, works afterward. Until one believes, he does not act, and in accordance with his faith, so will be his deeds.

Abraham, called of God, went forth in faith to establish a race and religion. It was faith that led Columbus to discover America, and faith again that conducted the early settlers to Jamestown, the Dutch to New York and the Pilgrims to Plymouth Rock. Faith has led the pioneer across deserts and through trackless forests, and faith has brought others in his footsteps to lay in our land the foundations of a civilization the highest that the world has known.

I might draw an illustration from the life of each one of you. You have faith in education, and that faith is behind your study; you have faith in this institution, and that faith brought you here; your parents and friends have had faith in you and have helped you to your present position. And back of all these manifestations of faith is your faith in God, in His Word and in His Son. We are told that without faith it is impossible to please God, and I may add that without faith it is impossible to meet the expectations of those who are most interested in you. Let me present this subject under four heads.

First: You must have faith in yourselves. Not that you should carry confidence in yourselves to the point of displaying egotism, and yet, egotism is not the worst possible fault. My father was wont to say that if a man had the big head, you could whittle it down, but that if he had the little head, there was no hope for him. If you have the big head others will help you to reduce it, but if you have the little head, they cannot help you. You must believe that you can do things or you will not undertake them. Those who lack faith attempt nothing and therefore cannot possibly succeed; those with great faith attempt the seemingly impossible and by attempting prove what man can do.

But you cannot have faith in yourselves unless you are conscious that you are prepared for your work. If one is feeble in body, he cannot have the confidence in his physical strength that the athlete has, and, as physical strength is necessary, one is justified in devoting to exercise and to the strengthening of the body such time as may be necessary.

Intellectual training is also necessary, and more necessary than it used to be. When but few had the advantage of a college education, the lack of such advantages was not so apparent. Now when so many of the ministers, lawyers, physicians, journalists, and even business men, are college graduates, one cannot afford to be without the best possible intellectual preparation. When one comes into competition with his fellows, he soon recognizes his own intellectual superiority, equality or inferiority as compared with others. In China they have a very interesting bird contest. The singing lark is the most popular bird there, and as you go along the streets of a Chinese city you see Chinamen out airing their birds. These singing larks are entered in contests, and the contests are decided by the birds themselves. If, for instance, a dozen are entered, they all begin to sing lustily, but as they sing, one after another recognizes that it is outclassed and gets down off its perch, puts its head under its wing and will not sing any more. At last there is just one bird left singing, and it sings with enthusiasm as if it recognized its victory.

So it is in all intellectual contests. Put twenty men in a room and let them discuss any important question. At first all will take part in the discussion, but as the discussion proceeds, one after another drops out until finally two are left in debate, one on one side and one on the other. The rest are content to have their ideas presented by those who can present them best. If you are going to have faith, therefore, in yourselves, you must be prepared to meet your competitors upon an equal plane; if you are prepared, they will be conscious of it as well as you.

A high purpose is also a necessary part of your preparation. You cannot afford to put a low purpose in competition with a high one. If you go out to work from a purely selfish standpoint, you will be ashamed to stand in the presence of those who have higher aims and nobler ambitions. Have faith in yourselves, but to have faith you must be prepared for your work, and this preparation must be moral and intellectual as well as physical. The preacher should be the boldest of men because of the unselfish character of his work.

Second: Have faith in mankind. The great fault of our scholarship is that it is not sufficiently sympathetic. It holds itself aloof from the struggling masses. It is too often cold and cynical. It is better to trust your fellowmen and be occasionally deceived than to be distrustful and live alone. Mankind deserves to be trusted. There is something good in every one, and that good responds to sympathy. If you speak to the multitude and they do not respond, do not despise them, but rather examine what you have said. If you speak from your heart, you will speak to their hearts, and they can tell very quickly whether you are interested in them or simply in yourself. The heart of mankind is sound; the sense of justice is universal. Trust it, appeal to it, do not violate it. People differ in race characteristics, in national traditions, in language, in ideas of government, and in forms of religion, but at the heart they are very much alike. I fear the plutocracy of wealth; I respect the aristocracy of learning; but I thank God for the democracy of the heart. You must love if you would be loved. "They loved him because he first loved them"—this is the verdict pronounced where men have unselfishly labored for the welfare of the whole people. Link yourselves in sympathy with your fellowmen; mingle with them; know them and you will trust them and they will trust you. If you are stronger than others, bear heavier loads; if you are more capable than others, show it by your willingness to perform a larger service.

Third: If you are going to accomplish anything in this country, you must have faith in your form of government, and there is every reason why you should have faith in it. It is the best form of government ever conceived by the mind of man, and it is spreading throughout the world. It is best, not because it is perfect, but because it can be made as perfect as the people deserve to have. It is a people's government, and it reflects the virtue and intelligence of the people. As the people make progress in virtue and intelligence, the government ought to approach more and more nearly to perfection. It will never, of course, be entirely free from faults, because it must be administered by human beings, and imperfection is to be expected in the work of human hands.

Jefferson said a century ago that there were naturally two parties in every country, one which drew to itself those who trusted the people, the other which as naturally drew to itself those who distrusted the people. That was true when Jefferson said it, and it is true to-day. In every country there are those who are seeking to enlarge the participation of the people in government, and that group is growing. In every country there are those who are endeavoring to obstruct each step toward government, and that group is diminishing. In this country the tendency is constantly toward more popular government, and every effort which has for its object the bringing of the government into closer touch with the people is sure of ultimate triumph.

Our form of government is good. Call it a democracy if you are a democrat, or a republic if you are a republican, but help to make it a government of the people, by the people, and for the people. A democracy is wiser than an aristocracy because a democracy can draw from the wisdom of the people, and all of the people know more than any part of the people. A democracy is stronger than a monarchy, because, as the historian, Bancroft, has said: "It dares to discard the implements of terror and build its citadel in the hearts of men." And a democracy is the most just form of government because it is built upon the doctrine that men are created equal, that governments are instituted to protect the inalienable rights of the people and that governments derive their just powers from the consent of the governed.

We know that a grain of wheat planted in the ground will, under the influence of the sunshine and rain, send forth a blade, and then a stalk, and then the full head, because there is behind the grain of wheat a force irresistible and constantly at work. There is behind moral and political truth a force equally irresistible and always operating, and just as we may expect the harvest in due season, we may be sure of the triumph of the eternal forces that make for man's uplifting. Have faith in your form of government: it rests upon a growing idea, and if you will but attach yourself to that idea, you will grow with it.

Fourth: The subject presents itself in another aspect. You must not only have faith in yourselves, in humanity, and in the form of government under which we live, but if you would do a great work, you must have faith in God. I am not a preacher; I am a layman; yet, I am not willing that the minister shall monopolize the blessings of Christianity, and I do not know of any moral precept binding upon the preacher behind the pulpit that is not binding upon the Christian and whose acceptance would not be helpful to every one. I am not speaking from the minister's standpoint but from the observation of everyday life when I say that there is a wide difference between the desire to live so that men will applaud you and the desire to live so that God will be satisfied with you. Man needs the inner strength that comes from faith in God and belief in His constant presence.

Man needs faith in God, therefore, to strengthen him in his hours of trial, and he needs it to give him courage to do the work of life. How can one fight for a principle unless he believes in the triumph of right? How can he believe in the triumph of the right if he does not believe that God stands back of the truth and that God is able to bring victory to His side? He knows not whether he is to live for the truth or to die for it, but if he has the faith he ought to have, he is as ready to die for it as to live for it.

Faith will not only give you strength when you fight for righteousness, but your faith will bring dismay to your enemies. There is power in the presence of an honest man who does right because it is right and dares to do the right in the face of all opposition. That is true to-day, and has been true through all history.

If your preparation is complete so that you are conscious of your ability to do great things; if you have faith in your fellowmen and become a co-laborer with them in the raising of the general level of society; if you have faith in our form of government and seek to purge it of its imperfections so as to make it more and more acceptable to our own people and to the oppressed of other nations; and if, in addition, you have faith in God and in the triumph of the right, no one can set limits to your achievements. This is the greatest of all ages in which to live. The railroads and the telegraph wires have brought the corners of the earth close together, and it is easier to-day for one to be helpful to the whole world than it was a few centuries ago to be helpful to the inhabitants of a single valley. This is the age of great opportunity and of great responsibility. Let your faith be large, and let this large faith inspire you to perform a large service.

Discussion of "Faith"

The selection above is taken from a speech given by William Jennings Bryan (1860-1925) before the Union Theological Seminary of Virginia.

During his very active public life, no man in America was better known as an orator. He first called attention to himself in the Presidential campaign of 1888, and he was a force in American politics for the next thirty years.

While a good speech is usually distinguished by the same qualities of organization, style and content which can be found in effective writing, there is often a spontaniety and verve in notable speaking that survives transcription and sounds in a reader's ears.

Unfortunately, Bryan is best remembered today for a few inflammatory speeches which are not entirely typical. His style would probably be considered florid by today's restrained standards, but it was extremely effective in his own time and has not entirely lost its appeal. There is balance and cadence to what he says, but there is also careful discrimination and sensitive allusion. Above all, there is a sincerity that must be respected.

His courage in opposing America's participation in the events which led to our involvement in World War I was only matched by his loyal support of President Wilson's war measures when our active participation became inevitable. His oratory was always used in behalf of causes that he believed in, and he was not afraid to change his mind.

These causes are aptly illustrated in his comments on faith. Without false modesty and without egotism he believed in himself. His faith in others was equally intense. As Secretary of State he worked tirelessly to persuade nations to submit their disputes to arbitration, for he was convinced that most people could be trusted and that good will and good faith characterized both men and nations. As an active politician he was not blind to the weaknesses of his own government, but he believed it could function effectively and could be improved. The final overriding belief of his life was a simple faith in God and Christianity.

In the few pages above in which Bryan speaks to us again, we are less persuaded by his rhetoric than we are convinced by his sweet reasonableness. Yet he also speaks from the heart, and we find our own hearts echoing the firm, steady beat which has not weakened with the years.

omit

Jacob and the Indians

by Stephen Vincent Benét

It goes back to the early days—may God profit all who lived then—and the ancestors.

Well, America, you understand, in those days was different. It was a nice place, but you wouldn't believe it if you saw it today. Without busses, without trains, without states, without Presidents, nothing!

With nothing but colonists and Indians and wild woods all over the country and wild animals to live in the wild woods. Imagine such a place! In these days, you children don't even think about it; you read about it in the schoolbooks, but what is that? And I put in a call to my daughter, in California, and in three minutes I am saying "Hello, Rosie," and there is Rosie and she is telling me about the weather, as if I wanted to know! But things were not always that way. I remember my own days, and they were different. And in the times of my grandfather's grandfather, they were different still. Listen to the story.

My grandfather's grandfather was Jacob Stein, and he came from Rettelsheim, in Germany. To Philadelphia he came, an orphan in a sailing ship, but not a common man. He had learning—he had been to the chedar—he could have been a scholar among the scholars. Well, that is the way things happen in this bad world. There was a plague and a new grand duke—things are always so. He would say little of it afterward—they had left his teeth in his mouth, but he would say little of it. He did not have to say—we were children of the Dispersion—we know a black day when it comes.

Yet imagine—a young man with fine dreams and learning, a scholar with a pale face and narrow shoulders, set down in those early days in such a new country. Well, he must work, and he did. It was very fine, his learning, but it did not fill his mouth. He must carry a pack on his back and go from door to door with it. That was no disgrace; it was so that many began. But it was not expounding the Law, and at first he was very homesick. He would sit in his room at night, with the one candle, and read the preacher Koheleth, till the bitterness of the preacher rose in his mouth. Myself, I am sure that Koheleth was a great preacher, but if he had had a good wife he would have been a more cheerful man. They had too many wives in those old days—it confused them. But Jacob was young.

As for the new country where he had come, it was to him a

place of exile, large and frightening. He was glad to be out of the ship, but, at first, that was all. And when he saw his first real Indian in the street—well, that was a day! But the Indian, a tame one, bought a ribbon from him by signs, and after that he felt better. Nevertheless, it seemed to him at times that the straps of his pack cut into his very soul, and he longed for the smell of the chedar and the quiet streets of Rettelsheim and the good smoked goosebreast pious housewives keep for the scholar. But there is no going back—there is never any going back.

All the same, he was a polite young man, and a hardworking. And soon he had a stroke of luck—or at first it seemed so. It was from Simon Ettelsohn that he got the trinkets for his pack, and one day he found Simon Ettelsohn arguing a point of the Law with a friend, for Simon was a pious man and well thought of in the Congregation Mikveh Israel. Our grandfather's grandfather stood by very modestly at first—he had come to replenish his pack and Simon was his employer. But finally his heart moved within him, for both men were wrong, and he spoke and told them where they erred. For half an hour he spoke, with his pack still upon his shoulders, and never has a text been expounded with more complexity, not even by the great Reb Samuel. Till, in the end, Simon Ettelsohn threw up his hands and called him a young David and a candle of learning. Also, he allowed him a more profitable route of trade. But, best of all, he invited young Jacob to his house, and there Jacob ate well for the first time since he had come to Philadelphia. Also he laid eyes upon Miriam Ettelsohn for the first time, and she was Simon's youngest daughter and a rose of Sharon.

After that, things went better for Jacob, for the protection of the strong is like a rock and a well. But yet things did not go altogether as he wished. For, at first, Simon Ettelsohn made much of him, and there was stuffed fish and raisin wine for the young scholar, though he was a peddler. But there is a look in a man's eyes that says "H'm? Son-in-law?" and that look Jacob did not see. He was modest—he did not expect to win the maiden overnight, though he longed for her. But gradually it was borne in upon him what he was in the Ettelsohn house—a young scholar to be shown before Simon's friends, but a scholar whose learning did not fill his mouth. He did not blame Simon for it, but it was not what he had intended. He began to wonder if he would ever get on in the world at all, and that is not good for any man.

Nevertheless, he could have borne it, and the aches and pains of his love, had it not been for Meyer Kappelhuist. Now, there was a pushing man! I speak no ill of anyone, not even of your Aunt

Cora, and she can keep the DeGroot silver if she finds it in her heart to do so; who lies down in the straw with a dog, gets up with fleas. But this Meyer Kappelhuist! A big, red-faced fellow from Holland with shoulders the size of a barn door and red hair on the back of his hands. A big mouth for eating and drinking and telling stories—and he talked about the Kappelhuists, in Holland, till you'd think they were made of gold. The crane says, "I am really a peacock—at least on my mother's side." And yet, a thriving man—that could not be denied. He had started with a pack, like our grandfather's grandfather, and now he was trading with the Indians and making money hand over fist. It seemed to Jacob that he could never go to the Ettelsohn house without meeting Meyer and hearing about those Indians. And it dried the words in Jacob's mouth and made his heart burn.

For, no sooner would our grandfather's grandfather begin to expound a text or a proverb, than he would see Meyer Kappelhuist looking at the maiden. And when Jacob had finished his expounding, and there should have been a silence, Meyer Kappelhuist would take it upon himself to thank him, but always in a tone that said: "The Law is the Law, and the Prophets are the Prophets, but prime beaver is also prime beaver, my little scholar!" It took the pleasure from Jacob's learning and the joy of the maiden from his heart. Then he would sit silent and burning, while Meyer told a great tale of Indians, slapping his hands on his knees. And in the end he was always careful to ask Jacob how many needles and pins he had sold that day; and when Jacob told him, he would smile and say very smoothly that all things had small beginnings, till the maiden herself could not keep from a little smile. Then, desperately, Jacob would rack his brains for more interesting matter. He would tell of the wars of the Maccabees and the glory of the Temple. But even as he told them, he felt they were far away. Whereas Meyer and his accursed Indians were there, and the maiden's eyes shone at his words.

Finally he took his courage in both hands and went to Simon Ettelsohn. It took much for him to do it, for he had not been brought up to strive with men, but with words. But it seemed to him now that everywhere he went he heard of nothing but Meyer Kappelhuist and his trading with the Indians, till he thought it would drive him mad. So he went to Simon Ettelsohn in his shop.

"I am weary of this narrow trading in pins and needles," he said, without more words.

Simon Ettelsohn looked at him keenly; for while he was an ambitious man, he was kindly as well.

"Nu," he said. "A nice little trade you have and the people like you. I myself started in with less. What would you have more?"

"I would have much more," said our grandfather's grandfather stiffly. "I would have a wife and a home in this new country. But how shall I keep a wife? On needles and pins?"

"Nu, it has been done," said Simon Ettelsohn, smiling a little. "You are a good boy, Jacob, and we take an interest in you. Now, if it is a question of marriage, there are many worthy maidens. Asher Levy, the baker has a daughter. It is true that she squints a little, but her heart is of gold." He folded his hands and smiled.

"It is not of Asher Levy's daughter I am thinking," said Jacob, taken aback. Simon Ettelsohn nodded his head and his face grew grave.

"Nu, Jacob," he said. "I see what is in your heart. Well, you are a good boy, Jacob, and a fine scholar. And if it were in the old country, I am not saying. But here I have one daughter married to a Seixas and one to a Da Silva. You must see that makes a difference." And he smiled the smile of a man well pleased with his world.

"And if I were such a one as Meyer Kappelhuist?" said Jacob, bitterly.

"Now—well, that is a little different," said Simon Ettelsohn sensibly. "For Meyer trades with the Indians. It is true, he is a little rough. But he will die a rich man."

"I will trade with the Indians too," said Jacob, and trembled.

Simon Ettelsohn looked at him as if he had gone out of his mind. He looked at his narrow shoulders and his scholar's hands.

"Now Jacob," he said soothingly, "do not be foolish. A scholar you are, and learned, not an Indian trader. Perhaps in a store you would do better. I can speak to Aaron Copras. And sooner or later we will find you a nice maiden. But to trade with Indians—well, that takes a different sort of man. Leave that to Meyer Kappelhuist."

"And your daughter, that rose of Sharon." Shall I leave her, too, to Meyer Kappelhuist?" cried Jacob.

Simon Ettelsohn looked uncomfortable.

"Nu, Jacob," he said, "Well, it is not settled, of course. But—"

"I will go forth against him as David went against Goliath," said our grandfather's grandfather wildly. "I will go forth into the wilderness. And God should judge the better man!"

Then he flung his pack on the floor and strode from the shop. Simon Ettelsohn called out after him, but he did not stop for that. Nor was it in his heart to go and seek the maiden. Instead, when he was in the street, he counted the money he had. It was not much. He had meant to buy his trading goods on credit from Simon Ettelsohn, but now he could not do that. He stood in the sunlit street of Philadelphia, like a man bereft of hope.

Nevertheless, he was stubborn—though how stubborn he did not yet know. And though he was bereft of hope, he found his feet taking him to the house of Raphael Sanchez.

Now, Raphael Sanchez could have bought and sold Simon Ettelsohn twice over. An arrogant old man he was, with fierce black eyes, and a beard that was whiter than snow. He lived apart, in his big house with his granddaughter, and men said he was very learned, but also very disdainful, and that to him a Jew was not a Jew who did not come of the pure sephardic strain.

Jacob had seen him, in the Congregation Mikveh Israel, and to Jacob he had looked like an eagle, and fierce as an eagle. Yet now, in his need, he found himself knocking at that man's door.

It was Raphael Sanchez himself who opened. "And what is for sale today, peddler?" he said, looking scornfully at Jacob's jacket where the pack straps had worn it.

"A scholar of the Law is for sale," said Jacob in his bitterness, and he did not speak in the tongue he had learned in this country, but in Hebrew.

The old man stared at him a moment.

"Now am I rebuked," he said. "For you have the tongue. Enter, my guest," and Jacob touched the scroll by the doorpost and went in.

They shared the noon meal at Raphael Sanchez's table. It was made of dark, glowing mahogany, and the light sank into it as sunlight sinks into a pool. There were many precious things in that room, but Jacob had no eyes for them. When the meal was over and the blessing said, he opened his heart and spoke, and Raphael Sanchez listened, stroking his beard with one hand. When the young man had finished, he spoke.

"So, Scholar," he said, though mildly, "you have crossed an ocean that you might live and not die, and yet all you see is a girl's face."

"Did not Jacob serve seven years for Rachel?" said our grandfather's grandfather.

"Twice seven, Scholar," said Raphael Sanchez dryly, "but that was in the blessed days." He stroked his beard again. "Do you know why I came to this country?" he said.

"No," said Jacob Stein.

"It was not for the trading," said Raphael Sanchez. "My house has lent money to kings. A little fish, a few furs—what are they to my house? No, it was for the promise—the promise of Penn—that this land should be an habitation and a refuge, not only for the Gentiles. Well, we know Christian promises. But so far, it has been kept. Are you spat upon in the street here, Scholar of the Law?"

"No," said Jacob. "They call me Jew, now and then. But the Friends, though Gentile, are kind."

"It is not so in all countries," said Raphael Sanchez, with a terrible smile.

"No," said Jacob quietly, "it is not."

The old man nodded. "Yes, one does not forget that," he said. "The spittle wipes off the cloth, but one does not forget. One does not forget the persecutor or the persecuted. That is why they think me mad, in the Congregation Mikveh Israel, when I speak what is in my mind. For, look you"—and he pulled a map from a drawer—"Here is what we know of these colonies, and here and here our people make a new beginning, in another air. But here is New France—see it—and down the great river come the French traders and their Indians."

"Well?" said Jacob in puzzlement.

"Well?" said Raphael Sanchez. "Are you blind? I do not trust the King of France—the king before him drove out the Huguenots, and who knows what he may do? And if they hold the great rivers against us, we shall never go westward."

"We?" said Jacob in bewilderment.

"We," said Raphael Sanchez. He struck his hand on the map. "Oh, they cannot see it in Europe—not even their lords in parliament and their ministers of state," he said. "They think this is a mine, to be worked as the Spaniards worked Potosi, but it is not a mine. It is something beginning to live, and it is faceless and nameless yet. But it is our lot to be part of it—remember that in the wilderness, my young scholar of the Law. You think you are going there for a girl's face, and that is well enough. But you may find something there you did not expect to find."

He paused and his eyes had a different look.

"You see, it is the trader first," he said. "Always the trader, before the settled man. The Gentiles will forget that, and some of our own folk too. But one pays for the land of Canaan; one pays in blood and sweat."

Then he told Jacob what he would do for him and dismissed him, and Jacob went home to his room with his head buzzing strangely. For at times it seemed to him that the Congregation Mikveh Israel was right in thinking Raphael Sanchez half mad. And at other times it seemed to him that the old man's words were a veil, and behind them moved and stirred some huge and unguessed shape. But chiefly he thought of the rosy cheeks of Miriam Ettelsohn.

It was with the Scotchman, McCampbell, that Jacob made his first trading journey. A strange man was McCampbell, with grim features and cold, blue eyes, but strong and kindly, though silent, except when he talked of the Ten Lost Tribes of Israel. For it was his contention that they were the Indians beyond the Western Mountains, and on this subject he would talk endlessly.

Indeed, they had much profitable conversation, McCampbell quoting the doctrines of a rabbi called John Calvin, and our grandfather's grandfather replying with Talmud and Torah till McCampbell would almost weep that such a honey-mouthed scholar should be destined to eternal damnation. Yet he did not treat our grandfather's grandfather as one destined to eternal damnation, but as a man, and he, too, spoke of cities of refuge as a man speaks of realities, for his people had also been persecuted.

First they left the city behind them, and then the outlying towns and, soon enough, they were in the wilderness. It was very strange to Jacob Stein. At first he would wake at night and lie awake listening, while his heart pounded, and each rustle in the forest was the step of a wild Indian, and each screech of an owl in the forest the whoop before the attack. But gradually this passed. He began to notice how silently the big man, McCampbell, moved in the woods; he began to imitate him. He began to learn many things that even a scholar of the Law, for all his wisdom, does not know—the girthing of a packsaddle and the making of fires, the look of dawn in the forest and the look of evening. It was all very new to him, and sometimes he thought he would die of it, for his flesh weakened. Yet always he kept on.

When he saw his first Indians—in the woods, not in the town—his knees knocked together. They were there as he had dreamt of them in dreams, and he thought of the spirit, Iggereth-beth-Mathlan, and her seventy-eight dancing demons, for they were painted and in skins. But he could not let his knees knock together, before heathens and a Gentile, and the first fear passed. Then he found they were grave men, very ceremonious and silent at first, and then when the silence had been broken, full of curiosity. They knew McCampbell, but him they did not know, and they discussed him and his garments with the frankness of children, till Jacob felt naked before them, and yet not afraid. One of them pointed to the bag that hung at Jacob's neck—the bag in which, for safety's sake, he carried his phylactery—then McCampbell said something and the brown hand dropped quickly, but there was a buzz of talk.

Later on, McCampbell explained to him that they, too, wore little bags of deerskin and inside them sacred objects—and they thought, seeing him, that he must be a person of some note. It made him wonder. It made him wonder more to eat deer meat with them, by a fire.

It was a green world and a dark one that he had fallen in—dark with the shadow of the forest, green with its green. Through it ran trails and paths that were not yet roads or highways—that did not have the dust and smell of the cities of men, but another scent, another look. These paths Jacob noted carefully, making a map, for that was one of the instructions of Raphael Sanchez. It seemed a great labor and difficult and for no purpose; yet, as he had promised, so he did. And as they sank deeper and deeper into the depths of the forest, and he saw pleasant streams and wide glades, untenanted but by the deer, strange thoughts came over him. It seemed to him that the Germany he had left was very small and crowded together; it seemed to him that he had not known there was so much width to the world.

Now and then he would dream back—dream back to the quiet fields around Rettelsheim and the red-brick houses of Philadelphia, to the stuffed fish and the raisin wine, the chanting in the chedar and the white twisted loaves of calm Sabbath, under the white cloth. They would seem very close for the moment, then they would seem very far away. He was eating deer's meat in a forest and sleeping beside embers in the open night. It was so that Israel must have slept in the wilderness. He had not thought of it as so, but it was so.

Now and then he would look at his hands—they seemed tougher and very brown, as if they did not belong to him anymore. Now and then he would catch a glimpse of his own face, as he drank at a stream. He had a beard, but it was not the beard of a scholar—it was wild and black. Moreover, he was dressed in skins now; it seemed strange to be dressed in skins at first, and then not strange.

Now all this time, when he went to sleep at night, he would think of Miriam Ettelsohn. But, queerly enough, the harder he tried to summon up her face in his thoughts, the vaguer it became.

He lost track of time—there was only his map and the trading and the journey. Now it seemed to him that they should surely turn back, for their packs were full. He spoke of it to McCampbell, but McCampbell shook his head. There was a light in the Scotchman's eyes now—a light that seemed strange to our grandfather's grandfather—and he would pray long at night, sometimes too loudly. So they came to the banks of the great river, brown and great, and saw it, and the country beyond it, like a view across Jordan. There was no end to that country—it stretched to the limits of the sky and Jacob saw it with his eyes. He was almost afraid at first, and then he was not afraid.

It was there that the strong man, McCampbell, fell sick, and there that he died and was buried. Jacob buried him on a bluff overlooking the river and faced the grave to the west. In his death sickness, McCampbell raved of the Ten Lost Tribes again and swore they were just across the river and he would go to them. It took all of Jacob's strength to hold him—if it had been at the beginning of the journey, he would not have had the strength. Then he turned back, for he, too, had seen a Promised Land, not for his seed only, but for nations yet to come.

Nevertheless, he was taken by the Shawnees, in a season of bitter cold, with his last horse dead. At first, when misfortune began to fall upon him, he had wept for the loss of the horses and the good beaver. But, when the Shawnees took him, he no longer wept; for it seemed to him that he was no longer himself, but a man he did not know.

He was concerned when they tied him to the stake and piled the wood around him, for it seemed to him still that it must be happening to another man. Nevertheless he prayed, as was fitting, chanting loudly; for Zion in the wilderness he prayed. He could smell the smell of the chedar and hear the voices that he knew—Reb Moses and Reb Nathan, and through them the curious voice of Raphael Sanchez, speaking in riddles. Then the smoke took him and he coughed. His throat was hot. He called for drink, and though they could not understand his words, all men know the sign of thirst, and they brought him a bowl filled. He put it to his lips eagerly and drank, but the stuff in the bowl was scorching hot and burned his mouth. Very angry then was our grandfather's grandfather, and without so much as a cry he took the bowl in both hands and flung it straight in the face of the man who had brought it, scalding him. Then there was a cry and a murmur from the Shawnees and, after some moments, he felt himself unbound and knew that he lived.

It was flinging the bowl at the man while yet he stood at the stake that saved him, for there is an etiquette about such matters. One does not burn a madman, among the Indians; and to the

Shawnees, Jacob's flinging the bowl proved that he was mad, for a sane man would not have done so. Or so it was explained to him later, though he was never quite sure that they had not been playing cat-and-mouse with him, to test him. Also they were much concerned by his chanting his death song in an unkown tongue and by the phylactery that he had taken from its bag and bound upon brow and arm for his death hour, for these they thought strong medicine and uncertain. But in any case they released him, though they would not give him back his beaver, and that winter he passed in the lodges of the Shawnees, treated sometimes like a servant and sometimes like a guest, but always on the edge of peril. For he was strange to them, and they could not quite make up their minds about him, though the man with the scalded face had his own opinion, as Jacob could see.

Yet when the winter was milder and the hunting better than it had been in some seasons, it was he who got the credit of it, and the holy phylactery also; and by the end of the winter he was talking to them of trade, though diffidently at first. Ah, our grandfather's grandfather, selig, what woes he had! And yet it was not all woe, for he learned much woodcraft from the Shawnees and began to speak in their tongue.

Yet he did not trust them entirely; and when spring came and he could travel, he escaped. He was no longer a scholar then, but a hunter. He tried to think what day it was by the calendar, but he could only remember the Bee Moon and the Berry Moon. Yet when he thought of a feast he tried to keep it, and always he prayed for Zion. But when he thought of Zion, it was not as he had thought of it before—a white city set on a hill—but a great and open landscape, ready for nations. He could not have said why his thought had changed, but it had.

I shall not tell all, for who knows all? I shall not tell of the trading post he found deserted and the hundred and forty French louis in the dead man's money belt. I shall not tell of the halfgrown boy, McGillvray, that he found in the fringes of settlement—the boy who was to be his partner in the days to come—and how they traded again with the Shawnees and got much beaver. Only this remains to be told, for this is true.

It was a long time since he had even thought of Meyer Kappelhuist—the big pushing man with red hairs on the backs of his hands. But now they were turning back toward Philadelphia, he and McGillvray, their packhorses and their beaver; and as the paths began to grow familiar, old thoughts came into his mind. Moreover, he would hear now and then, in the outposts of the wilderness, of a red-haired trader. So when he met the man himself, not thirty miles from Lancaster, he was not surprised.

Now, Meyer Kappelhuist had always seemed a big man to our grandfather's grandfather. But he did not seem such a big man, met in the wilderness by chance, and at that Jacob was amazed. Yet the greater surprise was Meyer Kappelhuist's, for he stared at our grandfather's grandfather long and puzzledly before he cried out, "But it's the little scholar!" and clapped his hand on his knee. Then they greeted each other civilly and Meyer Kappelhuist drank liquor at the meeting, but Jacob drank nothing. For, all the time, they were talking, he could see Meyer Kappelhuist's eyes fixed greedily upon his pack of beaver, and he did not like that. Nor did he like the looks of the three tame Indians who traveled with Meyer Kappelhuist and, though he was a man of peace, he kept his hand on his arms, and the boy, McGillvray, did the same.

Meyer Kappelhuist was anxious that they should travel on together, but Jacob refused, for, as I say, he did not like the look in the red-haired man's eyes. So he said he was taking another road and left it at that.

"And the news you have of Simon Ettelsohn and his family—it is good, no doubt, for I know you are close to them," said Jacob, before they parted.

"Close to them?" said Meyer Kappelhuist, and he looked black as thunder. Then he laughed a forced laugh. "Oh, I see them no more," he said. "The old rascal has promised his daughter to a cousin of the Seixas, a greeny, just come over, but rich, they say. But to tell you the truth, I think we are well out of it, Scholar—she was always a little too skinny for my taste," and he laughed coarsely.

"She was a rose of Sharon and a lily of the valley," said Jacob respectfully, and yet not with the pang he would have expected at such news, though it made him more determined than ever not to travel with Meyer Kappelhuist. And with that they parted and Meyer Kappelhuist went his way. Then Jacob took a fork in the trail that McGillvray knew of and that was as well for him. For when he got to Lancaster, there was news of the killing of a trader by the Indians who traveled with him; and when Jacob asked for details, they showed him some thing dried on a willow hoop. Jacob looked at the thing and saw the hairs upon it were red.

"Sculped all right, but we got it back," said the frontiersman, with satisfaction. "The red devil had it on him when we caught him. Should have buried it, too, I guess, but we'd buried him already and it didn't seem feasible. Thought I might take it to Philadelphy, sometime—might make an impression on the governor.

Say, if you're going there, you might—after all, that's where he came from. Be a sort of memento to his folks."

"And it might have been mine, if I had traveled with him," said Jacob. He stared at the thing again, and his heart rose against touching it. Yet it was well the city people should know what happened to men in the wilderness, and the price of blood. "Yes, I will take it," he said.

Jacob stood before the door of Raphael Sanchez, in Philadelphia. He knocked at the door with his knuckles, and the old man himself peered out at him.

"And what is your business with me, Frontiersman?" said the old man, peering.

"The price of blood for a country," said Jacob Stein. He did not raise his voice, but there was a note in it that had not been there when he first knocked at Raphael Sanchez's door.

The old man stared at him soberly. "Enter, my son," he said at last, and Jacob touched the scroll by the doorpost and went in.

He walked through the halls as a man walks in a dream. At last he was sitting by the dark mahogany table. There was nothing changed in the room—he wondered greatly that nothing in it had changed.

"And what have you seen, my son?" said Raphael Sanchez.

"I have seen the land of Canaan, flowing with milk and honey," said Jacob, Scholar of the Law. "I have brought back grapes from Eshcol, and other things that are terrible to behold," he cried, and even as he cried he felt the sob rise in his throat. He choked it down. "Also there are eighteen packs of prime beaver at the warehouse and a boy named McGillvray, a Gentile, but very trusty," he said. "The beaver is very good and the boy under my protection. And McCampbell died by the great river, but he had seen the land and I think he rests well. The map is not made as I would have it, but it shows new things. And we must trade with the Shawnees. There are three posts to be established—I have marked them on the map—and later, more. And beyond the great river there is country that stretches to the end of the world. That is where my friend McCampbell lies, with his face turned west. But what is the use of talking? You would not understand."

He put his head on his arms, for the room was too quiet and peaceful, and he was very tired. Raphael Sanchez moved around the table and touched him on the shoulder.

"Did I not say, my son, that there was more than a girl's face to be found in the wilderness?" he said.

"A girl's face?" said Jacob. "Why, she is to be married and,

I hope will be happy, for she was a rose of Sharon. But what are girls' faces beside this?" and he flung something on the table. It rattled dryly on the table, like a cast snakeskin, but the hairs upon it were red.

"It was Meyer Kappelhuist," said Jacob childishly, "and he was a strong man. And I am not strong, but a scholar. But I have seen what I have seen. And we must say Kaddish for him."

"Yes, yes," said Raphael Sanchez. "It will be done. I will see to it."

"But you do not understand," said Jacob. "I have eaten deer's meat in the wilderness and forgotten the month and the year. I have been a servant to the heathen and held the scalp of my enemy in my hand. I will never be the same man."

"Oh, you will be the same," said Sanchez. "And no worse a scholar, perhaps. But this is a new country."

"It must be for all," said Jacob. "For my friend McCampbell died also, and he was a Gentile."

"Let us hope," said Raphael Sanchez and touched him again upon the shoulder. Then Jacob lifted his head and he saw that the light had declined and the evening was upon him. And even as he looked, Raphael Sanchez's granddaughter came in to light the candles for Sabbath. And Jacob looked upon her, and she was a dove, with dove's eyes.

Discussion of "Jacob and the Indians"

Stephen Vincent Benét (1898-1943) was represented in Volume 2 of *Out of the Best Books* with a tragic story of young love entitled "Too Early Spring." In "Jacob and the Indians" we encounter a tale that is far more typical of Benét, for no theme is so attractive to this prolific writer as the American dream becoming a reality.

The full diapason of faith is sounded in "Jacob and the Indians." Young Jacob Stein must learn to believe in himself, and for the shy young scholar this is an ordeal. He doesn't find out who he is or what he is all at once, but as his experiences mature him he learns to see himself not only as a person with unexpected strengths and continuing weaknesses but as part of something bigger than self.

He learns to believe in men who do not share his personal commitment. His first companion on the frontier is a Calvinist with religious convictions which are almost diametrically opposed to Jacob's Hebraic teachings. But McCampbell has much to teach the young Jewish scholar, and Jacob learns well. After McCampbell dies, another Gentile becomes his partner, and his final words to Raphael Sanchez are an assertion that the country he has seen must be made available to all.

Jacob's developing faith in the country he travels through cannot be separated from his growing belief in himself and the people who both befriend and test him. But it is his belief in the religion that has nurtured him which gives Jacob both courage and determination when his problems seem overwhelming.

By the time he returns to his patron in Philadelphia Jacob's vision of his own and other's destiny has grown to match the vastness of the lands he has seen and the mountains he has crossed. Yet the language he uses to speak his vision are the words of the Bible and he still wants to be known as a Scholar of the Law. In the final, charming lines of this moving story, the language is from the Song of Solomon. What drove him in the beginning and sustained him in trial is now providing new opportunities for faith in the future.

The Tide of Faith

by George Eliot

So faith is strong
Only when we are strong, shrinks when we shrink.
It comes when music stirs us, and the chords,
Moving on some grand climax, shake our souls
With influx new that makes new energies.
It comes in swellings of the heart and tears
That rise at noble and at gentle deeds.
It comes in moments of heroic love,
Unjealous joy in joy not made for us;
In conscious triumph of the good within,
Making us worship goodness that rebukes.
Even our failures are a prophecy.
Even our yearnings and our bitter tears
After that fair and true we cannot grasp.
Presentiment of better things on earth
Sweeps in with every force that stirs our souls
To admiration, self-renouncing love.

Discussion of "The Tide of Faith"

George Eliot was the pen-name of Mary Ann Evans (1819-1880). Self-educated for the most part, she read widely and became proficient enough in languages to translate both Feuerbach and Spinoza. For a time she was an editor on the *Westminister Review,* and by 1858 had written her first prose fiction. With *Adam Bede,* in 1859, she became famous. A series of novels followed which enhanced her reputation if they did not always show continuing development as a novelist.

Despite her unquestioned success as a writer of prose she persisted in writing poetry, and a small number of her poems were printed. Today, only the famous line, "O, might I join the choir invisible" is widely remembered from her poetic work.

"The Tide of Faith" abounds in implicit praise of Christian virtues without identifying too closely with their formulation in a specific creed. Like Arnold, Miss Evans felt the strength of religious motives all her life, but the harsh religious discipline of her youth apparently drove her away from active participation in established churches.

A Good Night

by Francis Quarles

Close now thine eyes and rest secure;
Thy soul is safe enough, thy body sure;
He that loves thee, he that keeps
And guards thee, never slumbers, never sleeps.
The smiling conscience in a sleeping breast
Has only peace, has only rest.
The music and the mirth of kings
Are all but very discords, when she sings;
Then close thine eyes and rest secure;
No sleep so sweet as thine, no rest so sure.

Discussion of "A Good Night"

Little is known of the life of Francis Quarles (1592-1644). We do know that he matriculated at Christ's College, Cambridge, and that he began the study of law at Lincoln's Inn when his years at the university were over. Later, he was connected with the court as cupbearer to Princess Elizabeth and spent a number of years in Ireland as secretary to Archbishop Ussher.

The advent of eighteen children after his marriage in 1618 apparently did not deter his voluminous writing—although it may be worth noting that he admits to beginning his day at 3 a.m.! His poetry, particularly the *Emblems* of 1635, was immensely popular in a day when the King James Bible was the book which many people had easiest access to.

There is a quiet affirmation and trust in "A Good Night" that has kept this poem in print while many of the scriptural paraphrases for which Quarles was most famous during his lifetime have long since been forgotten. It is not the tone alone that recommends this poem, however. Note the long vowel sounds which help set a mood of peace and the repetition of the same ending words in the first and last couplets. All the rhymes inside these opening and closing lines are exact, and thereby restful, but to have the same words open and close the poem give a sense of completeness and control that *is* the meaning of this simple verse. Here is faith that fairly exudes from the page. A work such as "A Good Night" doesn't have to mention faith; it demonstrates it.

The Will To Believe

by William James

Science says things are; morality says some things are better than other things; and religion says essentially two things.

First, she says that the best things are the most eternal things, the overlapping things, the things in the universe that throw the last stone, so to speak, and say the final word. "Perfection is eternal,"—this phrase of Charles Secrétan seems a good way of putting this first affirmation of religion, an affirmation which obviously cannot yet be verified scientifically at all.

The second affirmation of religion is that we are better off even now if we believe her first affirmation to be true.

Now, let us consider what the logical elements of this situation are in case the religious hypothesis in both its branches be really true. (Of course, we must admit that possibility at the outset. If we are to discuss the question at all, it must involve a living option. If for any of you religion be an hypothesis that cannot, by any living possibility be true, then you need go no farther. I speak to the 'saving remnant' alone.) So proceeding, we see, first, that religion offers itself as a momentous option. We are supposed to gain, even now, by our belief, and to lose by our non-belief, a certain vital good. Secondly, religion is a forced option, so far as that good goes. We cannot escape the issue by remaining skeptical and waiting for more light, because, although we do avoid error in that way if religion be untrue, we lose the good, if it be true, just as certainly as if we positively chose to disbelieve. It is as if a man should hesitate indefinitely to ask a certain woman to marry him because he was not perfectly sure that she would prove an angel after he brought her home. Would he not cut himself off from that particular angel-possibility as decisively as if he went and married some one else? Skepticism, then, is not avoidance of option; it is option of a certain particular kind of risk. Better risk loss of truth than chance of error,—that is your faith-vetoer's exact position. He is actively playing his stake as much as the believer is; he is backing the field against the religious hypothesis, just as the believer is backing the religious hypothesis against the field. To preach skepticism to us as a duty until 'sufficient evidence' for religion be found, is tantamount therefore to telling us, when in presence of the religious hypothesis, that to yield to our fear of its being error is wiser and better than to yield to our hope that it may be true. It is not intellect against all passions, then; it is only intellect with one passion laying down its law. And by what, forsooth, is the supreme wisdom of this passion warranted? Dupery for dupery, what proof is there that dupery through hope is so much worse than dupery through fear? I, for one, can see no proof; and I simply refuse obedience to the scientist's command to imitate his kind of option, in a case where my own stake is important enough to give me the right to choose my own form of risk. If religion be true and the evidence for it still insufficient, I do not wish, by putting your extinguisher upon my nature (which feels to me as if it had after all some business in this matter), to forfeit my sole chance in life of getting upon the winning side,—that chance depending, of course, on my willingness to run the risk of acting as if my passional need of taking the world religiously might be prophetic and right.

Discussion of "The Will to Believe"

The Philosophical Clubs of Yale and Brown universities were the first groups to hear what has now become a classical defense of faith. Unlike many philosophical statements, "The Will to Believe" makes use of few technical terms; it is meant to be understood by laymen.

The author of this remarkable statement (we have here reproduced only a small part of an eighteen page treatise) belonged to an unusually gifted family. The father, Henry James Sr. was a highly original philosopher and theologian who was equally devoted to the life of the mind and the education of his children. A man of independent means, he was able to give his family extraordinary opportunities for development, but the formal education of his five children was sporadic and irregular.

A younger son, Henry James Jr., became the distinguished author of novels which are widely praised for psychological subtlety and refinement in style. William, the oldest, became a renowned philosopher and a leading figure in the school of philosophy known as pragmatism. After receiving his M.D. from Harvard Medical School in 1869 James was too ill to begin practicing. From his birth in 1842 he had been a sickly child, and it was only after his marriage in 1873 that the James we know so well today begins to become evident.

Between 1893 and 1903 all his studies were concerned with one aspect or another of religion and religious experience. "The Will to Believe" was published in 1897 and is James at the height of his powers. Instead of arguing foregone conclusions, he goes directly to religious experience to probe the nature of God. Instead of dismissing faith as beyond analysis he looks freshly at what may be required to assess faith.

If the argument James is pursuing in the selection we have reprinted seems a bit difficult to follow, it repays close reading. For it refuses to put faith on the defensive. When the skeptic insists that we must withhold belief until the evidence is irrefutable, he is not testing faith; he is simply denying it. James demands for the believer the same opportunity available to the skeptic. Faith can be tested only by standards which are appropriate to it. To see faith defended upon logical grounds may be a little disconcerting at first, but James demonstrates that the true scientist is scrupulously fair. Faith may finally be a gift from God, but our preparation to receive the gift may be as exacting as the most rigorous logic.

SECTION SEVEN

Charity Out of A Pure Heart

by Robert K. Thomas

"Le Benedicite"

by Jean Baptiste Simeon Chardin (1699-1779)
(Louvre Museum, Paris, France)

Commentary by
Floyd E. Breinholt, Associate Professor of Art, Brigham Young University

The artist Chardin lived in France at a time when a number of artists were changing the subject matter in art from the painting of the nobility, the pomp and gaiety of the court and its extravagance, to the quaint homely scene of everyday life. Paintings small enough and with subject matter fitting to a more humble setting were becoming more desirable. Chardin insisted on painting the everyday things of life and is said to have become more popular than the great artists who painted the nobility. His paintings told a story that the common people, the middle classes, could understand and identify with. This painting "Le Bénédicté" is such a work.

His purpose may have been to say that to be grateful is to be wise. A wise man discovers his own true relationship and place in the pattern of life. He discovers that gratitude is prerequisite to learning to love. As in Timothy, "the end of the commandment is charity out of a pure heart."

To illustrate this noble idea, Chardin shows a small child in the attitude of giving thanks with an implied faith in those who taught her and a simple faith in a divine province. Thus portraying, through gratitude, love out of a pure heart.

The story is told with astonishing naturalness and dignity. He had no use for tinsel or artificiality, but expressed himself in an unassuming and straightforward manner. This was unusual in his day, but his paintings influenced subsequent art.

When the color in his work was being criticized by another artist he said, "And who told you, Sir, that one paints with color? One makes use of colors, but one paints with emotions."

In Chardin's paintings we seem to be looking through a window, watching people live their private lives, always with a feeling of love and understanding.

There are those who would call this painting sentimental. The writer Venturi says, "A painting to be art must have feeling. But genuine feeling is a living approach to reality while sentimentality is a will to convince through sentiment, and a mistake in taste. And a will to sentiment destroys natural feeling." We leave the reader to decide whether sentiment is used in this case to convince, or whether the honest feeling of the artist thus expressed is paramount.

CHARITY OUT OF A PURE HEART

"The end of the commandment is charity out of a pure heart."
—I Timothy 1:5

Introductory Comments

There are few utterances in scripture as beautifully phrased as Paul's description of charity in I Corinthians 13. In fact these verses have such felicitous balance and cadence that it is possible to speak them impressively without plumbing their significance or to hear them with more pleasure than understanding.

Many readers may be aware that some English translators substitute the word *love* for *charity* in this chapter, but such a shift is not very illuminating unless we are aware of the problems involved in translating terms which do not appear to have exact equivalents.

The Greek word which we translate as love or charity is *agape*. Unfortunately, English does not have a single word which carries all the connotations of the original. In Greek there are at least three words which can accurately be translated as love in English: *eros, philia* and *agape*. If those terms share a generalized meaning, they differ sharply in emphasis. *Eros* is usually selfish, as in our English word erotic. *Philia* suggests brotherly love, as in Philadelphia. *Agape* is selfless, unconditional love. It is this term which is used to describe God's love for the world in John 3:16, and it is this concept which Jesus is apparently trying to get Peter to understand in John 21.

Since the Latin word *caritas* is a reasonably precise rendering of *agape*, it is easy to see how *charity* was chosen by the King James translators to stand for a type of love so profound and encompassing that it could be asserted to be a more basic precept in Christianity than faith itself. Unfortunately, generations of readers to whom such an exalted view of love had little meaning soon reduced the idea of charity to alms-giving. It is in such a narrow sense that we commonly think of this principle today.

It should be noted that charity surely includes concern for the physical needs of others. But we slight one of the fundamental truths of the Gospel if we fail to sound the full significance of this concept. "Charity never faileth" should be more than a motto for mutual aid; it should assert the practical validity and necessity for loving God and all His children wholeheartedly.

The person who is striving to put his life into accord with this precept will no longer be working for a reward, nor will he gauge his love of others by their love for him. In loving others with all the intensity he once reserved for himself, he begins to understand the *Book of Mormon* scripture which tells him that "Charity is the pure love of Christ."

The selections which make up this section on charity try to avoid the most obvious ways in which this principle can be demonstrated. "Giving" by Kahlil Gibran quickly points out that the donation of possession—no matter how worthy the cause—is far less significant than the bestowal of love, for only as you bestow love do you give your life. "The Christmas Guest" of Selma Lagerlöf lets us see that charity carries with it some risk. Under what conditions will innocence save the corrupted, and when will corruption destroy innocence?

The long story, "Bartleby the Scrivener" by Herman Melville is an especially perceptive study of charity. Bartleby's employer is surely not heartless; his concern for Bartleby is real and consistent under the most trying of circumstances. He is even aware that he is acting "charitably," and works at it. Yet what is lacking here is the *unconditional* aspect of real charity. Only after Bartleby has died does his employer catch a glimpse of the need that went hopelessly unfulfilled in Bartleby's life.

No theme which we have considered in the three volumes of *Out of the Best Books* is more basic to human happiness and heavenly exaltation than the topic examined in this lesson. In epic understatement, Moroni of old sounded its fundamental importance when he says "whoso is found possessed of [charity] at the last day, it shall be well with him."

"Giving" from "The Prophet"

by Kahlil Gibran

Then said a rich man, Speak to us of Giving.

And he answered:

You give but little when you give of your possessions.

It is when you give of yourself that you truly give.

For what are your possessions but things you keep and guard for fear you may need them tomorrow?

And tomorrow, what shall tomorrow bring to the overprudent dog burying bones in the trackless sand as he follows the pilgrims to the holy city?

And what is fear of need but need itself?

Is not dread of thirst when your well is full, the thirst that is unquenchable?

There are those who give little of the much which they have—and they give it for recognition and their hidden desire makes their gifts unwholesome.

And there are those who have little and give it all.

These are the believers in life and the bounty of life, and their coffer is never empty.

There are those who give with joy, and that joy is their reward.

And there are those who give with pain, and that pain is their baptism.

And there are those who give and know not pain in giving, nor do they seek joy, nor give with mindfulness of virtue;

They give as in yonder valley the myrtle breathes its fragrance into space.

Through the hands of such as these God speaks, and from behind their eyes He smiles upon the earth.

It is well to give when asked, but it is better to give unasked, through understanding;

And to the open-handed the search for one who shall receive is joy greater than giving.

And is there aught you would withhold?

All you have shall some day be given;

Therefore give now, that the season of giving may be yours and not your inheritors'.

You often say, "I would give, but only to the deserving."

The trees in your orchard say not so, nor the flocks in your pasture.

They give that they may live, for to withhold is to perish.

Surely he who is worthy to receive his days and his nights, is worthy of all else from you.

And he who has deserved to drink from the ocean of life deserves to fill his cup from your little stream.

And what desert greater shall there be, than that which lies in the courage and the confidence, nay the charity, of receiving?

And who are you that men should rend their bosom and unveil their pride, that you may see their worth naked and their pride unabashed?

See first that you yourself deserve to be a giver, and an instrument in giving.

For in truth it is life that gives unto life—while you, who deem yourself a giver, are but a witness.

And you receivers—and you are all receivers—assume no weight of gratitude, lest you lay a yoke upon yourself and upon him who gives.

Rather rise together with the giver on his gifts as on wings;

For to be overmindful of your debt, is to doubt his generosity who has the free-

hearted earth for mother, and God for
father.

Discussion of "Giving"

When Kahlil Gibran (1883-1931) died at the age of forty-eight in New York City, this Lebanese-American mystic was at work on a book of parables which were issued posthumously and which enjoyed the continuing popularity which all of his work in English has done. What is not generally known is that his earlier literary work, particularly his prose poems and plays, were known to the entire Arabic world.

As a child he displayed precocity in both drawing and writing. At the age of fourteen and a half he entered a Syrian college, and for a time he studied drawing at the Ecole des Beaux Arts in Paris. Before he was twenty he adopted English exclusively as his medium of expression, and his acceptance as artist and writer by the English-speaking world has been phenomenal. *The Prophet,* especially, has been reprinted a number of times. First published in 1923, it went through its thirty-fifth edition by 1936.

Many critics have tried to assess the appeal and importance of Gibran's work. While there is little agreement as to its importance—some feeling that he is more rephraser than thinker—most agree that its appeal is based on its mystical vision, metrical beauty, and a simple and fresh approach to the so-called problems of life.

"Giving" is typical of Gibran's style and method. The rather standard assertion that it is when you "give of yourself that you truly give" is followed by the striking metaphor of the "overprudent dog burying bones in the trackless sand as he follows the pilgrims to the holy city." The second stanza of this prose poem also begins with the obvious but quickly—and gracefully—moves to a deepening perspective. As various facets of giving, and receiving, are uncovered we remember King Benjamin's address in the *Book of Mormon*. Now as then, these words appeal to us because they speak to our actual condition. We know how we should both give and receive; our failures are not due to ignorance, and when we are reminded in language whose beauty reinforces its message, we resolve to do better.

A Christmas Guest

by Selma Lagerlöf

One of those who had lived the life of a pensioner at Ekeby was little Ruster, who could transpose music and play the flute. He was of low origin and poor, without home and without relations. Hard times came to him when the company of pensioners were dispersed.

He then had no horse nor carriole, no fur coat nor red-painted luncheon-basket. He had to go on foot from house to house and carry his belongings tied in a blue striped cotton handkerchief. He buttoned his coat all the way up to his chin, so that no one should need to know in what condition his shirt and waistcoat were, and in its deep pockets he kept his most precious possessions: his flute taken to pieces, his flat brandy bottle, and his music-pen.

His profession was to copy music, and if it had been as in the old days, there would have been no lack of work for him. But with every passing year music was less practised in Värmland. The guitar, with its moldy, silken ribbon and its worn screws, and the dented horn, with faded tassels and cord, were put away in the lumber-room in the attic, and the dust settled inches deep on the long-iron-bound violin boxes. Yet the less little Ruster had to do with flute and music-pen, so much the more must he turn to the brandy flask, and at last he became quite a drunkard. It was a great pity.

He was still received at the manor-houses as an old friend, but there were complaints when he came and joy when he went. There was an odor of dirt and brandy about him, and if he had only a couple of glasses of wine or one toddy, he grew confused and told unpleasant stories. He was the torment of the hospitable houses.

One Christmas he came to Löfdala, where Liljekrona, the great violinist, had his home. Liljekrona had also been one of the pensioners of Ekeby, but after the death of the major's wife, he returned to his quiet farm and remained there. Ruster came to him a few days before Christmas, in the midst of all the preparations, and asked for work. Liljekrona gave him a little copying to keep him busy.

"You ought to have let him go immediately," said his wife; now he will certainly take so long with that that we will be obliged to keep him over Christmas."

"He must be somewhere," answered Liljekrona.

And he offered Ruster toddy and brandy, sat with him, and lived over again with him the whole Ekeby time. But he was out of spirits and disgusted by him, like everyone else, although he would not let it be seen, for old friendship and hospitality were sacred to him.

In Liljekrona's house for three weeks now they had been preparing to receive Christmas. They had been living in discomfort and bustle, had sat up with dip-lights and torches till their eyes grew red, had been frozen in the out-house with the salting of meat and in the brew-house with the brewing of the beer. But both the mistress and the servants gave themselves up to it all without grumbling.

When all the preparations were done and the holy evening came, a sweet enchantment would sink down over them. Christmas would loosen all tongues, so that jokes and jests, rhymes and merriment would flow of themselves without effort. Everyone's feet would wish to twirl in the dance, and from memory's dark corners words and melodies would rise, although no one could believe that they were there. And then everyone was so good, so good!

Now when Ruster came the whole household at Löfdola thought that Christmas was spoiled. The mistress and the older children and the old servants were all of the same opinion. Ruster caused them a suffocating disgust. They were moreover afraid that when he and Liljekrona began to rake up the old memories, the artist's blood would flame up in the great violinist and his home would lose him. Formerly he had not been able to remain long at home.

No one can describe how they loved their master on the farm, since they had had him with them a couple of years. And what he had to give! How much he was to his home especially at Christmas! He did not take his place on any sofa or rocking stool, but on a high narrow wooden bench in the corner of the fireplace. When he was settled there he started off on adventures. He traveled about the earth, climbed up to the stars, and even higher. He played and talked by turns, and the whole household gathered about him and listened. Life grew proud and beautiful when the richness of that one soul shone on it.

Therefore they loved him as they loved Christmas time, pleasure, the spring sun. And when little Ruster came, their Christmas peace was destroyed. They had worked in vain if he was coming to tempt away their master. It was unjust that the drunkard should sit at the Christmas table in a happy house and spoil the Christmas pleasure.

On the forenoon of Christmas eve little Ruster had his music written out, and he said something about going, although of course he meant to stay.

Liljekrona had been influenced by the general feeling, and

therefore said quite lukewarmly and indifferently that Ruster had better stay where he was over Christmas.

Little Ruster was inflammable and proud. He twirled his mustache and shook back the black artist's hair that stood like a dark cloud over his head. What did Liljekrona mean? Should he stay because he had nowhere else to go? Oh, only think how they stood and waited for him in the big iron-works in the parish of Bro! The guest-room was in order, the glass of welcome filled. He was in great haste. He only did not know to which he ought to go first.

"Very well," answered Liljekrona "you may go if you will."

After dinner little Ruster borrowed horse and sleigh, coat and furs. The stable-boy from Löfdala was to take him to some place in Bro and drive quickly back, for it threatened snow.

No one believed that he was expected, or that there was a single place in the neighborhood where he was welcome. But they were so anxious to be rid of him that they put the thought aside and let him depart. "He wished it himself," they said; and then they thought that now they would be glad.

But when they gathered in the dining-room at five o'clock to drink tea and to dance round the Christmas tree, Liljekrona was silent and out of spirits. He did not seat himself on the bench; he touched neither tea nor punch; he could not remember any polka; the violin was out of order. Those who could play and dance had to do it without him.

Then his wife grew uneasy; the children were discontented, everything in the house went wrong. It was the most lamentable Christmas Eve.

The porridge turned sour; the candles sputtered; the wood smoked; the wind stirred up the snow and blew bitter cold into the rooms. The stable-boy who had driven Ruster did not come home. The cook wept; the maids scolded.

Finally Liljekrona remembered that no sheaves had been put out for the sparrows, and he complained aloud of all the women about him who abandoned old customs and were new-fangled and heartless. They understood well enough that what tormented him was remorse that he had let little Ruster go away from his home on Christmas Eve.

After a while he went to his room, shut the door, and began to play as he had not played since he had ceased roaming. It was full of hate and scorn, full of longing and revolt. "You thought to bind me, but you must forge new fetters. You thought to make me as small-minded as yourselves, but I turn to larger things, to the open.

Commonplace people, slaves of the home, hold me prisoner if it is in your power!"

When his wife heard the music, she said: "Tomorrow he is gone, if God does not work a miracle in the night. Our inhospitableness has brought on what we thought we could avoid."

In the meantime little Ruster drove about in the snowstorm. He went from one house to the other and asked if there was any work for him to do, but he was not received anywhere. They did not even ask him to get out of the sledge. Some had their houses full of guests, others were going away on Christmas Day. "Drive to the next neighbor," they all said.

He could come and spoil the pleasure of an ordinary day, but not of Christmas Eve. Christmas Eve came but once a year, and the children had been rejoicing in the thought of it all the autumn. They could not put that man at a table where there were children. Formerly they had been glad to see him, but not since he had become a drunkard. Where should they put the fellow, moreover? The servants' room was too plain and the guest-room too fine.

So little Ruster had to drive from house to house in the blinding snow. His wet mustache hung limply down over his mouth; his eyes were bloodshot and blurred, but the brandy was blown out of his brain. He began to wonder and to be amazed. Was it possible, was it possible that no one wished to receive him?

Then all at once he saw himself. He saw how miserable and degraded he was, and he understood that he was odious to people. "It is the end of me," he thought. "No more copying of music, no more flute-playing. No one on earth needs me; no one has compassion on me."

The storm whirled and played, tore apart the drifts and piled them up again, took a pillar of snow in its arms and danced out into the plain, lifted one flake up to the clouds and chased another down into a ditch. "It is so, it is so," said little Ruster; "while one dances and whirls it is play, but when one must be buried in the drift and forgotten, it is sorrow and grief." But down they all have to go, and now it was his turn. To think that he had now come to the end!

He no longer asked where the man was driving him; he thought that he was driving in the land of death.

Little Ruster made no offerings to the gods that night. He did not curse flute-playing or the life of a pensioner; he did not think that it had been better for him if he had ploughed the earth or sewn shoes. But he mourned that he was now a worn-out instrument, which pleasure could no longer use. He complained of no one, for he knew that when the horn is cracked and the guitar will not stay in tune, they must go. He became all at once a very humble man. He understood that it was the end of him, on this Christmas Eve. Hunger and cold would destroy him, for he understood nothing, was good for nothing, and had no friends.

The sledge stops, and suddenly it is light about him, and he hears friendly voices, and there is some one who is helping him into a warm room, and some one who is pouring warm tea into him. His coat is pulled off him, and several people cry that he is welcome, and warm hands rub life into his benumbed fingers.

He was so confused by it all that he did not come to his senses for nearly a quarter of an hour. He could not possibly comprehend that he had come back to Löfdala. He had not been at all conscious that the stable-boy had grown tired of driving about in the storm and had turned home.

Nor did he understand why he was now so well received in Liljekrona's house. He could not know that Liljekrona's wife understood what a weary journey he had made that Christmas Eve, when he had been turned away from every door where he had knocked. She felt such compassion on him that she forgot her own troubles.

Liljekrona went on with the wild playing up in his room; he did not know that Ruster had come. The latter sat meanwhile in the dining-room with the wife and the children. The servants, who used also to be there on Christmas Eve, had moved out into the kitchen away from their mistress' trouble.

The mistress of the house lost no time in setting Ruster to work. "You hear, I suppose," she said, "that Liljekrona does nothing but play all the evening, and I must attend to setting the table and the food. The children are quite forsaken. You must look after these two smallest."

Children were the kind of people with whom little Ruster had had least intercourse. He had met them neither in the bachelor's wing nor in the campaign tent, neither in wayside inns nor on the highways. He was almost shy of them, and did not know what he ought to say that was fine enough for them.

He took out his flute and taught them how to finger the stops and holes. There was one of four years and one of six. They had a lesson on the flute and were deeply interested in it. "This is A," he said, "and this is C," and then he blew the notes Then the young people wished to know what kind of an A and C it was that was to be played.

Ruster took out his score and made a few notes.

"No," they said, "that is not right." And they ran away for an A B C book.

Little Ruster began to hear their alphabet. They knew it and they did not know it. What they knew was not very much. Ruster grew eager; he lifted the little boys up, each on one of his knees, and began to teach them. Liljekrona's wife went out and in and listened quite in amazement. It sounded like a game, and the children were laughing the whole time, but they learned.

Ruster kept on for a while, but he was absent from what he was doing. He was turning over the thoughts from out in the storm. It was good and pleasant, but nevertheless, it was the end of him. He was worn out. He ought to be thrown away. And all of a sudden he put his hands before his face and began to weep.

Liljekrona's wife came quickly up to him.

"Ruster," she said, "I can understand that you think that all is over for you. You cannot make a living with your music, and you are destroying yourself with brandy. But it is not the end, Ruster."

"Yes," sobbed the little flute-player.

"Do you see that to sit as tonight with the children, that would be something for you? If you would teach children to read and write you would be welcomed everywhere. There is no less important an instrument on which to play, Ruster, than flute and violin. Look at them, Ruster!"

She placed the two children in front of him, and he looked up blinking as if he had looked at the sun. It seemed as if his little blurred eyes could not meet those of the children, which were big, clear, and innocent.

"Look at them, Ruster!" repeated Liljekrona's wife.

"I dare not," said Ruster, for it was like a purgatory to look through the beautiful child eyes to the unspotted beauty of their souls.

Liljekrona's wife laughed loud and joyously.

"Then you must accustom yourself to them, Ruster. You can stay in my house as schoolmaster this year."

Liljekrona heard his wife laugh and came out of his room.

"What is it?" he said. "What is it?"

"Nothing," she answered, "but that Ruster has come again, and that I have engaged him as schoolmaster for our little boys."

Liljekrona was quite amazed. "Do you dare?" he said, "do you dare." Has he promised to give up—"

"No," said the wife; "Ruster has promised nothing. But there is much about which he must be careful when he has to look little children in the eyes every day. If it had not been Christmas, perhaps I would not have ventured; but when our Lord dared to place a little child who was His own son among us sinners, so can I also dare to let my little children try to save a human soul."

Liljekrona could not speak, but every feature and wrinkle in his face twitched and twisted as always when he heard anything noble.

Then he kissed his wife's hand as gently as a child who asks for forgiveness and cried aloud: "All the children must come and kiss their mother's hand."

They did so, and then they had a happy Christmas in Liljekrona's house.

Discussion of "A Christmas Guest"

"A Christmas Guest" is from a book of short stories by Selma Lagerlöf (1858-1940) which was translated into English in 1899. A third of a century later Miss Lagerlöf was still writing vigorously. Along the way she became the first woman to win the Nobel prize for literature, was given the gold medal of the Swedish Academy and was later elected to be its first female member. As the years passed, Miss Lagerlöf lived more and more in retirement, although her fiftieth birthday was celebrated nationally in her native Sweden, and her seventieth was internationally acclaimed.

To critics of a later generation her philosophy often seems overly simple and her outlook a bit limited. Yet this is her great strength. She belongs to the small group of writers who have reached the world through an art deeply rooted in the provincial. In giving permanent expression to a local culture, she chooses universal themes which stir the imagination and aspirations of people everywhere.

"A Christmas Guest" is Scandinavian in locale and dated in time, yet it manages to speak freshly to anyone who sets himself to help another. Probably all of us would find it both convenient and satisfying to aid the attractively destitute, the deserving poor. But real want has often had such a negative effect on those who undergo it that helping them is neither appealing nor easy.

Ruster, in this story, is such a person. He seems to be partly a victim of circumstances but mostly a willing accomplice to his own misfortune. To begin with, Liljekrona's wife is annoyed to think that her family's Christmas must include such an uninviting—and uninvited—guest. But when Ruster is eased out of the house, both husband and wife suffer remorse.

When the pitiful little flute player is brought back, it is the mistress of the house who first understands that compassion which is selective has already lost its central meaning. Ruster is not much more attractive now than he was earlier. He does realize his shortcomings but seems powerless to do anything about them. In an intuitive decision, Mrs. Liljekrona decides to unite the innocence and purity of her children with her own compassion in a concerted effort to save him. If there is risk in such an attempt, it appears to be both justified and prefigured in the Lord's sending "a little child who was His own son" to redeem mankind.

Bartleby, the Scrivener

by Herman Melville

I am a rather elderly man. The nature of my avocations, for the last thirty years, has brought me into more than ordinary contact with what would seem an interesting and somewhat singular set of men, of whom, as yet, nothing, that I know of, has ever been written—I mean, the law-copyists, or scriveners. I have known very many of them, professionally and privately, and, if I pleased, could relate divers histories, at which good-natured gentlemen might smile, and sentimental souls might weep. But I waive the biographies of all other scriveners, for a few passages in the life of Bartleby, who was a scrivener, the strangest I ever saw, or heard of. While, of other lawcopyists, I might write the complete life, of Bartleby nothing of that sort can be done. I believe that no materials exist, for a full and satisfactory biography of this man. It is an irreparable loss to literature. Bartleby was one of those beings of whom nothing is ascertainable, except from the original sources, and, in his case, those are very small. What my own astonished eyes saw of Bartleby, that is all I know of him, except, indeed, one vague report, which will appear in the sequel.

Ere introducing the scrivener, as he first appeared to me, it is fit I make some mention of myself, my employes, my business, my chambers, and general surroundings; because some such description is indispensable to an adequate understanding of the chief character about to be presented. Imprimis: I am a man who, from his youth upwards, has been filled with a profound conviction that the easiest way of life is the best. Hence, though I belong to a profession proverbially energetic and nervous, even to turbulence, at times, yet nothing of that sort have I ever suffered to invade my peace. I am one of those unambitious lawyers who never address a jury, or in any way draw down public applause; but, in the cool tranquility of a snug retreat, do a snug business among rich men's bonds, and mortgages, and title-deeds. All who know me, consider me an eminently safe man. The late John Astor, a personage little given to poetic enthusiasm, had no hesitation in pronouncing my first grand point to be prudence; my next, method. I do not speak it in vanity, but simply record the fact, that I was not unemployed in my profession by the late John Jacob Astor, a name which I admit, I love to repeat; for it hath a rounded and orbicular sound to it, and rings like unto bullion. I will freely add, that I was not insensible to the late John Jacob Astor's good opinion.

Some time prior to the period at which this little history begins, my avocations had been largely increased. The good old office, now extinct, in the State of New York, of a Master in Chancery, had been conferred upon me. It was not a very arduous office, but very pleasantly remunerative. I seldom lose my temper; much more seldom indulge in dangerous indignation at wrongs and outrages; but I must be permitted to be rash here and declare, that I consider the sudden and violent abrogation of the office of Master in Chancery, by the new Constitution, as a—premature act; inasmuch as I had counted upon a life-lease of the profits, whereas I only received those of a few short years. But this is by the way.

My chambers were up stairs, at No. .... Wall Street. At one end, they looked upon the white wall of the interior of a spacious sky-light shaft, penetrating the building from top to bottom.

This view might have been considered rather tame than otherwise, deficient in what landscape painters call "life." But, if so, the view from the other end of my chambers offered, at least, a contrast, if nothing more. In that direction, my windows commanded an unobstructed view of a lofty brick wall, black by age and everlasting shade; which wall required no spyglass to bring out its lurking beauties, but, for the benefit of all near-sighted spectators, was pushed up to within ten feet of my window-panes. Owing to the great height of the surrounding buildings, and my chambers being on the second floor, the interval between this wall and mine not a little resembled a huge square cistern.

At the period just preceding the advent of Bartleby, I had two persons as copyists in my employment, and a promising lad as an office-boy. First, Turkey; second, Nippers; third, Ginger Nut. These may seem names, the like of which are not usually found in the Directory. In truth, they were nicknames, mutually conferred upon each other by my three clerks, and were deemed expressive of their respective persons or characters. Turkey was a short, pursy Englishman, of about my own age—that is, somewhere not far from sixty. In the morning one might say, his face was of a fine florid hue, but after twelve o'clock, meridian—his dinner hour—it blazed like a grate full of Christmas coals; and continued blazing—but, as it were, with a gradual wane—till six o'clock, p.m., or thereabouts; after which, I saw no more of the proprietor of the face, which, gaining its meridian with the sun, seemed to set with it, to rise, culminate, and decline the following day, with the like regularity and undiminished glory. There are many singular coincidences I have known in the course of my life, not the least among which was the fact, that, exactly when Turkey displayed his fullest beams from his red and radiant countenance, just then, too, at that critical moment began the daily period when I considered his business capacities as seriously disturbed for the remainder of the twenty-four hours. Not that he was absolutely idle, or averse to business then; far from it. The difficulty was, he was apt to be altogether too energetic. There was a strange, inflamed, flurried, flighty recklessness of activity about him. He would be incautious in dipping his pen into his inkstand. All his blots upon my documents were dropped there after twelve o'clock, meridian. Indeed, not only would he be reckless, and sadly given to making blots in the afternoon, but, some days, he went further, and was rather noisy. At such times, too, his face flamed with augumented blazonry, as if cannel coal had been heaped on anthracite. He made an unpleasant racket with his chair; spilled his sand-box; in mending his pens, impatiently split them all to pieces, and threw them on the floor in a sudden passion; stood up, and leaned over his table, boxing his papers about in a most indecorous manner, very sad to behold in an elderly man like him. Nevertheless, as he was in many ways a most valuable person to me, and all the time before twelve o'clock, meridian, was the quickest, steadiest creature, too, accomplishing a great deal of work in a style not easily to be matched —for these reasons, I was willing to overlook his eccentricities, though, indeed, occasionally, I remonstrated with him. I did this very gently, however, because, though the civilest, nay, the blandest and most reverential of men in the morning, yet, in the afternoon, he was disposed, upon provocation, to be slightly rash with his tongue—in fact, insolent. Now, valuing his morning services as I did, and resolved not to lose them—yet, at the same time, made uncomfortable by his inflamed ways after twelve o'clock—and being a man of peace, unwilling by my admonitions to call forth unseemly retorts from him, I took upon me, one Saturday noon (he was always worse on Saturdays) to hint to him, very kindly, that, perhaps, now that he was growing old, it might be well to abridge his labors; in short, he need not come to my chambers after twelve o'clock, but, dinner over, had best go home to his lodgings, and rest himself till tea-time. But no; he insisted upon his afternoon devotions. His countenance became intolerably fervid, as he oratorically assured me—gesticulating with a long ruler at the other end of the room— that if his services in the morning were useful, how indispensable, then, in the afternoon?

"With submission, sir," said Turkey, on this occasion, "I consider myself your right-hand man. In the morning I but marshal and deploy my columns; but in the afternoon I put myself at their head, and gallantly charge the foe, thus"—and he made a violent thrust with the ruler.

"But the blots, Turkey," intimated I.

"True; but, with submission, sir, behold these hairs! I am getting old. Surely, sir, a blot or two of a warm afternoon is not to be severely urged against gray hairs. Old age—even if it blot the page—is honorable. With submission, sir, we both are getting old."

This appeal to my fellow-feeling was hardly to be resisted. At all events, I saw that go he would not. So, I made up my mind to let him stay, resolving, nevertheless, to see to it that, during the afternoon, he had to do with my less important papers.

Nippers, the second on my list, was a whiskered, sallow, and upon the whole, rather piratical-looking young man, of about five-and twenty. I always deemed him the victim of two evil powers—ambition and indigestion. The ambition was evinced by a certain impatience of the duties of a mere copyist, an unwarrantable usurpation of strictly professional affairs, such as the original drawing up of legal documents. The indigestion seemed betokened in an occasional nervous testiness and grinning irritability, causing the teeth to audibly grind together over mistakes committed in copying; unnecessary maledictions, hissed, rather than spoken, in the heat of business; and especially by a continual discontent with the height of the table where he worked. Though of a very ingenious mechanical turn, Nippers could never get this table to suit him. He put chips under it, blocks of various sorts, bits of pasteboard, and at last went so far as to attempt an exquisite adjustment, by final pieces of folded blotting-paper. But no invention would answer. If, for the sake of easing his back, he brought the table-lid at a sharp angle well up towards his chin, and wrote there like a man using the steep roof of a Dutch house for his desk, then he declared that it stopped the circulation in his arms. If now he lowered the table to his waist band, and stooped over it in writing, then there was a sore aching in his back. In short, the truth of the matter was, Nippers knew not what he wanted. Or, if he wanted anything, it was to be rid of a scrivener's table altogether. Among the manifestations of his diseased ambition was a fondness he had for receiving visits from certain ambiguous-looking fellows in seedy coats, whom he called his clients. Indeed, I was aware that not only was he, at times, considerable of a ward-politician, but he occasionally did a little business at the Justices' courts, and was not unknown on the steps of the Tombs. I have good reason to believe, however, that one individual who called upon him at my chambers, and who, with a grand sir, he insisted was his client, was no other than a dun, and the alleged title-deed, a bill.

But, with all his failings, and annoyances he caused me, Nippers, like his compatriot Turkey, was a very useful man to me; wrote a neat, swift hand; and, when he chose, was not deficient in a gentlemanly sort of deportment. Added to this, he always dressed in a gentlemanly sort of way; and so, incidentally, reflected credit upon my chambers. Whereas, with respect to Turkey, I had much ado to keep him from being a reproach to me. His clothes were apt to look oily, and smell of eating-houses. He wore his pantaloons very loose and baggy in summer. His coats were execrable; his hat not to be handled. But while the hat was a thing of indifference to me, inasmuch as his natural civility and deference, as a dependent Englishman, always led him to doff it the moment he entered the room, yet his coat was another matter. Concerning his coats, I reasoned with him; but no effect. The truth was, I suppose, that a man with so small an income could not afford to sport such a lustrous face and lustrous coat at one and the same time. As Nippers once observed, Turkey's money went chiefly for red ink. One winter day, I presented Turkey a highly respectable-looking coat of my own—a padded gray coat, of a most comfortable warmth, and which buttoned straight up from the knee to the neck. I thought Turkey would appreciate the favor, and abate his rashness and obstreperousness of afternoons. But no; I verily believe that buttoning himself up in so downy and blanket-like a coat had a pernicious effect upon him—upon the same principle that too much oats are bad for horses. In fact, precisely as a rash, restive horse is said to feel his oats, so Turkey felt his coat. It made him insolent. He was a man whom prosperity harmed.

Though, concerning the self-indulgent habits of Turkey, I had my own private surmises, yet touching Nippers, I was well persuaded that, whatever might be his faults in other respects, he was, at least, a temperate young man. But, indeed, nature herself seemed to have been his vintner, and, at his birth, charged him so thoroughly with an irritable, brandy-like disposition, that all subsequent potations were needless. When I consider how, amid the stillness of my chambers, Nipper would sometimes impatiently rise from his seat, and stooping over his table, spread his arms wide apart, seize the whole desk, and move it, and jerk it, with a grim, grinding motion on the floor, as if the table were a perverse voluntary agent, intent on thwarting and vexing him, I plainly perceive that, for Nippers, brandy-and-water were altogether superfluous.

It was fortunate for me that, owing to its peculiar cause—indigestion—the irritability and consequent nervousness of Nippers were mainly observable in the morning while in the afternoon he was comparatively mild. So that, Turkey's paroxysms only coming on about twelve o'clock, I never had to do with their eccentricities at one time. Their fits relieved each other, like guards. When Nipper's was on, Turkey's was off; and vice versa. This was a good natual arrangement, under the circumstances.

Ginger Nut, the third of my list, was a lad, some twelve years old. His father was a carman, ambitious of seeing his son on the bench instead of a cart, before he died. So he sent him to my office, as student at law, errand-boy, cleaner and sweeper, at the rate of one dollar a week. He had a little desk to himself, but he did not use it much. Upon inspection, the drawer exhibited a great array of the shells of various sorts of nuts. Indeed, to this quickwitted youth, the whole noble science of the law was contained in a nutshell. Not the least among the employments of Ginger Nut, as well as one which he discharged with the most alacrity, was his duty as cake and apple purveyor for Turkey and Nippers. Copying law-papers being proverbially a dry, husky sort of business, my two scriveners were fain to moisten their mouths very often with Spitzenbergs, to be had at the numerous stalls nigh the Custom House and Post Office. Also, they sent Ginger Nut very frequently for that peculiar cake—small, flat, round, and very spicy—after which he had been named by them. Of a cold morning, when business was but dull, Turkey would gobble up scores of these cakes, as if they were wafers—indeed, they sell them at the rate of six or eight for a penny—the scrape of his pen blending with the crunching of the crisp particles in his mouth. Of all the fiery afternoon blunders and flurried rashnesses of Turkey, was his moistening a gingercake between his lips, and clapping it on a mortgage, for a seal. I came within an ace of dismissing him then. But he mollified me by making an oriental bow, and saying—

"With submission, sir, it was generous of me to find you in stationery on my own account."

Now my original business—that of a conveyancer and title hunter, and drawer-up of recondite documents of all sorts—was considerably increased by receiving the Master's office. There was now great work for scriveners. Not only must I push the clerks already with me, but I must have additional help.

In answer to my advertisement, a motionless young man one morning stood upon my office threshold, the door being open, for it was summer. I can see that figure now—pallidly neat, pitiably respectable, incurably forlorn! It was Bartleby.

After a few words touching his qualifications, I engaged him, glad to have among my corps of copists a man of so singularly sedate an aspect, which I thought might operate beneficially upon the flighty temper of Turkey, and the fiery one of Nippers.

I should have stated before that groundglass folding-doors divided my premises into two parts, one of which was occupied by my scriveners, the other by myself. According to my humor, I threw open these doors, or closed them. I resolved to assign Bartleby a corner by the folding-doors, but on my side of them, so as to have this quiet man within easy call, in case any trifling thing was to be done. I placed his desk close up to a small side-window in that part of the room, a window which originally had afforded a lateral view of certain grimy backyards and bricks, but which, owing to subsequent erections, commanded at present no view at all, though it gave some light. Within three feet of the panes was a wall, and the light came down from far above, between two lofty buildings, as from a very small opening in a dome: Still farther to a satisfactory arrangement, I procured a high green folding screen, which might entirely isolate Bartleby from my sight, though not remove him from my voice. And thus, in a manner, privacy and society were conjoined.

At first, Bartleby did an extraordinary quantity of writing. As if long famishing for something to copy, he seemed to gorge himself on my documents. There was no pause for digestion. He ran a day and night line, copying by sunlight and by candlelight. I should have been quite delighted with his application, had he been cheerfully industrious. But wrote on silently palely, mechanically.

It is, of course, an indispensable part of a scrivener's business to verify the accuracy of his copy, word by word. Where there are two or more scriveners in an office, they assist each other in this examination, one reading from the copy, the other holding the original. It is a very dull, wearisome, and lethargic affair. I can readily imagine that, to some sanguine temperaments, it would be altogether intolerable. For example, I cannot credit that the mettlesome poet, Byron, would have contentedly sat down with Bartleby to examine a law document of, say five hundred pages, closely written in a crimpy hand.

Now and then, in the haste of business, it has been my habit to assist in comparing some brief documents myself, calling Turkey or Nipper for this purpose. One object I had, in placing Bartleby so handy to me behind the screen, was, to avail myself of his services on such trivial occasions. It was on the third day, I think, of his being with me, and before my necessity had arisen for having his own writing examined, that being much hurried to complete a small affair I had in hand, I abruptly called to Bartleby. In my haste and natural expectancy of instant compliance, I sat with my head bent over the original on my desk, and my right hand sideways, and somewhat nervously extended with the copy, so that, immediately upon emerging from his retreat, Bartleby might snatch it and proceed to business without the least delay.

In this very attitude did I sit when I called to him, rapidly stating what it was I wanted him to do—namely, to examine a small paper with me. Imagine my surprise, nay, my consternation, when, without moving from his privacy, Bartleby, in a singularly mild, firm voice, replied, "I would prefer not to."

I sat awhile in perfect silence, rallying my stunned facilities. Immediately it occurred to me that my ears had decieved me, or Bartleby had entirely misunderstood my meaning. I repeated my request in the clearest tone I could assume; but in quite as clear a one came the previous reply, "I would prefer not to."

"Prefer not to," echoed I, rising in high excitement, and crossing the room with a stride. 'What do you mean? Are you moonstruck" I want you to help me compare this sheet here—take it," and I thrust it toward him.

"I would prefer not to," said he.

I looked at him steadfastly. His face was leanly composed; his gray eye dimly calm. Not a wrinkle of agitation rippled him. Had there been the least uneasiness, anger, impatience or impertinence in his manner, in other words, had there been anything ordinarily human about him, doubtless I should have violently dismissed him from the premises. But as it was, I should have as soon thought of turning my pale plaster-of-paris bust of Cicero out of doors. I stood gazing at him awhile, as he went on with his own writing, and then reseated myself at my desk. This is very strange, thought I. What had one best do? But my business hurried me. I concluded to forget the matter for the present, reserving it for my future leisure. So, calling Nippers from the other room, the paper was speedily examined.

A few days after this, Bartleby concluded four lengthly documents, being quadruplicates of a week's testimony taken before me in my High Court of Chancery. It became necessary to examine them. It was an important suit, and great accuracy was imperative. Having all things arranged, I called Turkey, Nippers and Ginger Nut, from the next room, meaning to place the four copies in the hands of my four clerks, while I should read from the original. Accordingly, Turkey, Nippers, and Ginger Nut had taken their seats in a row, each with his document in his hand, when I called to Bartleby to join this interesting group.

"Bartleby! quick, I am waiting."

I heard a slow scrape of his chair legs on the uncarpeted floor, and soon he appeared standing at the entrance of his hermitage.

"What is wanted?" said he, mildly.

"The copies, the copies," said I, hurriedly. We are going to examine them. There"—and I held towards him the fourth quadruplicate.

"I would prefer not to," he said, and gently disappeared behind the screen.

For a few moments I was turned into a pillar of salt, standing at the head of my seated column of clerks. Recovering myself, I advanced towards the screen, and demanded the reason for such extraordinary conduct.

"Why do you refuse?"

"I would prefer not to."

With any other man I should have flown outright into a dreadful passion, scorned all further words, and thrust him ignominiously from my presence. But there was something about Bartleby that not only strangely disarmed me, but, in a wonderful manner, touched and disconcerted me. I began to reason with him.

"There are your own copies we are about to examine. It is labor saving to you, because one examination will answer for your four papers. It is common usage. Every copyist is bound to help examine his copy. Is it not so? Will you not speak? Answer!"

"I prefer not to," he replied in a flutelike tone. It seemed to me that, while I had been addressing him, he carefully revolved every statement that I made; fully comprehended the meaning; could not gainsay the irresistible conclusion; but, at the same time, some paramount consideration prevailed with him to reply as he did.

"You are decided, then, not to comply with my request—a request made according to common usage and common sense?"

He briefly gave me to understand, that on that point my judgment was sound. Yes: his decision was irreversible.

It is not seldom the case that, when a man is browbeaten in some unprecedented and violently unreasonable way, he begins to stagger in his own plainest faith. He begins, as it were, vaguely to surmise that, wonderful as it may be, all the justice and all the reason is on the other side. Accordingly, if any disinterested persons are present, he turns to them for some reinforcement for his own faltering mind.

"Turkey," said I, "what do you think of this? Am I not right?"

"With submission, sir," said Turkey, in his blandest tone, "I think that you are."

"Nippers," said I, "what do you think of it?"

"I think I should kick him out of the office."

(The reader of nice perceptions will here perceive that, it being morning, Turkey's answer is couched in polite and tranquil terms, but Nippers replies in ill-tempered ones. Or, to repeat a previous sentence, Nippers' ugly mood was on duty, and Turkey's off.)

"Ginger Nut," said I, willing to enlist the smallest suffrage in my behalf, "what do you think of it?"

"I think, sir, he's a little luny," replied Ginger Nut, with a grin.

"You hear what they say," said I, turning towards the screen, "come forth and do your duty."

But he vouchsafed no reply. I pondered a moment in sore perplexity. But once more business hurried me. I determined again to postpone the consideration of this dilemma to my future leisure. With a little trouble we made out to examine the papers without Bartleby, though at every page or two Turkey deferentially dropped his opinion, that this proceeding was quite out of the common; while Nippers, twitching in his chair with a dyspeptic nervousness, ground out, between his set teeth, occasional hissing maledictions against the stubborn oaf behind the screen. And for his (Nipper's) part, this was the first and the last time he would do another man's business without pay.

Meanwhile Bartleby sat is his hermitage, oblivious to everything but his own peculiar business there.

Some days passed, the scrivener being employed upon another lengthy work. His late remarkable conduct led me to regard his way narrowly. I observed that he never went to dinner; indeed, that he never went anywhere. As yet I had never, of my personal knowledge, known him to be outside of my office. He was a perpetual sentry in the corner. At about eleven o'clock though, in the morning, I noticed that Ginger Nut would advance toward the opening in Bartleby's screen, as if silently beckoned thither by a gesture invisible to me where I sat. The boy would then leave the office, jingling a few pence, and reappear with a handful of ginger-nuts, which he delivered in the hermitage, receiving two of the cakes for his trouble.

He lives, then, on ginger-nuts, thought I; never eats a dinner, properly speaking; he must be a vegetarian, then, but no; he never eats even vegetables, he eats nothing but ginger-nuts. My mind then ran on in reveries concerning the probable effects upon the human constitution of living entirely on ginger-nuts. Ginger-nuts are so called, because they contain ginger as one of their peculiar constituents, and the final flavoring one. Now, what was ginger? A hot, spicy thing. Was Bartleby hot and spicy? Not at all. Ginger, then, had no effect upon Bartleby. Probably he preferred it should have none.

Nothing so aggravates an earnest person as passive resistance. If the individual so resisted be of a not inhumane temper, and the resisting one perfectly harmless in his passivity, then, in the better moods of the former, he will endeavor charitably to construe to his imagination what proves impossible to be solved by his judgment. Even so, for the most part, I regarded Bartleby and his ways. Poor fellow! thought I, he means no mischief; it is plain he intends no insolence; his aspect sufficiently evinces that his eccentricities are involuntary. He is useful to me. I can get along with him. If I turn him away, the chances are he will fall in with some less indulgent employer, and then he will be rudely treated, and perhaps driven forth miserably to starve. Yes. Here I can cheaply purchase a delicious self-approval. To befriend Bartleby; to humor him in his strange wilfulness, will cost me little or nothing, while I lay up in my soul what will eventually prove a sweet morsel for my conscience. But this mood was not invariable with me. The passiveness of Bartleby sometimes irritated me. I felt strangely goaded on to encounter him in new opposition—to elicit some angry spark from him answerable to my own. But, indeed, I might as well have essayed to strike fire with my knuckles against a bit of Windsor soap. But one afternoon the evil impulse in me mastered me, and the following little scene ensued:

"Bartleby," said I, "when those papers are all copied, I will compare them with you."

"I would prefer not to."

"How? Surely you do not mean to persist in that mulish vagary?"

No answer.

I threw open the folding-doors near by, and, turning upon Turkey and Nippers, exclaimed:

"Bartleby a second time says, he won't examine his papers. What do you think of it, Turkey?"

It was afternoon, be it remembered. Turkey sat glowing like a brass boiler; his bald head steaming; his hands reeling among his blotted papers.

"Think of it?" roared Turkey. "I think I'll just step behind his screen, and black his eyes for him!"

So saying, Turkey rose to his feet and threw his arms into a pugilistic position. He was hurrying away to make good his promise, when I detained him, alarmed at the effect of incautiously arousing Turkey's combativeness after dinner.

"Sit down, Turkey," said I, "and hear what Nippers has to say. What do you think of it, Nippers? Would I not be justified in immediately dismissing Bartleby?"

"Excuse me, that is for you to decide, sir. I think his conduct quite unusual, and, indeed, unjust as regards Turkey and myself. But it may only be a passing whim."

"Ah," exclaimed I, "you have strangely changed your mind, then—you speak very gently of him now."

"All beer," cried Turkey, "gentleness is effects of beer—Nippers and I dined together to-day. You see how gentle I am, sir. Shall I go and black his eyes?"

"You refer to Bartleby, I suppose. No, not to-day, Turkey," I replied; "pray, put up your fists."

I closed the doors and again advanced towards Bartleby. I felt additional incentives tempting me to my fate. I burned to be rebelled against again. I remembered that Bartleby never left the office.

"Bartleby," said I, "Ginger Nut is away; just step around to the Post Office, won't you?" (it was but a three minutes' walk) "and see if there is anything for me."

"I would prefer not to."

"You will not?"

"I prefer not."

I staggered to my desk, and sat there in a deep study. My blind inveteracy returned. Was there any other thing in which I could procure myself to be ignominiously repulsed by this lean, penniless wight?—my hired clerk? What added thing is there, perfectly reasonable, that he will be sure to refuse to do?

"Bartleby!"

No answer.

"Bartleby," I roared.

Like a very ghost, agreeably to the laws of magical invocation, at the third summons, he appeared at the entrance of his hermitage.

"Go to the next room, and tell Nippers to come to me."

"I prefer not to," he respectfully and slowly said, and mildly disappeared.

"Very good, Bartleby," said I, in a quiet sort of serenely-severe self-possessed tone, intimating the unalterable purpose of some terrible retribution very close at hand. At the moment I half intended something of the kind. But upon the whole, as it was drawing towards my dinner-hour, I thought it best to put on my hat and walk home for the day, suffering much from perplexity and distress of mind.

Shall I acknowledge it? The conclusion of this whole business was, that it soon became a fixed fact of my chambers, that a pale young scrivener, by the name of Bartleby, had a desk there; that he copied for me at the usual rate of four cents a folio (one hundred words); but he was permanently exempt from examining the work done by him, that duty being transferred to Turkey and Nippers, out of compliment, doubtless, to their superior acuteness; moreover, said Bartleby was never, on any account, to be dispatched on the most trivial errand of any sort; and that even if entreated to take upon him such a matter, it was generally understood that he would "prefer not to"—in other words, that he would refuse point-blank.

As days passed on, I became considerably reconciled to Bartleby. His steadiness, his freedom from all dissipation, his incessant industry (except when he chose to throw himself into a standing revery behind his screen), his great stillness, his unalterableness of demeanor under all circumstances, made him a valuable acquisition. One prime thing was this—he was always there—first in the morning, continually through the day, and the last at night. I had a singular confidence in his honesty. I felt my most precious papers perfectly safe in his hands. Sometimes, to be sure, I could not, for the very soul of me, avoid falling into sudden spasmodic passions with him. For it was exceeding difficult to bear in mind all the time those strange peculiarities, privileges, and unheard-of exemptions, forming the tacit stipulations on Bartleby's part under which he remained in my office. Now and then, in the eagerness of dispatching pressing business, I would inadvertently summon Bartleby, in a short, rapid tone, to put his finger, say, on the incipent tie of a bit of red tape with which I was about compressing some papers. Of course, from behind the screen the usual answer, "I prefer not to ," was sure to come; and then, how could a human creature, with the common infirmities of our nature, refrain from bitterly exclaiming upon such perverseness—such unreasonableness? However, every added repulse of this sort which I received only tended to lessen the probability of my repeating the inadvertence.

Here it must be said, that, according to the custom of most legal gentlemen occupying chambers in densely-populated law buildings, there were several keys to my door. One was kept by a woman residing in the attic, which person weekly scrubbed and daily swept and dusted my apartments. Another was kept by Turkey for convenience sake. The third I sometimes carried in my own pocket. The fourth I knew not who had.

Now, one Sunday morning I happened to go to Trinity Church, to hear a celebrated preacher, and finding myself rather early on the ground I thought I would walk round to my chambers for a while. Luckily I had my key with me; but upon applying it to the lock, I found it resisted by something inserted from the inside. Quite surprised, I called out; when to my consternation a key was turned from within; and thrusting his lean visage at me, and holding the door ajar, the apparition of Bartleby appeared, in his shirt-sleeves, and otherwise in a strangely tattered deshabille, saying quietly that he was sorry, but he was deeply engaged just then, and—preferred not admitting me at present. In a brief word or two, he moreover added, that perhaps I had better walk round the block two or three times, and by that time he would probably have concluded his affairs.

Now, the utterly unsurmised appearance of Bartleby, tenanting my law-chambers of a Sunday morning, with his cadaverously gentlemanly nonchalance, yet withal firm and self-possessed, had such a strange effect upon me, that incontinently I slunk away from my own door, and did as desired. But not without sundry twinges of impotent rebellion against the mild effrontery of this unaccountable scrivener. Indeed, it was his wonderful mildness chiefly, which not only disarmed me, but unmanned me, as it were. For I considered that one, for the time, is a sort of unmanned when he tranquilly permits his hired clerk to dictate to him, and order him away from his own premises. Furthermore, I was full of uneasiness as in my office in his shirt-sleeves, and in an otherwise dismantled condition of a Sunday morning. Was anything amiss going on? Nay, that was out of the question. It was not to be thought of for a moment that Bartleby was an immoral person. But what could he be doing there?—copying? Nay again, whatever might be his eccentricities, Bartleby was an eminently decorous person. He would be the last man to sit down to his desk in any state approaching to nudity. Besides, it was Sunday; and there was something about Bartleby that forbade the supposition that he would by any secular occupation violate the proprieties of the day.

Nevertheless, my mind was not pacified; and full of a restless curiosity, at last I returned to the door. Without hindrance I inserted my key, opened it, and entered. Bartleby was not to be seen. I looked round anxiously, peeped behind his screen; but it was very plain that he was gone. Upon more closely examining the place, I surmised that for an indefinite period Bartleby must have ate, dressed, and slept in my office, and that too without plate, mirror, or bed. The cushioned seat of a rickety old sofa in one corner bore the faint impress of a lean reclining form. Rolled away under his desk, I found a blanket; under the empty grate, a blacking box and brush; on a chair, a tin basin, with soap and a ragged towel; in a newspaper a few crumbs of ginger-nuts and a morsel of cheese. Yes, thought I, it is evident enough that Bartleby has been making his home here, keeping bachelor's hall all by himself. Immediately then the thought came sweeping across me, what miserable friendlessness and loneliness are here revealed! His poverty is great; but his solitude, how horrible! Think of it. Of a Sunday, Wall Street is deserted as Petra; and every night of every day it is an emptiness. This building, too, which of week-days hums with industry and life, at nightfall echoes with sheer vacancy, and all through Sunday is forlorn. And here Bartleby makes his home; sole spectator of a solitude which he has seen all populous—a sort of innocent and transformed Marius brooding among the ruins of Carthage!

For the first time in my life a feeling of overpowering stinging melancholy seized me. Before, I had never experienced aught but a not unpleasing sadness. The bond of a common humanity now drew me irresistibly to gloom. A fraternal melancholy! For both I and Bartleby were sons of Adam. I remembered the bright silks and sparkling faces I had seen that day, in gala trim, swan-like sailing down the Mississippi of Broadway; and I contrasted them with the pallid copyist, and thought to myself, Ah, happiness courts the light, so we deem the world is gay; but misery hides aloof, so we deem that misery there is none. These sad fancyings—chimeras, doubtless, of a sick and silly brain—led on to other and more special thoughts, concerning the eccentricities of Bartleby. Presentiments of strange discoveries hovered round me. The scrivener's pale form appeared to me laid out, among uncaring strangers, in its shivering winding-sheet.

Suddenly I was attracted by Bartleby's closed desk, the key in open sight left in the lock.

I mean no mischief, seek the gratification of no heartless curiosity, thought I; besides, the desk is mine, and its contents, too, so I will make bold to look within. Everything was methodically arranged, the papers smoothly placed. The pigeon-holes were deep, and removing the files of documents, I groped into their recesses. Presently I felt something there, and dragged it out. It was an old bandanna handkerchief, heavy and knotted. I opened it, and saw it was a saving's bank.

I now recalled all the quiet mysteries which I had noted in the man. I remembered that he never spoke but to answer; that, though at intervals he had considerable time to himself, yet I had never seen him reading—no, not even a newspaper; that for long periods he would stand looking out, at his pale window behind the screen, upon the dead brick wall; I was quite sure he never visited any refectory or eating-house; while his pale face clearly indicated that he never drank beer like Turkey, or tea and coffee even, like other men; that he never went anywhere in particular that I could learn; never went out for a walk, unless, indeed, that was the case at present; that he had declined telling who he was, or whence he came, or whether he had any relatives in the world; that though so thin and pale, he never complained of ill-health. And more than all, I remembered a certain unconscious air of pallid—how shall I call it?—of pallid haughtiness, say, or rather an austere reserve about him, which had positively awed me into my tame compliance with his eccentricities, when I had feared to ask him to do the slightest incidental thing for me, even though I might know, from his long-continued motionlessness, that behind his screen he must be standing in one of those dead-wall reveries of his.

Revolving all these things, and coupling them with the recently discovered fact, that he made my office his constant abiding place and home, and not forgetful of his morbid moodiness; revolving all these things, a prudential feeling began to steal over me. My first emotions had been those of pure melancholy and sincerest pity; but just in proportion as the forlornness of Bartleby grew and grew to my imagination, did that same melancholy merge into fear, that pity into repulsion. So true it is, and so terrible, too, that up to a certain point the thought or sight of misery enlists our best affections; but, in certain special cases, beyond that point it does not. They err who would assert that invariably this is owing to the inherent selfishness of the human heart. It rather proceeds from a certain hopelessness of remedying excessive and organic ill. To a sensitive being, pity is not seldom pain. And when at last it is perceived that such pity cannot lead to effectual succor, common sense bids the soul be rid of it. What I saw that morning persuaded me that the scrivener was the victim of innate and incurable disorder. I might give alms to his body; but his body did not pain him; it was his soul that suffered, and his soul I could not reach.

I did not accomplish the purpose of going to Trinity Church that morning. Somehow, the things I had seen disqualified me for the time from church-going. I walked homeward, thinking what I would do with Bartleby. Finally, I resolved upon this—I would put certain calm questions to him the next morning, touching his history, etc., and if he declined to answer them openly and unreservedly (and I supposed he would prefer not), then to give him a twenty dollar bill over and above whatever I might owe him, and tell him his services were no longer required; but that if in any other way I could assist him, I would be happy to do so, especially if he desired to return to his native place, wherever that might be,

I would willingly help to defray the expenses. Moreover, if, after reaching home, he found himself at any time in want of aid, a letter from him would be sure of a reply.

The next morning came.

"Bartleby," said I, gently calling to him behind his screen.

No reply.

"Bartleby," said I, in a still gentler tone, "come here; I am not going to ask you to do anything you would prefer not to do—I simply wish to speak to you."

Upon this he noiselessly slid into view.

"Will you tell me, Bartleby, where you were born?"

"I would prefer not to."

"But what reasonable objection can you have to speak to me? I feel friendly towards you."

He did not look at me while I spoke, but kept his glance fixed upon my bust of Cicero, which, as I then sat, was directly behind me, some six inches above my head.

"What is your answer, Bartleby?" said I, after waiting a considerable time for a reply, during which his countenance remained immovable, only there was the faintest conceivable tremor of the white attenuated mouth.

"At present I prefer to give no answer," he said, and retired into his hermitage.

It was rather weak in me I confess, but his manner, on this occasion, nettled me. Not only did there seem to lurk in it a certain calm disdain, but his perverseness seemed ungrateful, considering the undeniable good usage and indulgence he had received from me.

Again I sat ruminating what I should do. Mortified as I was at his behavior, and resolved as I had been to dismiss him when I entered my office, nevertheless I strangely felt something superstitious knocking at my heart, and forbidding me to carry out my purpose, and denouncing me for a villain if I dared to breathe one bitter word against this forlornest of mankind. At last, familiarly drawing my chair behind his screen, I sat down and said: "Bartleby, never mind, then, about revealing your history; but let me entreat you, as a friend, to comply as far as may be with the usages of this office. Say now, you will help to examine papers tomorrow or next day: in short, say now, that in a day or two you will begin to be a little reasonable:—say so, Bartleby."

"At present I would prefer not to be a little reasonable," was his mildly cadaverous reply.

Just then the folding-doors opened, and Nippers approached. He seemed suffering from an unusually bad night's rest, induced by severer indigestion than common. He overheard those final words of Bartleby.

"Prefer not, eh?" gritted Nippers—"I'd prefer him, if I were you sir," addressing me— "I'd prefer him; I'd give him preferences, the stubborn mule! What is it, sir, pray, that he prefers not to do now?"

Bartleby moved not a limb.

"Mr. Nippers," said I, "I'd prefer that you would withdraw for the present."

Somehow, of late, I had got into the way of involuntarily using this word "prefer" upon all sorts of not exactly suitable occasions. And I trembled to think that my contact with the scrivener had already and seriously affected me in a mental way. And what further and deeper aberration might it not yet produce? This apprehension had not been without efficacy in determining me to summary measures.

As Nippers, looking very sour and sulky, was departing, Turkey blandly and deferentially approached.

"With submission, sir," said he, "yesterday I was thinking about Bartleby here, and I think that if he would but prefer to take a quart of good ale every day, it would do much towards mending him, and enabling him to assist in examining his papers."

"So you have got the word, too," said I, slightly excited.

"With submission, what word, sir?" asked Turkey, respectfully crowding himself into the contracted space behind the screen, and by so doing, making me jostle the scrivener. "What word, sir?"

"I would prefer to be left alone here," said Bartleby, as if offended at being mobbed in his privacy.

"That's the word, Turkey," said I—"thats it."

"Oh, prefer? oh yes—queer word. I never use it myself. But, sir, as I was saying, if he would but prefer—"

"Turkey," interrupted I, "you will please withdraw."

"Oh certainly, sir, if you prefer that I should."

As he opened the folding-door to retire, Nippers at his desk caught a glimpse of me, and asked whether I would prefer to have a certain paper copied on blue paper or white. He did not in the least roguishly accent the word "prefer." It was plain that it involuntarily rolled from his tongue. I thought to myself, surely I must get rid of a demented man, who already has in some degree turned the tongues, if not the heads of myself and clerks. But I thought it prudent not to break the dismission at once.

The next day I noticed that Bartleby did nothing but stand at his window in his dead-wall revery. Upon asking him why he did not write, he said that he had decided upon doing no more writing.

"Why, how now? what next?" exclaimed I, "do no more writing?"

"No more."

"And what is the reason?"

"Do you not see the reason for yourself?" he indifferently replied.

I looked steadfastly at him, and perceived that his eyes looked dull and glazed. Instantly it occurred to me, that his unexampled diligence in copying by his dim window for the first weeks of his stay with me might have temporarily impaired his vision.

I was touched. I said something in condolence with him. I hinted that of course he did wisely in abstaining from writing for a while; and urged him to embrace that opportunity of taking wholesome exercise in the open air. This, however, he did not do. A few days after this, my other clerks being absent, and being in a great hurry to dispatch certain letters by the mail, I thought that, having nothing else earthly to do, Bartleby would surely be less inflexible than usual, and carry these letters to the post office. But he blankly declined. So, much to my inconvenience, I went myself.

Still added days went by. Whether Bartleby's eyes improved or not, I could not say. To all appearance, I thought they did. But when I asked him if they did, he vouchsafed no answer. At all events, he would do no copying. At last, in reply to my urgings, he informed me that he had permanently given up copying.

"What!" exclaimed I; "suppose your eyes should get entirely well—better than ever before—would you not copy then?"

"I have given up copying," he answered, and slid aside.

He remained as ever, a fixture in my chamber. Nay—if that were possible—he became still more of a fixture than before. What was to be done? He would do nothing in the office; why should he stay there? In plain fact, he had now become a millstone to me, not only useless as a necklace, but afflictive to bear. Yet I was sorry for him. I speak less than truth when I say that, on his own account, he occasioned me uneasiness. If he would but have named a single relative or friend, I would instantly have written, and urged their taking the poor fellow away to some convenient retreat. But he seemed alone, absolutely alone in the universe. A bit of wreck in the mid-Atlantic. At length, necessities connected with my business tyrannized over all other considerations. Decently as I could, I told Bartleby that in six days' time he must unconditionally leave the office. I warned him to take measures, in the interval, for procuring some other abode. I offered to assist him in this endeavor, if he himself would but take the first step towards a removal. "And when you finally quit me, Bartleby," added I, "I shall see that you go not away entirely unprovided. Six days from this hour, remember."

At the expiration of that period, I peeped behind the screen, and lo! Bartleby was there.

I buttoned up my coat, balanced myself, advanced slowly towards him, touched his shoulder, and said, "The time has come; you must quit this place; I am sorry for you; here is money; but you must go."

"I would prefer not," he replied, with his back towards me.

"You must."

He remained silent.

Now I had an unbounded confidence in this man's common honesty. He had frequently restored to me sixpences and shillings carelessly dropped upon the floor, for I am apt to be very reckless in such shirtbutton affairs. The proceeding, then, which followed will not be deemed extraordinary.

"Bartleby," said I, "I owe you twelve dollars on account; here are thirty-two; the odd twenty are yours—Will you take it?" and I handed the bills towards him.

But he made no motion.

"I will leave them here, then," putting them under a weight on the table. Then taking my hat and cane and going to the door, I tranquilly turned and added—"After you have removed your things from these offices, Bartleby, you will of course lock the door—since every one is now gone for the day but you—and if you please, slip your key underneath the mat, so that I may have it in the morning. I shall not see you again; so good-bye to you. If, hereafter, in your new place of abode, I can be of any service to you, do not fail to advise me by letter. Good-bye, Bartleby, and fare you well."

But he answered not a word; like the last column of some ruined temple, he remained standing mute and solitary in the middle of the otherwise deserted room.

As I walked home in a pensive mood, my vanity got the better of my pity. I could not but highly plume myself on my masterly management in getting rid of Bartleby. Masterly I call it, and such it must appear to any dispassionate thinker. The beauty of my procedure seemed to consist in its perfect quietness. There was no vulgar bullying, no bravado of any sort, no choleric hectoring, and striding to and fro across the apartment, jerking out vehement commands for Bartleby to bundle himself off with his beggarly traps. Nothing of the kind. Without loudly bidding Bartleby depart—as an inferior genius might have done—I assumed the ground that depart he must; and upon that assumption built all I had to say. The more I thought over my procedure, the more I was charmed with it. Nevertheless, next morning, upon awakening, I had my doubts—I had somehow slept off the fumes of vanity. One of the coolest and wisest hours a man has, is just after he awakes in the morning. My procedure seemed as sagacious as ever—but only in theory. How it would prove in practice—there was the rub. It was truly a beautiful thought to have assumed Bartleby's departure; but, after all, that assumption was simply my own, and none of Bartleby's. The great point was, not whether I had assumed that he would quit me, but whether he would prefer so to do. He was more a man of preferences than assumptions.

After breakfast, I walked down town, arguing the probabilities pro and con. One moment I thought it would prove a miserable failure, and Bartleby would be found all alive at my office as usual; the next moment it seemed certain that I should find his chair empty. And so I kept veering about. At the corner of Broadway and Canal Street, I saw quite an excited group of people standing in earnest conversation.

"I'll take odds he doesn't," said a voice as I passed.

"Doesn't go?—done!" said I, "put up your money."

I was instinctively putting my hand in my pocket to produce my own, when I remembered that this was an election day. The words I had overheard bore no reference to Bartleby, but to the success or non-success of some candidate for the mayoralty. In my intent frame of mind, I had, as it were, imagined that all Broadway shared in my excitement, and were debating the same question with me. I passed on, very thankful that the uproar of the street screened my momentary absent-mindedness.

As I had intended, I was earlier than usual at my office door. I stood listening for a moment. All was still. He must be gone. I tried the knob. The door was locked. Yes, my procedure had worked to a charm; he indeed must be vanished. Yet a certain melancholy mixed with this: I was almost sorry for my brilliant success. I was fumbling under the door mat for the key, which Bartleby was to have left there for me, when accidentally my knee knocked against a panel, producing a summoning sound, and in response a voice came to me from within—"Not yet; I am occupied."

It was Bartleby.

I was thunderstruck. For an instant I stood like the man who, pipe in mouth, was killed one cloudless afternoon long ago in Virginia, by summer lightning; at his own warm open window he was killed, and remained leaning out there upon the dreamy afternoon, till some one touched him, when he fell.

"Not gone!" I murmured at last. But again obeying that wondrous ascendancy which the inscrutable scrivener had over me, and from which ascendancy, for all my chafing, I could not completely escape, I slowly went down stairs and out into the street, and while walking round the block, considered what I should next do in this unheard-of perplexity. Turn the man out by an actual thrusting I could not; to drive him away by calling him hard names would not do; calling in the police was an unpleasant idea; and yet, permit him to enjoy his cadaverous triumph over me—this, too, I could not think of. What was to be done? or, if nothing could be done, was there anything further that I could assume in the matter? Yes, as before I had prospectively assumed that Bartleby would depart, so now I might retrospectively assume that departed he was. In the legitimate carrying out of this assumption, I might enter my office in a great hurry, and pretending not to see Bartleby at all, walk straight against him as if he were air. Such a proceeding would in a singular degree have the appearance of a home-thrust. It was hardly possible that Bartleby could withstand such an application of the doctrine of assumptions. But upon second thoughts the success of the plan seemed rather dubious. I resolved to argue the matter over with him again.

"Bartleby," said I, entering the office, with a quietly severe expression, "I am seriously displeased. I am pained, Bartleby. I had thought better of you. I had imagined you of such a gentlemanly organization, that in any delicate dilemma a slight hint would suffice—in short, an assumption. But it appears I am deceived. Why," I added, unaffectedly starting, "you have not even touched that money yet," pointing to it, just where I had left it the evening previous.

He answered nothing.

"Will you, or will you not, quit me?" I now demanded in a sudden passion, advancing close to him.

"I would prefer not to quit you," he replied, gently emphasizing the not.

"What earthly right have you to stay here? Do you pay any rent? Do you pay my taxes? Or is this property yours?"

He answered nothing.

"Are you ready to go on and write now? Are your eyes recovered? Could you copy a small paper for me this morning? or help examine a few lines? or step round to the post-office? In a word, will you do anything at all, to give a coloring to your refusal to depart the premises?"

He silently retired into his hermitage.

I was now in such a state of nervous resentment that I thought it but prudent to check myself at present from further demonstrations. Bartleby and I were alone. I remembered the tragedy of the unfortunate Adams and the still more unfortunate Colt in the solitary office of the latter; and how poor Colt, being dreadfully incensed by Adams, and imprudently permitting himself to get wildly excited, was at unawares hurried into his fatal act—an act which certainly no man could possibly deplore more than the actor himself. Often it had occurred to me in my ponderings upon the subject that had that altercation taken place in the public street, or at a private residence, it would not have terminated as it did. It was the circumstance of being alone in a solitary office, upstairs, of a building entirely unhallowed by humanizing domestic associations—an uncarpeted office, doubtless, of a dusty, haggard sort of appearance—that it must have been, which greatly helped to enhance the irritable desperation of the hapless Colt.

But when this old Adam of resentment rose in me and tempted me concerning Bartleby, I grappled him and threw him. How? Why, simply by recalling the divine injunction: "A new commandment give I unto you, that ye love one another." Yes, this it was that saved me. Aside from higher considerations, charity often operates as a vastly wise and prudent principle—a great safeguard to its possessor. Men have committed murder for jealousy's sake, and anger's sake, and hatred's sake, and selfishness' sake, and spiritual pride's sake; but no man, that ever I heard of, ever committed a diabolical murder for sweet charity's sake. Mere self-interest, then, if no better motive can be enlisted, should, especially with high-tempered men, prompt all beings to charity and philanthropy. At any rate, upon the occasion in question, I strove to drown my exasperated feelings towards the scrivener by benevolent construing his conduct. Poor fellow, poor fellow! thought I, he don't mean anything; and besides, he has seen hard times, and ought to be indulged.

I endeavored, also, immediately to occupy myself, and at the same time to comfort my despondency. I tried to fancy, that in the course of the morning, at such time as might prove agreeable to him, Bartleby, of his own free accord, would emerge from his hermitage and take up some decided line of march in the direction of the door. But no. Half-past twelve o'clock came; Turkey began to glow in the face, overturn his inkstand, and became generally obstreperous:

Nippers abated down into quietude and courtesy; Ginger Nut munched his noon apple; and Bartleby remained standing at his window in one of his profoundest dead-wall reveries. Will it be credited? Ought I to acknowledge it? That afternoon I left the office without saying one further word to him.

Some days now passed, during which, at leisure intervals I looked a little into "Edwards on the Will," and "Priestly on Necessity." Under the circumstances, those books induced a salutary feeling. Gradually I slid into the persuasion that these troubles of mine, touching the scrivener, had been all predestinated from eternity, and Bartleby was billeted upon me for some mysterious purpose of an all-wise Providence, which it was not for a mere mortal like me to fathom. Yes, Bartleby, stay there behind your screen, thought I; I shall persecute you no more; you are harmless and noiseless as any of these old chairs; in short, I never feel so private as when I know you are here. At last I see it, I feel it; I penetrate to the predestinated purpose of my life. I am content. Others may have loftier parts to enact; but my mission in this world, Bartleby, is to furnish you with office-room for such period as you may see fit to remain.

I believe that this wise and blessed frame of mind would have continued with me, had it not been for the unsolicited and uncharitable remarks obtruded upon me by my professional friends who visited the rooms. But thus it often is, that the constant friction of illiberal minds wears out at least the best resolves of the more generous. Though to be sure, when I reflected upon it, it was not strange that people entering my office should be struck by the peculiar aspect of the unaccountable Bartleby, and so be tempted to throw out some sinister observations concerning him. Sometimes an attorney, having business with me, and calling at my office, and finding no one but the scrivener there, would undertake to obtain some sort of precise information from him touching my whereabouts; but without heeding his idle talk, Bartleby would remain standing immovable in the middle of the room. So after contemplating him in that position for a time, the attorney would depart, no wiser than he came.

Also, when a reference was going on, and the room full of lawyers and witnesses, and business driving fast, some deeply-occupied legal gentleman present, seeing Bartleby wholly unemployed, would request him to run round to his (the legal gentleman's) office and fetch some papers for him. Thereupon, Bartleby would tranquilly decline, and yet remain idle as before. Then the lawyer would give a great stare, and turn to me. And what could I say? At last I was made aware that all through the circle of my professional acquaintance, a whisper of wonder was running round, having reference to the strange creature I kept at my office. This worried me very much. And as the idea came upon me of his possibly turning out a long-lived man, and keep occupying my chambers, and denying my authority; and perplexing my visitors; and scandalizing my professional reputation; and casting a general gloom over the premises; keeping soul and body together to the last upon his savings (for doubtless he spent but half a dime a day), and in the end perhaps outlive me, and claim possession of my office by right of his perpetual occupancy: as all these dark anticipations crowded upon me more and more, and my friends continually intruded their relentless remarks upon the apparition in my room; a great change was wrought in me. I resolved to gather all my faculties together, and forever rid me of this intolerable incubus.

Ere revolving any complicated project, however, adapted to this end, I first simply suggested to Bartleby the propriety of his permanent departure. In a calm and serious tone, I commended the idea to his careful and mature consideration. But, having taken three days to meditate upon it, he apprised me, that his original determination remained the same; in short that he still preferred to abide with me.

What shall I do? I now said to myself, buttoning up my coat to the last button. What shall I do? what ought I to do? what does conscience say I should do with this man, or, rather, ghost. Rid myself of him, I must; go, he shall. But how? You will not thrust him, the poor, pale, passive mortal—you will not thrust such a helpless creature out of your door? you will not dishonor yourself such cruelty? No, I will not, I cannot do that. Rather would I let him live and die here, and then mason up his remains in the wall. What, then, will you do? For all your coaxing, he will not budge. Bribes he leaves under your own paperweight on your table; in short, it is quite plain that he prefers to cling to you.

Then something severe, something unusual must be done. What! surely you will not have him collared by a constable, and commit his innocent pallor to the common jail? And upon what ground could you procure such a thing to be done?—a vagrant, is he? What! he a vagrant, a wanderer, who refuses to budge? It is because he will not be a vagrant, then, that you seek to count him as a vagrant. That is too absurd. No visible means of support: that I have him. Wrong again: for indubitably he does support himself, and that is the only unanswerable proof that any man can show of his possessing the means so to do. No more, then. Since he will not quit me, I must quit him. I will change my offices; I will move elsewhere, and give him fair notice, that if I find him on my new premises I will then proceed against him as a common trespasser.

Acting accordingly, next day I thus addressed him: "I find these chambers too far from the City Hall, the air is unwholesome. In a word, I propose to remove my offices next week, and shall no longer require your services. I tell you this now, in order that you may seek another place."

He made no reply, and nothing more was said.

On the appointed day I engaged carts and men ,proceeded to my chambers, and, having but little furniture, everything was removed in a few hours. Throughout, the scrivener remained standing behind the screen, which I directed to be removed the last thing. It was withdrawn; and, being folded up like a huge folio, left him the motionless occupant of a naked room. I stood in the entry watching him a moment, while something from within me upbraided me.

I re-entered, with my hand in my pocket—and—and my heart in my mouth.

"Good-bye, Bartleby; I am going—good-bye, and God some way bless you; and take that," slipping something in his hand. But it dropped upon the floor, and then—strange to say—I tore myself from him whom I had so longed to be rid of.

Established in my new quarters, for a day or two I kept the door locked, and started at every footfall in the passage. When I returned to my rooms, after any little absence, I would pause at the threshold for an instant, and attentively listen, ere applying my key. But these fears were needless. Bartleby never came nigh me.

I thought all was going well, when a perturbed-looking stranger visited me, inquiring whether I was the person who had recently occupied rooms at No. — Wall Street.

Full of forebodings, I replied that I was.

"Then sir," said the stranger, who proved a lawyer, "you are responsible for the man you left there. He refuses to do any copying; he refuses to do anything; he says he prefers not to; and he refuses to quit the premises."

"I am very sorry, sir," said I, with assumed tranquillity, but an inward tremor, "but, really, the man you allude to is nothing to me—he is no relation or apprentice of mine, that you should hold me responsible for him."

"In mercy's name, who is he?"

"I certainly cannot inform you. I know nothing about him. Formerly I employed him as a copyist; but he has done nothing for me now for some time past."

"I shall settle him, then—good morning, sir."

Several days passed, and I heard nothing more; and though I often felt a charitable prompting to call at the place and see poor

Bartleby, yet a certain squeamishness, of I know not what, withheld me.

All is over with him, by this time thought I, at last, when, through another week, no further intelligence reached me. But, coming to my room the day after, I found several persons waiting at my door in a high state of nervous excitement.

"That's the man—here he comes," cried the foremost one, whom I recognized as the lawyer who had previously called upon me alone.

"You must take him away, sir, at once," cried a portly person among them, advancing upon me, and whom I knew to be the landlord of No. — Wall Street. "These gentlemen, my tenants, cannot stand it any longer; Mr. B———," pointing to the lawyer, "has turned him out of his room, and he now persists in haunting the building generally, sitting upon the banisters of the stairs by day, and sleeping in the entry by night. Everybody is concerned; clients are leaving the offices; some fears are entertained of a mob; something you must do, and that without delay."

Aghast at this torrent, I fell back before it, and would fain have locked myself in my new quarters. In vain I persisted that Bartleby was nothing to me—no more than to any one else. In vain—I was the last person known to have anything to do with him, and they held me to the terrible account. Fearful, then, of being exposed in the papers (as one person present obscurely threatened), I considered the matter, and, at length, said, that if the lawyer would give me a confidential interview with the scrivener, in his (the lawyer's own room, I would, that afternoon, strive my best to rid them of the nuisance they complained of.

Going up stairs to my old haunt, there was Bartleby silently sitting upon the bannister at the landing.

"What are you doing here, Bartleby?" said I.

"Sitting upon the banister," he mildly replied.

I motioned him into the lawyer's room, who then left us.

"Bartleby," said I, "are you aware that you are the cause of great tribulation to me, by persisting in occupying the entry after being dismissed from the office?"

No answer.

"Now one of two things must take place. Either you must do something, or something must be done to you. Now what sort of business would you like to engage in? Would you like to re-engage in copying for some one?"

"Would you like a clerkship in a drygoods store?"

"There is too much confinement about that. No, I would not like a clerkship; but I am not particular."

"Too much confinement," I cried, "why, you keep yourself confined all the time!"

"I would prefer not to take a clerkship," he rejoined, as if to settle that little item at once.

"How would a bar-tender's business suit you? There is no trying of the eyesight in that."

"I would not like it at all; though, as I said before, I am not particular."

His unwonted wordiness inspirited me. I returned to the charge.

"Well, then, would you like to travel through the country collecting bills for the merchants? That would improve your health."

"No, I would prefer to be doing something else."

"How, then, would going as a companion to Europe, to entertain some young gentleman with your conversation—how would that suit you?"

"Not at all. It does not strike me that there is anything definite about that. I like to be stationary. But I am not particular."

"Stationary you shall be, then," I cried, now losing all patience, and, for the first time in all my exasperating connection with him, fairly flying into a passion. "If you do not go away from these premises before night, I shall feel bound—indeed, I am bound—to—to—to quit the premises myself!" I rather absurdly concluded, knowing not with what possible threat to try to frighten his immobility into compliance. Despairing of all further efforts, I was precipitately leaving him, when a final thought occurred to me—one which had not been wholly unindulged before.

"Bartleby," said I, in the kindest tone I could assume under such exciting circumstances, "will you go home with me now—not to my office, but my dwelling— and remain there till we can conclude upon some convenient arrangement for you at our leisure? Come, let us start now, right away."

"No: at present I would prefer not to make any change at all."

I answered nothing; but, effectually dodging every one by the suddenness and rapidity of my flight, rushed from the building jumping into the first omnibus, was soon removed from pursuit. As soon as tranquility returned, I distinctly perceived that I had now done all that I possibly could, both in respect to the demands of the landlord and his tenants, and with regard to my own desire and sense of duty, to benefit Bartleby, and shield him from rude persecution. I now strove to be entirely care-free and quiescent; and my conscience justified me in the attempt; though, indeed, it was not so successful as I could have wished. So fearful was I of being again hunted out by the incensed landlord and his exasperated tenants, that, surrendering my business to Nippers, for a few days, I drove about the upper part of the town and through the suburbs, in my rockaway; crossed over to Jersey City and Hoboken, and paid fugitive visits to Manhattenville and Astoria. In fact, I almost lived in my rockaway for the time.

When again I entered my office, lo, a note from the landlord lay upon the desk. I opened it with trembling hands. It informed me that the writer had sent to the police, and had Bartleby removed to the Tombs as a vagrant. Moreover, since I knew more about him than any one else, he wished me to appear at that place, and make a suitable statement of the facts. These tidings had a conflicting effect upon me. At first I was indignant; but, at last, almost approved. The landlord's energetic, summary disposition, had led him to adopt a procedure which I do not think I would have decided upon myself; and yet, as a last resort, under such peculiar circumstances, it seemed the only plan.

As I afterwards learned, the poor scrivener, when told that he must be conducted to the Tombs, offered not the slightest obstacle, but, in his pale, unmoving way, silently acquiesced.

Some of the compassionate and curious by-standers joined the party; and headed by one of the constables arm-in-arm with Bartleby, the silent procession filed its way through all the noise, and heat, and joy of the roaring thoroughfares at noon.

The same day I received the note, I went to the Tombs, or, to speak more properly, the Halls of Justice. Seeking the right officer, I stated the purpose of my call, and was informed that the individual I described was, indeed, within. I then assured the functionary that Bartleby was a perfectly honest man, and greatly to be compassionated, however, unaccountably eccentric. I narrated all I knew, and closed by suggesting the idea of letting him remain in as indulgent confinement as possible, till something less harsh might be done—though, indeed, I hardly knew what. At all events, if nothing else could be decided upon, the alms-house must receive him. I then begged to have an interview.

Being under no disgraceful charge, and quite serene and harmless in all his ways, they had permitted him freely to wander about the prison, and, especially, in the inclosed grass-platted yards thereof. And so I found him there, standing all alone in the quietest of the yards, his face towards a high wall, while all around, from the narrow slits of the jail windows, I thought I saw peering out upon him the eyes of murderers and thieves.

"Bartleby!"

"I know you," he said, without looking around—"and I want nothing to say to you."

"It was not I that brought you here, Bartleby," said I, keenly pained at his implied suspicion. "And to you, this should be so vile a place. Nothing reproachful attaches to you by being here. And see, it is not so sad a place as one might think. Look, there is the sky, and here is the grass."

"I know where I am," he replied, but would say nothing more, and so I left him.

As I entered the corridor again, a broad meat-like man, in an apron, accosted me, and, jerking his thumb over his shoulder, said—"Is that your friend?"

"Yes."

"Does he want to starve? If he does, let him live on the prison fare, that's all."

"Who are you?" said I, not knowing what to make of such an unofficially speaking person in such a place.

"I am the grub-man. Such gentlemen as have friends here, hire me to provide them with something good to eat."

"Is this so?" said I, turning to the turnkey.

He said it was.

"Well, then," said I, slipping some silver into the grub-man's hands (for so they called him), "I want you to give particular attention to my friend there; let him have the best dinner you can get. And you must be as polite to him as possible."

"Introduce me, will you?" said the grub-man, looking at me with an expression which seemed to say he was all impatience for an opportunity to give a specimen of his breeding.

Thinking it would prove of benefit to the scrivener, I acquiesced; and, asking the grub-man his name, went up with him to Bartleby.

"Bartleby, this is a friend; you will find him very useful to you."

"Your servant, sir, your servant," said the grub-man, making a low salutation behind his apron. "Hope you find it pleasant here, sir; nice grounds—cool apartments—hope you'll stay with us some time—try to make it agreeable. What will you have for dinner to-day?"

"I prefer not to dine to-day," said Bartleby, turning away. "It would disagree with me; I am unused to dinners." So saying, he slowly moved to the other side of the inclosure, and took up a position fronting the dead-wall.

"How's this?" said the grub-man, addressing me with a stare of astonishment. "He's odd, ain't he?"

"I think he is a little deranged," said I, sadly.

"Deranged? deranged is it? Well, now, upon my word, I thought that friend of yourn was a gentleman forger; they are always pale and genteel-like, them forgers. I can't help pity 'em—can't help it, sir. Did you know Monroe Edwards?" he added, touchingly, and paused. Then, laying his hand piteously on my shoulder, sighed, "he died of consumption at Sing-Sing. So you weren't acquainted with Monroe?"

"No, I was never socially acquainted with any forgers. But I cannot stop longer. Look to my friend yonder. You will not lose by it. I will see you again."

Some few days after this, I again obtained admission to the Tombs, and went through the corridors in quest of Bartleby; but without finding him.

"I saw him coming from his cell not long ago," said a turnkey, "may be he's gone to loiter in the yards."

So I went in that direction.

"Are you looking for the silent man?" said another turnkey, passing me. "Yonder he lies—sleeping in the yard there. 'Tis not twenty minutes since I saw him lie down."

The yard was entirely quiet. It was not accessible to the common prisoners. The surrounding walls, of amazing thickness, kept off all sounds behind them. The Egyptian character of the masonry weighed upon me with its gloom. But a soft imprisoned turf grew under foot. The heart of the eternal pyramids, it seemed, wherein, by some strange magic, through the clefts, grass-seed, dropped by birds, had sprung.

Strangely huddled at the base of the wall, his knees drawn up, and lying on his side, his head touching the cold stones, I saw the wasted Bartleby. But nothing stirred. I paused; then went close up to him; stooped over, and saw that his dim eyes were open; otherwise he seemed profoundly sleeping. Something prompted me to touch him. I felt his hand, when a tingling shiver ran up my arm and down my spine to my feet.

The round face of the grub-man peered upon me now. "His dinner is ready. Won't he dine to-day, either? Or does he live without dining?"

"Lives without dining," said I, and closed the eyes.

"Eh!—He's asleep, ain't he?"

"With kings and counselors," murmured I.

* * *

There would seem little need for proceeding further in this history. Imagination will readily supply the meagre recital of poor Bartleby's interment. But, ere parting with the reader, let me say, that if this little narrative has sufficiently interested him, to awaken curiosity as to who Bartleby was, and what manner of life he led prior to the present narrator's making his acquaintance, I can only reply, that in such curiosity I fully share, but am wholly unable to gratify it. Yet here I hardly know whether I should divulge one little item of rumor, which came to my ear a few months after the scrivener's decease. Upon what basis it rested, I could never ascertain; and hence, how true it is I cannot now tell. But, inasmuch as this vague report has not been without a certain suggestive interest to me, however sad, it may prove the same with some others; and so I will briefly mention it. The report was this: that Bartleby had been a subordinate clerk in the Dead Letter Office at Washington, from which he had been suddenly removed by a change in the administration. When I think over this rumor, hardly can I express the emotions which seize me. Dead letters! does it not sound like dead men? Conceive a man by nature and misfortune prone to a pallid hopelessness, can any business seem more fitted to heighten it than that of continually handling these dead letters, and assorting them for the flames? For by the cart-load they are annually burned. Sometimes from out the folded paper the pale clerk takes a ring—the finger it was meant for, perhaps, moulders in the grave; a bank-note sent in swiftest charity—he whom it would relieve, nor eats nor hungers any more; pardon for those who died despairing; hope for those who died unhoping; good tidings for those who died stifled by unrelieved calamities. On errands of life, these letters speed to death.

Ah, Bartleby! Ah, humanity!

Discussion of "Bartleby, the Scrivener"

His father's bankruptcy compelled Herman Melville (1819-1891) to begin work at the age of fifteen. After a few years of clerking and farming, he sailed as a cabin-boy to England in 1837. From then until 1844 he spent most of his time at sea, first on a whaler and later in the U.S. navy. His sailing days ended, Melville won moderate success as a writer with half-fanciful accounts of his voyages in novels such as *Typee* (1846) and *White-Jacket* (1850).

Dissatisfied with the income he was receiving from his works and unwilling to write the kind of work that would sell, he retired to his uncle's farm in Massachusetts and wrote his masterpiece, *Moby Dick*. The difficult symbolism of this book alienated many readers, and when Melville followed this novel with others even more opaque, he lost his audience entirely. In 1866 he accepted a post in the New York Customs House where he remained until shortly before his death.

"Bartleby the Scrivener" was written in 1853 and collected in *The Piazza Tales* in 1856. Although one of Melville's triumphs in the field of short fiction, the tale is a highly ambiguous one. Bartleby the copyist who will neither work nor leave has been interpreted as Melville's comment upon his contemporary Henry David Thoreau, and he has also been taken to be a symbolic representation of Melville himself, misunderstood by his employer (or his readers) and rejected by the world at large. In either case Bartleby's excessive individualism seems to be both negative and futile. Yet the stubborn scrivener remains a human being who cannot be callously ignored. As the narrator of the story observes, both he and Bartleby are sons of Adam, and this basic and universal bond cannot be dissolved.

Few readers feel that they ever really understand Bartleby, but most of us find ourselves identified with his employer to some extent. Here is a man who is both practical and amiable. Through the use of first person narration we get a sense of the lawyer's education, his humor, his prudence and his morality.

Another kind of man would have dismissed and dispossessed Bartleby at once. But this lawyer is not only orderly; he is also compassionate. He is shocked to find Bartleby in the office on Sunday, but he is even more struck by what must be the terrifying loneliness of having no other place to go. In this state of mind he resolves to do the charitable thing, which in this case would mean to do nothing.

But the lawyer's comments on charity are very revealing. He sees clearly that there are "higher considerations" in charity than self-interest, but his life is not attuned to these higher realms. He salves his conscience by insisting that even self-interest can "prompt all beings to charity and philanthropy." In the light of the introductory comments to this section, such a line should alert us to the lawyer's essential problem. *Philanthropy* has as its root *phila,* not *agape*. The narrator may talk of charity, but he is not willing to practice it.

Immediate evidence of this is seen when his resolve to leave Bartleby alone is overwhelmed by fear that clients and colleagues are criticizing his generous decision. He is still unwilling to take violent action to get rid of Bartleby, but is nevertheless determined to see him go. When the unresisting copyist is finally taken to jail as a vagrant, the lawyer tries everything short of an *unconditional* effort to help Bartleby. At the very end of the story, the lawyer seems to suggest that a tragedy such as this is inevitable, a part of the price one pays for being human.

We are left, as Melville intended we should be left, with the uncomfortable feeling that no one in this tale cared enough. Bartleby is hopelessly and obviously focused upon himself. But the lawyer is no less ego-centered. He would like the trappings of charitable behavior but not its central core. Like other precepts of the New Testament, charity cannot be diluted or rationalized. Principles are not quantitative; half-love is only mockery and an illusion.

Index of References to Authors

Index of Selections Quoted